Praise for *Outlaw*

" [An] engaging cultural history . . . a fascinating chronicle." —*Washington Post*

"A biting, in-depth chronicle of Nashville's most tumultuous era told through the voices of iconic artists who used their music to accomplish significant changes in the music industry."
—*Kirkus Reviews* (starred review)

"The author of two Johnny Cash books, Michael Streissguth goes widescreen with this look at the social and musical ferment that produced the Seventies outlaw-country movement—a transformational break from the past that brought the post-hippie singer-songwriter ethos to superstraight Music Row. He skillfully portrays Sixties Nashville's studio politics and their gradual loosening up, alongside a city where post-Sixties social change took its time arriving. Streissguth shores his story up by cramming it with loving details—like when he lets on that Kris Kristofferson's 'Me and Bobby McGee' was inspired by Fellini's *La Strada*." —*Rolling Stone*

"Offers a look at how the 'outlaw' music of Waylon Jennings, Willie Nelson, and Kris Kristofferson shook up Nashville in the late '60s and '70s. . . . Author Streissguth has country music bona fides: He also wrote *Johnny Cash: The Biography*." —*USA Today*

"A riveting look at how three Texans joined forces to liberate Nashville from its company-town ways in the 1970s. It is a small group portrait, tightly focused and well told by Michael Streissguth."
—*Wall Street Journal*

"*Outlaw* is an entertaining, authoritative account of Nashville's rebel years." —*PopMatters.com*

"In this compulsively readable book, music historian Streissguth describes the contrast between the staid Nashville music scene of the late '60s and early '70s, and the dynamic new music filtering into the city from Los Angeles (Emmylou Harris), Texas (Willie Nelson, Billy Joe Shaver, Waylon Jennings), and South Carolina (Marshall Chapman)." —*Publishers Weekly* (starred review)

"Streissguth makes a compelling, intelligent, and elegant case for an outlaw zeitgeist, and he draws the main characters—Willie, Waylon, Kris, and 'the boy' (and a few girls)—with depth and truth. If God is in the details and art is in the specifics, Streissguth has created a beautiful document of the uniquely specific." —Rosanne Cash

"A unique and significant book. It paints a poignant picture of Nashville's Music Row in the 1960s and 1970s, when it was inhabited by songwriters, strange characters, heroes (sung and unsung), and talented, troubled, deathbound passengers of life full of words and music, which taken together sometimes makes dreams." —Kinky Friedman

"Think what you want about Nashville. Back in the 1960s, a seismic shift was taking place, beyond the purview of the Music Row mainstream, led by three singer-songwriters who didn't quite fit in. Michael Streissguth lifts up the rug and shows how the outsiders became the ultimate insiders and saved country music from itself." —Joe Nick Patoski, author of *Willie Nelson: An Epic Life* and *The Dallas Cowboys: The Outrageous History of the Biggest, Loudest, Most Hated, Best Loved Football Team in America*

"The outlaw scene was a cultural upheaval in a company town, spurred largely by outsiders—in its way, not unlike punk. Full of period color and surprising details (who knew 'Me and Bobby McGee' was inspired by Fellini's *La Strada*?), St̶ ̶ ̶ ̶ ̶ ̶t, as in the best country music, continues to repeat itself." ̶s, author of
Love Goes to Buildings on Fire: ̶usic Forever

ALSO BY MICHAEL STREISSGUTH

Nonfiction

Always Been There: Rosanne Cash, the List, and the Spirit of Southern Music

Voices of the Country: Interviews with Classic Country Performers

Johnny Cash: The Biography

Johnny Cash at Folsom Prison: The Making of a Masterpiece

Ring of Fire: The Johnny Cash Reader

OUTLAW

Waylon, Willie, Kris, and the Renegades of Nashville

Michael Streissguth

*it***books**

AN IMPRINT OF HARPERCOLLINS*PUBLISHERS*

*it*books

HarperCollins books may be purchased for educational, business, or sales promotional use. For information please e-mail the Special Markets Department at SPsales@harpercollins.com.

A hardcover edition of this book was published in 2013 by It Books, an imprint of HarperCollins Publishers.

FIRST IT BOOKS PAPERBACK PUBLISHED 2014.

Designed by Shannon Plunkett

The Library of Congress has catalogued the hardcover edition as follows:

Streissguth, Michael.
    Outlaw: Waylon, Willie, Kris and the Renegades of Nashville / Michael Streissguth. — First edition.
       pages ; cm
    Includes bibliographical references.
    Summary: "A definitive look at the outlaw country music movement, *Outlaw* follows the stories of three legendary icons—Willie Nelson, Waylon Jennings, and Kris Kristofferson—as they redefined country music in the late 1960s and early 1970s, set in the rich backdrop of Nashville"—Provided by publisher.
    ISBN 978-0-06-203818-0 (hardcover) — ISBN 978-0-06-203819-7 (pbk.) — ISBN 978-0-06-203820-3 (ebook) — ISBN 978-0-06-226349-0 (audio)
    1. Country music—History and criticism. I. Title.
    ML3524.S76 2013
    781.64209768'55—dc23

                    2012043490

ISBN 978-0-06-203819-7 (pbk.)

HB 07.06.2023

CONTENTS

*I just don't think that any of us thought we would spend
ten years banging our heads against walls and not come
out in good shape on the other side. If we had, I don't
know if we would have had the spirit for it.*

—**Dianne Davidson**

★ *Introduction*

THE LAST LIGHT of a November day in Nashville crept out of
the room where Kris Kristofferson, in a black coat and scuffed boots,
grappled with my questions. Over his shoulder, leaves on an old oak
tree pressed against the window, turning from yellow to orange according to the retreating sun's intensity, until they at last disappeared in
the darkness. Meanwhile, Kristofferson frowned and stared at the floor
as he searched for names and sensations from the late 1960s and early
1970s, when he was the most talked about man in this country music
town. "It was like everybody was in love with music," he finally offered.
"Everybody was in love with the creative part. And that's the only part
I ever had anything to do with. I've often felt that I was so lucky that I
got here at that time, because there were people like Mickey Newbury
and John Hartford. 'Gentle on My Mind' was just a revolutionary song
to me. It was light-years ahead of the stock, old-time songs. And I don't
think the lines even rhyme in it!"

Outside, Vanderbilt University football fans ambled down Seventeenth Avenue South after their team's embarrassing loss to Florida,
their guffaws and occasional complaints trailing off toward the neighborhood bars. Kristofferson, his carriage still suggestive of his own days

on the college gridiron, gestured toward the neighborhood outside, the West End, which used to be his home, admitting that the town and its music industry seemed more real in his memories. "I wish I could sometimes go back to that time. It was just so creative. All the time. And our hearts and souls were totally committed to the songwriting."

KRISTOFFERSON AND HIS friends were outlaws, servants of the songs, who chased the music the way it sounded in their heads. They resisted the music industry's unwritten rules, which prescribed the length, the meter, and the lyrical content of songs as well as how those songs were recorded in the studio. In time, the music industry bowed to their vision, shedding the old ways and accepting songs with peculiar names, like "Jesus Was a Capricorn" or "Devil in a Sleepin' Bag" or "The Battle of Laverne and Captain Flint." Kristofferson's songs, particularly, explored sensual love and desperate negotiations with personal devils in a rambling ballad style that sharply contrasted with the strictly tempered verse that had dominated country music for decades. He engendered a freedom of expression in Nashville's music business, and, in his wake, other freedoms emerged.

Waylon Jennings and Willie Nelson became outlaws in country music when they won the right to record with any producer and studio musicians they preferred. For decades the record companies made such decisions, but in the early 1970s Waylon and Willie began crafting a narrative that condemned their first RCA producer, Chet Atkins, the legendary guitarist who ran RCA's Nashville offices. Few people had contributed more to Nashville's ascent as a recording center in the 1950s and 1960s than the beloved Atkins, but in the eyes of Waylon and Willie he was the man who dictated their sound and their repertory. In the outlaw story, Chet had to be removed in order to liberate Waylon and Willie.

One could pin outlaw patches on dozens of men and women who

discarded Nashville's old recipes in the late 1960s and early 1970s—such as recording artists Roger Miller and Bobby Bare and producers Fred Foster and Jack Clement—but Kristofferson, Jennings, and Nelson became Stone Mountain in outlaw lore. Predictably, music executives capitalized on the excitement over the new independence and created a companion marketing label, "the outlaw movement," which in the minds of concert promoters and label bosses encompassed singers with cussed attitudes who dressed like Jesse James. Any one of them could have passed for a member of the Marshall Tucker Band, the southern rockers whom Waylon toured with and whose gold-record hit "Can't You See" he covered in 1976. Indeed, their solemn photos cranked up the appeal of RCA's *Wanted! The Outlaws*, a 1976 compilation featuring Waylon, Willie, Jessi Colter, and Tompall Glaser that became country music's first platinum album and introduced the outlaw label to the masses.

Save for Kristofferson's activism on behalf of the United Farm Workers and other causes, the scene proved vacuous politically, definitely more of a Jimmy Buffett invitation to hard partying than a call to social responsibility. But amid the hippie girls who stripped off their halter tops at Waylon's shows and magazine advertisements for Willie's belt buckles, the independence these men inspired rang through Nashville. As other recording artists took control of their own sessions, staff producers lost their jobs and record companies sold their Nashville studios; RCA, CBS, ABC, and the rest became packagers and marketers of Nashville-based artists, from Eddy Arnold to Tammy Wynette.

To nobody's surprise, the music made by the chief outlaws proved just as influential as their dilution of corporate control. Kristofferson inspired a singer-songwriter tide in the 1970s that swept up Rodney Crowell, Rosanne Cash, and Mary Chapin Carpenter, major stars in the 1980s, while the PG overtones of his songs echo still in today's country music. Kristofferson had arrived in Nashville in 1965 and struggled for years for recognition, working odd jobs while attempting to rein in a songwriting style that owed more to the English poet William Blake, whom he had studied in college, than to the honky-tonk king Hank Williams, whom he idolized. When Blake and Bocephus finally merged in Kristofferson's verse, song publisher and record company owner Fred Foster stepped forward to sign him. Plenty of observers—including Foster's business partners—believed Kristofferson belonged back on the Nashville streets, where he had rambled and drank and soaked up songs. But by 1970 he was the talk of Nashville: Johnny Cash, Roger Miller, and Ray Price recorded his songs and hip nightclubs on the coasts embraced him. Songwriters copied his style and explored his themes, and radio stations decided that a little modern maturity sung in a Dylan style could live in the country music format.

Of course, Waylon Jennings rarely missed a play on the country music airwaves. Ever since his first session with RCA in 1965, his records routinely hit the charts, although they rarely climbed very high. He'd come from West Texas by way of Phoenix, where he and his band, the Waylors, had hammered out a restless union of country and rock inspired by his association with Buddy Holly in the 1950s and the demands of young Beatles-influenced fans who flocked to Phoenix clubs to see him. However, Chet Atkins paid little mind to Waylon's rock-and-roll orientation: he plied him with songs from Nashville's songwriting machine and the contemporary folk catalog, all designed to appeal to pop audiences as well as country. Under Chet, Waylon tried Latin sounds, pop crooning, and a jaunty Marty Robbins imitation, until his original country-rock sound disappeared into a thousand discordant notes.

Finally, with a brash New York manager by his side, Waylon demanded control of his recording sessions in the early 1970s, and those dissonant elements in his music magically reorganized into a long lost country-rock style that culminated in the records "Are You Sure Hank Done It This Way" (1975) and "Are You Ready for the Country" (1976), which he borrowed from Neil Young's *Harvest* album. Although Waylon remained at RCA, he explored new studios, chose his own producers and songs, and polished an outlaw image that followed him until he died in 2002. His gutsy, throbbing sound (as well as his rebellious attitude) reverberated in Hank Williams Jr. and the supergroup Alabama during the 1980s and still glows today in the careers of Zac Brown, Gretchen Wilson, Toby Keith, Trace Adkins, and Jamey Johnson (who freely covers Waylon and Kris, references Waylon by name in his songs, and recently recorded with Willie).

While Waylon redefined country-rock, Willie rode his own long-neck rocket ship, blasting out of the 1970s and arriving at his own personal subgenre within country music. He may be the most significant musical and spiritual legacy of the outlaw movement. Like Waylon, he weathered a frustrating period at RCA in the 1960s despite his songwriting genius and smart vocal delivery. But then he, too, took up the outlaw truncheon, fleeing RCA for greater independence at Atlantic Records and, later, Columbia. Willie's outlaw association as well as the multimillion-selling albums *Red Headed Stranger* (1975) and *Stardust* (1978) supercharged his career and ensured his top-selling status into the early 1990s. And when his dizzying popularity finally calmed, Willie's remained the soul of country music, communicating a red-white-and-blue individuality and a back-to-basics ethos. He embodied the original pulse, the link to rural beginnings, to the classics "Crazy" and "Night Life," which he had penned in the 1960s, and to the rowdy outlaw vibe that invoked the Texas dance halls and honky-tonks where country music had lived for so long. In all the years since the outlaw movement faded, Willie has bridged the gaps between those all-too-few golden moments when country music meshes the present with tradition, like Johnny Cash's *American Recordings* of 1994, Marty Stuart's *Badlands* of 2005, and Jamey Johnson's *That Lonesome Song* of 2008. When country music sinks too deeply into gooey sentiment, rock and rap embellishments, and the cannibalization of teen singers, Willie remains onstage with a smile and a gut string.

*   *   *

WAYLON, WILLIE, AND Kris lived in an authentic and modern outlaw tradition that settled into Nashville beginning in the early 1960s, when civil rights protestors attacked segregation and led the way for Vanderbilt University students and other socially conscious people who later railed against the Vietnam War. By the late 1960s, young hippies from all over the country—themselves outlaws in the eyes of their parents and their government—streamed into Nashville's West End, transforming the area into a bohemian enclave, a glint of San Francisco in the buckle of the Bible Belt. Many of the pilgrims were inspired by the southern bluegrass music that had made its way to northern college campuses and the popular rock and folk music featured on the Nashville-based *Johnny Cash Show* on ABC-TV, and they found a vibrant underground cultural scene that coalesced around clubs such as the Red Dog Saloon, Bishop's American Pub, and the fabled Exit/In. "The thing about the Exit/In, it mirrored the general atmosphere of creativity in that underground group, that little outlaw group," says singer-songwriter Dianne Davidson, who came from nearby Camden, Tennessee, in 1970. "We pretty much believed that we were about free-form ideas, about creating what our souls told us to create, so, of course, if several of us got together and came up with an idea that we thought was great, the Exit/In would be the place to perform it."

Alive with political activism and musical experimentation, the West End became Nashville's very own Greenwich Village. It sheltered Kristofferson, who wandered the neighborhood like a goliard, auditioning his songs in taverns and publishing companies, and energized Waylon, who found a creative workshop in the Glaser Brothers Sound Studio, which rejected common business practices, like appointments and closing times.

Even Willie Nelson, so closely associated with Texas during this era, wiggled freely in Nashville's West End, clocking late-night hours with

Waylon at Glaser Brothers and lapping up adoration in the small bars and private clubs from fans who just knew that Willie's time would come.

The very idea of a Greenwich Village vibe in Nashville in the late 1960s and early 1970s clashes with the southern-backwater stereotype that some attach to the city. Certainly, Nashville tried its best to strangle desegregation and thoughtful urban renewal, to name two battle-grounds in the culture wars, but its nature also revealed a tolerance for change and experimentation. Those who agitated for civil rights crafted an outlaw template that Waylon, Willie, and Kris could be heir to, and the city's funky West End helped mold their careers. When they gained the freedom of navigation from Nashville's intransigent institutions, they created music that conformed to their own vision and introduced a country-rock chic that helped transform Nashville from merely a recording center to a cultural capital with all of its adjunct creative energy and vulgar excess.

This book tracks the outlaw paths of Waylon, Willie, and Kris from their arrival in Nashville in the 1960s through the 1970s, the decade of the outlaw movement. But despite their looming presence here, it also paints a broad portrait of the outlaw in Nashville, making room for underground travelers such as Rodney Crowell, Kinky Friedman, and Guy Clark, who also found prosperity without adhering to any particular expectations set forth by the music industry. All of them—Waylon and Willie, Rodney, and Guy—have in common their coming of age against the canvas of Nashville's wildly clashing notions about race, education, lifestyle, urban renewal, war, gender, corporate influence, and government interference, which sorted the outlaws—musical and otherwise—from the accommodationists.

Some readers will insist that the outlaw phenomenon in music was strictly Texas-based and that Nashville lacked the spark to ignite musical freedom. Of course, Texas burns wildly in the outlaw story: the lead riders were Texans by birth and nobody tapped that state's outlaw ethos more vigorously than Willie when he abandoned Nashville in the early

1970s and cantered into Austin's progressive music scene, where artists such as Jerry Jeff Walker, Michael Martin Murphey, and Doug Sahm fused country, rock, and folk. But Texas is only one part of the story; this book sets up camp in Nashville and considers the outlaw phenomenon as it lived there.

★   ★   ★

BACK IN THE West End, only a dim light from a desk lamp framed Kristofferson. The clatter of football fans had disappeared, and long silences punctuated the singer's responses to my questions. His eyes squinting as they do in the movies nowadays when he has an important line, he once more reached for the Nashville he knew forty years ago. "To me, the best thing about that time and the thing that I have the most gratitude for is that the integrity was there. Of wanting . . . not to be famous, though I'm sure people wanted to be! But belief in the quality of music that was coming out. I don't listen enough anymore to what's going on today, but I'm sure that there's guys out there that have as much respect for the music as we did."

*How remarkably lucky I was to have been there. I
have often thought that for me and my purposes and
aspirations, it was the best place in the world. I couldn't
want it to have been any different from what it was.*

—**Robert Penn Warren**

 One

The Newcomers

A NEW YORK jazz critic traveled down to Nashville in the 1960s on
assignment for a national magazine. He was supposed to focus on the
music industry there, but the city so offended his uptown sensibilities
that his disgust infected every paragraph. "Nashville is a pallid, tasteless
town," he complained as he took aim at the city's replica of the Parthenon in Centennial Park, and which to him symbolized hillbilly preten-
sion or, at the very least, a mind-boggling lack of imagination. And
then he attacked the quality of Nashville's food, urging visiting New
Yorkers to bring their own canned goods because the city's restaurant
fare soured the stomach.

Such criticism frequently rained on Nashville. Music executives visiting from New York and Los Angeles groused about its Bible Belt ban on
the sale of liquor by the glass. When veeps from RCA poured in for the
funeral of legendary country crooner Jim Reeves in 1964, hometown
singer Eddy Arnold had to pay a state trooper to fetch moonshine whiskey for their hotel room parties. Even folks from elsewhere in the South

raised an eyebrow at the city: writer Larry L. King, a native Texan, arrived at the Ryman Auditorium (home of the *Grand Ole Opry*) in 1968
and gasped at the surrounding neighborhood. "It is located in a section
of Nashville with much to be modest about: curio shops dealing in
Sweetheart Pillows and crockery painted with Kitchen Prayers; lunch
counters, garages, a barber college; and a series of beer parlors special-
izing in rollicking jukeboxes, dried-beef sticks, and thirty-cent suds."

While freelance writers snickered, sons and daughters of Nashville,
too, bristled from time to time: teens who watched the police's smother-
ing presence at local rock-and-roll shows; housewives who searched in
vain for food products advertised on national television but never available in their local grocery stores; and earnest music fans who groaned
about the boxed-in musical formats on daytime AM radio.

Young people who showed up for classes at the city's hallowed
Vanderbilt University marveled at campus concerts featuring passé artists such as the Platters and local country-pop princess Skeeter Davis,
when most of young America was discovering Jefferson Airplane and
Sly and the Family Stone. In the 1960s, Vanderbilt saw *pro*-Vietnam
demonstrations and expelled James Lawson, a black divinity student
who dared to act against desegregation in the city. "Nashville certainly
was no hotbed of liberal or progressive ideas," says a Vanderbilt alumnus
who attended in the 1960s and considered himself part of the counterculture. "In fact, it was the exact opposite. It was a very uptight town
and everything was completely kept under wraps. There was a huge
influence from the church. The Southern Baptist Convention was based
in Nashville. We tried to keep out of sight as much as possible."

But a few Nashvillians chanced to show themselves when it counted
most. Despite the dismissive magazine articles that appeared in national
magazines, and the conservative leadership at Vanderbilt University, a
modest social awakening took hold in Nashville in the 1960s. Some
middle-class white kids joined protests organized by the scrawny Nashville Committee for Alternatives to the War or slipped out to North

Nashville, the center of black life, to see why riots flared up there in 1967. Their black counterparts joined voter registration drives, and sat in and boycotted in pursuit of civil rights.

Contrary to popular memory, Nashville had long been relatively progressive on race, especially compared to Memphis, to the west, a city shaped by plantation traditions. The *Nashville Tennessean* newspaper had successfully railed against the poll tax, and blacks served on city council and the school board. And when public schools finally began desegregating on September 9, 1957—three years after *Brown v. Board of Education*—Nashville avoided most of the mob rule and political posturing that had descended on Little Rock, Arkansas, one week earlier. Still, mixing of the races in schools would plod along at the rate of one grade per year. A few segregationists in Nashville harassed black students, and on September 10, somebody in the night dynamited an integrated school in East Nashville, but nobody was killed or injured. Unlike Arkansas governor Orval Faubus, Nashville mayor Ben West publicly discouraged obstructionists who vowed to fight *Brown* to the last.

Some tied Nashville's relative tolerance in those days to its river-city tradition and hilly terrain, which means it accommodated newcomers and never depended on slavery as much as its neighbors to the south and west did. As author and one-time Nashville newspaper reporter David Halberstam pointed out, the city's segregation "was largely a soft kind, administered, it sometimes seemed, not with the passion of angry racist officials but more as a cultural leftover from the past."

While Nashville's schools desegregated, young civil rights activists, many of them students at the traditionally black Fisk University and Meharry Medical College, believed the dimes they spent on socks and chewing gum in Woolworth's, Walgreens, and other stores bought them a stool at their lunch counters, too. But those lunch counters shooed away black customers. So on February 13, 1960, John Lewis, a student from American Baptist College, Diane Nash from Fisk, and

James Lawson from Vanderbilt began staging lunch-counter sit-ins that would last for months. At first, Nashville resisted. Cruel whites seemingly uprooted from the streets of Little Rock gathered to intimidate and attack, while a few stores closed their counters rather than offend white customers. But black Nashville persisted: when police dragged away one band of would-be diners, another took its place.

As Nashville's winter disappeared into spring, the sit-ins became as regular and expected as the L&N freight trains that rumbled through town every day. But then a segregationist tossed a bomb onto the lawn of Z. Alexander Looby, a prominent black lawyer, inflicting only minor injuries. But the explosion made up in inspiration what it lacked in lethality. Alarmed by the violence, leaders of the sit-ins led thousands to the courthouse steps, where they met Mayor Ben West, who in front of newspaper reporters and photographers unexpectedly endorsed the righteousness of integration.

Courtesy of Nashville Public Library, The Nashville Room

On the courthouse steps: Mayor Ben West (in bow tie) and, left to right, civil rights workers Curtis Murphy (wearing sunglasses), Diane Nash, C. T. Vivian, and James Bevel.

By the end of 1960, most stores in downtown Nashville had integrated their lunch counters. And then segregated movie theaters and hotels budged. In the wake of such progress, Nash and Lewis graduated to the dangerous enterprise known as the Freedom Rides, which tested the U.S. Supreme Court's ruling that had struck down segregation in interstate travel. Their activism rooted in Nashville, Nash and Lewis invigorated the national civil rights movement. Indeed, they were among the city's first outlaws.

★   ★   ★

A FEW MONTHS before President Lyndon Baines Johnson signed the Voting Rights Act in August 1965, Captain Kris Kristofferson set down his duffel bag on the hot sidewalk outside Nashville's airport and looked around for his ride. Women in their pencil skirts glanced admiringly at him, as if William Holden in an army officer's uniform had just landed in middle Tennessee. Kristofferson neither knew nor cared about Nashville's recent civil rights progress; to him, the city was a songwriting mecca and nothing else.

At the moment, he was between commissions and had dispatched his wife and young daughter to family in California, so he could meet Marijohn Wilkin, a Nashville music publisher who also happened to be his platoon leader's cousin. He had little time to spend. A teaching assignment in British literature at West Point awaited him.

During his childhood in Brownsville, Texas, and later in California's San Francisco Bay area, Kris dreamed of Nashville while listening to Hank Williams on the *Grand Ole Opry* show, which beamed out of Nashville on the 50,000-watt radio station WSM. One can hardly imagine jet-age Californians communing with the *Opry*'s old-mountain sound, so Kristofferson must have been one of the few. "I had eleven years of growing up in Brownsville," he says. "They thought I was a shit-kicker." He wrote songs after hearing Williams and wrote more of them in an extraordinary career as a student at the exclusive Pomona

College in California and then at Oxford University, where he studied on a Rhodes scholarship.

At the airport, Kristofferson slid into a gleaming Alfa Romeo driven by Bucky Wilkin, Marijohn's son, and headed downtown. "I checked into this hotel," says Kristofferson, "and in my uniform walked up De-monbreun to Music Row, to Marijohn Wilkins's publishing house, and it was just like a magic day for me." Wilkins owned Buckhorn Music on Hawkins Street in Music Row and had cowritten one of country music's classics, "The Long Black Veil," a hit for Lefty Frizzell in 1959. She had taught school in Tulsa, Oklahoma, before coming to Nashville to play piano in Printer's Alley, the city's muted incarnation of Bourbon Street. She also drank like a man. One almost had to in Nashville's music busi-ness. It was like a nonstop fraternity party.

When Marijohn stood up to greet her visitor, she introduced him to three colleagues in the room: songwriters Billy Swan and Chris Gantry, and singer Johnny Darrell. Darrell had come around to show off his new record, "The Green, Green Grass of Home," a Curly Putnam com-position controlled by one of Marijohn's competitors, Tree Publishing. "It was his first record," recalls Kris. "We sat there at Marijohn's listen-ing to it, and then went over to Cowboy Jack Clement's and played it over there. We were walking out of there, and this guy said [to Johnny], 'Porter's in the studio right now covering your record.' I didn't even know the significance of it at that time." The bandit, of course, was Porter Wagoner, whose RCA recording would snuff out Darrell's new release. Only later would Kris realize the lesson: the big artists in town, like sharks in the ocean, snatched up the plumpest songs no matter who first laid claim to them.

After a few drinks at the Professional Club, a music industry hangout on Sixteenth Avenue South, Marijohn and Johnny left the newcomer in Clement's care. He couldn't have been in better hands: the producer and songwriter knew every back door and bar stool in town. "After everybody else fell off and went home," continues Kris, "he took me down to—now, this is my first day in Nashville—Audrey Williams's place, right next to the Professional Club." At this point, Kris probably deduced that everybody in Nashville owned a publishing company, an astonishing possibility. More astonishing, though, was the sight in front of him: the lanky Cajun fiddler Doug Kershaw hawking the rights to his hit "Louisiana Man" to the widow of Hank Williams. "I'm thinking, 'Wow, I'm here. This is happening.' And then Cowboy [Clement] took me down to the train station because he just loved trains. He'd get on them and ride to New Orleans and back, just to write. But it was pretty magical. I was so excited about it. I think I probably right then decided I was coming back here. It was so much, that little Professional Club, those two streets, the whole shooting match was right there.

"It seemed like every place we turned there was somebody I'd listened to since I was little," he says. Backstage at the Ryman Auditorium, the *Opry*'s home base, Kris squirmed as Clement introduced him to his dark, lean friend born in the cotton fields of Arkansas. "I shook his hand," says Kris of meeting Johnny Cash. "And it was like shaking hands with lightning. He was so wired up or something at the time. But he was what I imagined Hank Williams was like."

Captain Kristofferson left town after a few days, resigned his West Point commission, and arranged his family's move to Nashville. Marijohn warned that the business gobbled up wide-eyed rookies like Kris, and Jack saw only faint potential in his writing. It was "poetical stuff, and unsingable," he remarked.

When Kris returned for good in the summer of 1965, he gravitated to Willie Nelson, whose songwriting could seem as abstruse as his own. "We happened to be the guys who were just absolutely disciples of Willie Nelson," Kristofferson told writer Robert K. Oermann. "Every one of Willie's songs would be sung and analyzed for his emotion and his delivery and all this. It was a training ground for a whole bunch of us. We said, 'Willie will never make it because he's way too deep. He'll never make it because they don't understand him.'"

★   ★   ★

WILLIE CAME FIRST to Nashville in 1960, after a decade of dee-jaying, door-to-door sales, and playing the honky-tonks and dance halls in Texas. Down there, he had already written "Family Bible" and "The Party's Over," which nestled into his repertoire like princely cats, and "Night Life," later to be recorded by everybody from Ray Price to B.B. King. By the time Willie packed his wife, Martha, and three children into his old Buick and drove toward Nashville, "Family Bible," as recorded by Claude Gray, was soaring on the national country charts. Which put no cash in Willie's pocket. He had sold the rights to the song outright to a studio owner in Pasadena, Texas. All he could do was shrug, which is how Willie handled adversity. "The way I looked at it, songs for a songwriter were like paintings for a painter," he wrote in his 1988 autobiography. "You finish one and you sell it for whatever you can get and then you do another."

Willie told everybody he met in Nashville about "Family Bible," and he soon fell in with the city's songwriting pack, men like Harlan Howard and Roger Miller, who served up much of the raw material—the songs—fueling Nashville's explosion as a recording center. Howard's "Heartaches by the Number" and "I Fall to Pieces" and Miller's "Invitation to the Blues" and "When Two Worlds Collide" ranked among the solid building blocks in Nashville's rise. Mississippi-born songwriter Hank Cochran, a sometime cowriter with Howard, introduced Willie to Pamper Music, a song publishing company that hired Willie as a staff writer. He got fifty dollars a week against future writing royalties, enjoying for the first time a stake in music he composed.

In less than a year, Willie wrote three country-pop classics: "Crazy," "Hello Walls," and "Funny How Time Slips Away." The songs rode high on the country and pop charts and were recorded by the likes of Patsy Cline, Elvis Presley, Ray Charles, and Faron Young. That meant Willie could move from a trailer park to a farm in Ridgetop, Tennessee, about thirty miles outside Nashville. Willie also got himself a new woman, dropping Martha, with whom he savagely fought, for a singer named Shirley Collie, who was the wife of a deejay friend and happened to have caught his eye out in Nevada.

The Texan's songwriting also attracted recording contracts. In 1964, Fred Foster's Monument Records recorded Willie in a setting that predicted his spare *Red Headed Stranger* album of 1975, long considered Nelson's masterpiece. With only classical guitarist David Parker and three other musicians, Willie taped five songs, including the cold and mysterious "I Never Cared for You." Foster released it as a single, but against the rollicking honky-tonk sounds and string-laden arrangements popular in those days, its sparseness and poetic lyrics frightened the radio disc jockeys who could have made it a hit. *The sun is filled with ice and gives no warmth at all / The skies were never blue.*

Willie's stubborn streak—one of his core outlaw traits—emerged at Monument when a trade magazine ad that Foster had promised to run for Willie got bogged down in production. "I didn't get to tell him that his ad was going to be a week late," says Foster. "I tried to call him but I couldn't find him. Now some say he picked up the *Billboard* and saw that his ad wasn't in there and he got upset. I don't know. In his mind, his obligation to Monument was to come in and do the sessions he did. In his mind, he was free to go to RCA." Indeed, like one of those old delta blues singers, never bound by contracts, recording for whomever might pay him for sessions, Willie left Monument and ambled down the street to RCA.

Too fond of the scamp to sue him, Foster merely rolled his eyes while RCA rushed out Willie's self-penned single "Pretty Paper," the heart-tugging Christmas song about a blind man selling pencils, which Roy Orbison had released on Monument in 1963. If Willie's version was meant to undercut Orbison and Foster, his blade was dull and late to the game: Orbison's version reemerged on the Christmas charts in 1964 while Nelson's new release foundered. The fumbling new beginning predicted Willie's abysmal career with RCA.

For the next seven years, his appearances on the charts seemed like bit parts. Despite creating some of the smartest country music records to ever roll out of Nashville—"Healing Hands of Time" (1965), "The Party's Over" (1966), and "I Gotta Get Drunk" (1969) among them— he remained a second-tier artist. Perhaps some of his beer-drenched creations offended the new breed of country fan lulled by the syrupy Nashville Sound, or the lyrics proved too wry next to the Brill Building–like rhymes so common in country music. Or maybe it was RCA's fault, which was Willie's theory: "I couldn't get anybody on the executive end of it interested in promoting me as an artist," he complained in 1975. "They might have been hoping that one of my records might accidentally do something on its own without their having to spend a lot of money promoting it."

A FEW MONTHS after Willie's anemic debut on RCA, Waylon Jennings motored into town with an RCA contract just like Willie's. The two men had first crossed paths not long before in Phoenix, where Waylon dazzled the club audiences and Willie had stopped while on tour. "I went to catch his show," wrote Willie, "and afterwards we shared a bottle of tequila and he asked my advice on his career. 'Whatever you do, Waylon, stay away from Nashville,' I told him. 'Nashville ain't ready for you. They'll just break your heart.' Upon hearing my advice, Waylon did what any good songwriter would do. He went to Nashville."

Waylon and his band had landed that regular Phoenix gig in July 1964 at a club called J.D.'s. There was no place else like it: rock-and-roll music downstairs, country music upstairs, and go-go girls everywhere. And Waylon magnetized college kids and cowboys as if he were the region's very own Elvis Presley. "He was just king," said a fan. "From the little girls to the bouncers, it was all Waylon. I mean, he was their star and it was that way. . . . When people found out how great Waylon was—he drew all kinds of people. You would often see elderly people watching him with their shawls on. People were just fascinated by his music." Waylon's band packed J.D.'s dance floor with an electric guitar and a bass and rhythm guitar, but the increasingly rambunctious crowd demanded a drummer.

To answer the cry, Waylon hired Richie Albright, a native of Bradley, Oklahoma, who relished his chance with Waylon after playing for brutal honky-tonk audiences in Prescott, Arizona. "Waylon played lead," says Albright. "And his style of guitar playing was definitely different. We did Dylan songs. We did Beatles songs. We did all genres of music. Did a lot of country stuff. It was kind of a castoff of Buddy Holly's rhythm. It wasn't country really." They serenaded sweaty fans with a panoply of popular music: "What'd I Say," "Crying," "Jole Blon," "Love's Gonna Live Here."

"My reputation was growing throughout Arizona," wrote Waylon. "I was the hottest thing in town. I was making decent money for the first time, and paying the band. The crowds were listening to me, and I was getting to them. I could tell the girls liked me and the cowboys thought I was a good 'ol boy. But most important, in the middle of a set, I'd turn around and look at Richie and we'd be going off on this tangent, jamming, letting the song carry us along, and a smile of satisfaction would spread across our faces. I just knew musically we fit." Indeed, the fit was brotherly. Albright drummed the beat and held Waylon's hand for most of the next thirty years.

At the time, Waylon was signed to A&M Records in Los Angeles, which was also home to poet Rod McKuen and trumpeter Herb Alpert. Alpert was actually the "A" in the company name and his 1962 lounge hit "The Lonely Bull" was the vein of gold that fortified the label. Jerry Moss—who would go on to work with Burt Bacharach, Joe Cocker, and others—was the "M." Together, Alpert and Moss tempered Waylon's lion vocals, so prominent on the stage of J.D.'s, for ballads, folk songs, country novelties, and light rock tunes that they had chosen. However, they seemed most interested in folk. They paired Waylon with Ian Tyson's "Four Strong Winds," the traditional ballad "The House of the Rising Sun," and Bob Dylan's "Don't Think Twice, It's Alright." The results were pleasant, but hardly remarkable. Sensing the same, Waylon balked. "Herb kept looking for something in me that he couldn't find," he lamented. "It just wasn't there, really. He truly liked my singing, and he wanted me to make it, but even if you get a bigger hammer, you can't fit a round peg in a square hole. One night we tried 'Unchained Melody' countless times. I never understood . . . what [the song] was talking about. It was too far over my head."

In 1965, Jennings hitched up with Chet Atkins and RCA-Nashville. Chet had heard about Waylon from two trusted sources: comedian Don Bowman, a 1964 discovery of Chet's who had worked on radio in Lubbock, Texas, with Waylon in the late 1950s; and Bobby Bare, who had signed with RCA in 1962 and got his first dose of Waylon at J.D.'s in 1964. "Well, he always had that charisma," said Bare on meeting Waylon for the first time. "And he was doin' speed so he had that element of danger about him. Speed people do; you don't know what they're going to do next."

In March 1965, Waylon recorded twelve songs for Chet, including an arrangement of the old ballad "I'm a Man of Constant Sorrow." Chet was known for keeping a tight handle on the studio reins, choosing the session musicians and the songs, but on these sessions, he eased up. He let Waylon's band, the Waylors—bassist Paul Foster, guitarist Jerry Gropp, and drummer Richie Albright—dominate the instrumentation, and inexplicably gave Waylon the freedom to include five of his own songs, including "That's the Chance I'll Have to Take," his first number-one country record.

Chet was pushing Waylon to the folk-pop audience, which boomed on college campuses and in large urban centers. But Waylon's first recordings sounded more like a cross between Elvis Presley's post-army records and the pop troubadour Frankie Laine than the Kingston Trio. No matter. Chet merely stuck the title *Folk-Country* on the album and hoped for a cash bonanza. It never materialized. But Chet persevered. He believed he had signed the next Johnny Cash and was anxious to prove it.

★　★　★

EACH MAN HAD recorded elsewhere before they hit Nashville: Kris in Britain while at Oxford; Waylon in Texas and California; and Willie in Texas and Washington. But they forged a path to Nashville, an unimposing city that seemed far more accessible to young climbers than New York and Los Angeles. In that Tennessee town, music business doors swung open and a handful of smoky bars that served as industry haunts brokered connections for the uninitiated. In its studios, talented and efficient background musicians converged with powerful record company producers and publishing companies bulging with great songs. These forces, like departments at a Hollywood movie studio, created and sustained stars who sold millions of records and helped bring the music of Nashville to the world.

The wellspring of this Nashville Sound first percolated in the mid-1950s, when producers Chet Atkins at RCA and Owen Bradley at Decca fended off the threat of rock and roll by injecting country music with middle-of-the-road flavor (strings and crooning background vocals added to please pop listeners). The strategy produced some of the greatest recordings in twentieth-century popular music, including "She's Got You" by Patsy Cline, "He'll Have to Go" by Jim Reeves, and "Detroit City" by Bobby Bare, stirring up brisk demand for Nashville product.

Inasmuch as the music aspired to pop markets, the term *Nashville Sound* became forever linked to middle-of-the-road embellishments. But the engine also embraced the hard, traditional sound of country music as well as rock-and-roll flavorings. Even though Chet had declined to produce Elvis Presley in the 1950s because the Hillbilly Cat recorded too late at night, he wasn't above jacking up the bass or goosing the electric guitar man if he felt the market would like it. Owen Bradley, too, straddled the fence between rock and country, producing sessions by country queen Kitty Wells while propelling Brenda Lee to the high echelons of rock and roll. So the Nashville Sound paid no mind to musical genres—its studios and musicians could accommodate in a single day the likes of Connie Francis, Perry Como, and Porter Wagoner. Rather, it prided itself on the lockstep efficiency of the machine, which kept up with demand, occasionally produced music that echoed itself, and helped make country music a global commodity worth $60 million annually in the mid-1960s.

Producers mindful of corporate budgets had little choice but to work efficiently. Ideally, four songs emerged from a three-hour session, forcing background singers and instrumentalists to learn songs within minutes of walking in the door. The best of the musicians—drummer Buddy Harman, bassist Bob Moore, pianist Floyd Cramer, guitarist Harold Bradley, and others—circulated through the city's studios, while the two big vocal accompanists, the Jordanaires and the Anita Kerr Singers, hummed beside them.

Along with the musicians, the big publishing companies—Tree, Cedarwood, Acuff-Rose—always camped at the studios; their writers and pluggers could come and go as they pleased, often crashing recording sessions with their new songs in tow. With each major-label artist releasing two and sometimes three albums a year, demand for songs was constant, but the creative reservoirs of even the best writers were only so deep. When fifteen compositions by the legendary songwriter Harlan Howard appeared on the country charts at the same time in 1961, it was as much an indictment of the industry's parochialism as it was evidence of Howard's greatness.

The quality of Nashville's product also slipped when kickbacks in the form of shared writing credits for artists or outright cash payments from publishers to producers gave special prominence to underserving songs. To make matters worse, producers who kept their own publishing companies ran straight into the headwinds of ethical probity. Whom did they serve: their pocketbooks or their employer? In a 1996 interview, Chet Atkins responded to the manager of one of his 1960s artists who had wildy charged that he owned a piece of every song he ever produced: "That's the biggest fuckin' joke I've ever heard. I never owned a piece of any song anybody did. I had a little publishing company before I went on the payroll [with RCA]. I think Jim Reeves wanted me to publish one of his songs. [Running RCA-Nashville] was just a sideline for me. . . . I was making $50,000 or $100,000 a year in royalties off my guitar playing. So I didn't need that. Mr. Jim Denny of Cedarwood Publishing would send people over and say, 'If you record this, you get 10 percent.' And I said, 'You know, I don't do that.'"

Bar none, Chet Atkins remains Nashville's most beloved figure. For years, the city's musicians had dealt with visiting New Yorkers who came to supervise sessions, but Chet was a veritable local boy who had played all the roadhouses and dawn patrol radio shows that everybody else in town had played. And when he ascended at RCA-Nashville, he never seemed to change, propping his office door open to any old friend who happened to stop and taking his lunches in unassuming cafeterias that sat on every corner. In the studio, artists loved his soft touch. "Chet was so secure within himself and his own knowledge," says former RCA engineer Jim Malloy, "that he didn't have to be running around the studio like a chicken with his head cut off like some of these people do, hollering and screaming. Because Chet knew that the worst that could happen is that he could pick up the guitar himself and play the whole thing. Chet picked great musicians and he let them play and every so often Chet would rise up and hit the talk-back and [make a recommendation] and, sure enough, it was always better. Chet was brilliant."

Chet liked his scotch and spent his nights out in Printer's Alley, which made him part of a certain in-crowd, but Waylon Jennings, at least, found him to be something of a square, mostly on the topic of drugs. Although Chet never objected to pot, he lectured Waylon about the latter's liberal use of amphetamines, part of a long-standing feud on the subject that was summed up by Waylon during the 1960s, when a friend of his suggested that he record a song about pills. The sulky Texan replied that "Chet Atkins thinks it's a sin to even look at one."

Waylon could be just as dismissive of Chet's leadership, which the singer found intransigent. It was a rare broadside against the easygoing chief, but not one without some foundation. For the most part, Chet demanded that his artists record in Nashville even when leaving town might have invigorated their sound, but releasing an artist to another RCA studio in Los Angeles or New York was an admission of failure and, besides, Chet, in partnership with Owen and Harold Bradley, owned and collected rent on 806 Seventeenth Avenue South, the building that housed RCA's offices and its massive Studio A. It behooved him to keep the artists recording there.

Courtesy of Metropolitan Government Archives of Nashville and Davidson County

RCA at 806 Seventeenth Avenue South.

And Chet, his eye on the machine's fluid operation, by and large supported the virtual lock that Nashville session musicians had on recordings; that disappointed more than a few artists who would have preferred using their own band. After allowing Waylon to use members of his band on his first sessions, he promptly barred them. For a while,

Chet let Willie use drummer Johnny Bush and steel player Jimmy Day, who traveled with Willie, but he soon reversed course. "When we'd get to Nashville, Chet didn't like it," Bush told the country music historian Rich Kienzle. "He kept sayin' the drums weren't makin' it. If you hear some of Willie's recordings, he liked a little rhumba and a Bolero beat. That's what Willie wanted. Chet hated it." By the autumn of 1967, Chet prevailed. He expelled Bush *and* Day from Willie's sessions. "Chet had to have control, not Willie," moaned Bush.

Chet's obstinacy no doubt grew in part from his loyalty to his boss in New York, the portly Steve Sholes, who brought Elvis Presley to the label in 1955 and who must have been a father figure to Chet (whose own father was absent from his early childhood). "I worked for Steve," he said. "I didn't work for RCA." Sholes, who ran the division that oversaw country music, had given the struggling guitar player a recording contract in 1947 and made sure that he had plenty of session work. By and by, Chet became Sholes's eyes and ears in Nashville. Then, in 1955, Sholes officially put him in charge. It presented Chet with his lifelong dilemma: he had transcended his impoverished childhood and gained a tall measure of respectability in a growing industry, but his guitar increasingly lost out to his RCA responsibilities and he found himself negotiating with the big wheels in Nashville, a task for which his asthmatic, country childhood had left him royally unprepared. The position tied him in knots, and some say it was to blame for his long and ultimately losing battle with cancer, but he pressed on in order to please Sholes.

At any given time, thirty to thirty-five artists populated RCA-Nashville's stable, and even with a handful of staff producers at Chet's disposal, executive burdens tugged at him from every direction. "I spread myself too thin," he acknowledged. "But that's the way all the labels did it in those days. You'd make a bunch of records and just throw them out and see what stuck to the wall."

*A quiet place. . . . Nothing of the life here that gives color
and good variety to the cities in the East and West. Just a
good, ordinary, humdrum, business town.*

—O. Henry

 Two

Nashville Sounds

THE EMPIRE OF Texas laid claim to many of the music industry's outlaws, which may be more than coincidental. After all, few parts of the country boasted more fertile musical earth: from the hard blues of the Deep Ellum district in Dallas to the western swing that lit up the ballrooms and beer gardens of Houston to the rockabilly that sizzled along the highways from Lubbock to Longview. Latin rhythms floated up from the south and kissed the polka music that German and Czech immigrants brought with them in the nineteenth century. Gospel mingled with field hollers while country music inundated the radio airwaves and dance halls. The Lone Star State's spectacular roster of native talent included Ernest Tubb, Gene Autry, Lightnin' Hopkins, T-Bone Walker, Roger Miller, Janis Joplin, George Jones, Bob Wills, Ornette Coleman, Scott Joplin. And Waylon, Willie, and Kris.

Kristofferson was born to middle-class parents in Brownsville on June 22, 1936. One cannot drive south of Brownsville and still be in the United States. A major port of entry to Mexico, especially during

Prohibition, when Texans lined up to drink freely across the border, the city hummed during the difficult 1930s thanks to its busy port and verdant farms, which stretched over the Rio Grande valley as far as the eye could see.

Kris's memories of childhood linger on the Mexican music he heard, the old rancheros that were everywhere, and going to school barefoot. "I think there was something I wrote at the time, a list of dislikes," he says. "And I think mine were my sister and shoes! . . . But I always really loved Brownsville. Something about the feeling of it. Looking at it now, when I go back, it looks so much like it's south of the border. But it was definitely a good place to grow up."

Brownsville's first airport opened in the 1920s, and it would be the scene of separations and reunions in young Kris's life. His father, Henry, flew for Pan American World Airways in the 1930s and joined the army with the outbreak of the Second World War, where he rose to the rank of full colonel. "He was really a highly respected guy," says Kris. "First guy to fly over the Himalayas at night. And later on, when he was a major general, he was handling the Korean Airlift." His mother, Mary Ann, learned to be father and mother to Kris and his two siblings.

The family left Brownsville in 1947 and lived in a succession of states before settling in San Mateo, California, near San Francisco, where Henry had returned to the military, this time with the newly established U.S. Air Force. It was 1950, the beginning of Kris's high school years. As his father moved up the ranks, Kris lettered in football, led a number of student clubs and activities, and pulled impressive grades. In 1954, he entered Southern California's Pomona College, his mother's alma mater, where he continued his football career, joined ROTC, and majored in English. He proved passionate and masterful at creative writing, winning awards from the *Atlantic Monthly* for his short stories.

When Kris qualified for a Rhodes scholarship in 1958, nobody was surprised. "I thought I was special and I got conceited," he recalled in 1971. "But when I got to Oxford they had no respect for me at first.

They thought I was a cowboy. Then I showed them by getting the highest grades in philosophy." However, Oxford spelled the beginning of the end of his academic career. His prose writing and study of Romantic poet William Blake soon gave way to the call of Hank Williams. In London, he tried out his songs in coffeehouses and then won a talent contest that promised a deal with Top Rank Records. Kristofferson recorded a few tracks, but the gambit was voided by an obscure recording contract he had signed back in California. For the time being, flirtations with the music industry were exactly that. He left Oxford at Christmas break in 1960.

Kristofferson ignored his musical impulses long enough to join the army in the spring of 1961 and marry a former classmate named Frances Beer. By 1962, the couple had a child, and Kris was rising in the ranks. Taking to the sky like his dad, Kris flew helicopters and joined the admired Airborne Rangers, serving most of his stint in West Germany, like Elvis Presley and Johnny Cash before him. Like at least Cash before him, he drank like a frustrated novelist and played country music with a band of like-minded comrades. In the mid-1960s, Kristofferson received an assignment to teach literature at the U.S. Military Academy, at West Point, New York. "But I didn't want to do that," he says. "And I really didn't want to keep staying in the army. I didn't resent any of the time that I spent in there, but I didn't want to make a life of it. And I did want to be a creative writer. A songwriter. I had already fulfilled my commitment; I had been in the army for almost five years. I remember running into an officer that I knew when I was at the Pentagon, trying to get out of the army. And I was very lucky, because he got me out. They were sort of dragging their feet because nobody wanted somebody to get out of the army after you were selected to go teach at West Point! But I don't know . . . I'd done all I could in the army, I think."

★　　　★　　　★

AS KRISTOFFERSON'S BROWNSVILLE bustled in the 1930s, Waylon's hometown of Littlefield, Texas, hoped that drivers racing from nearby Lubbock to New Mexico might stop for coffee and gas. Sitting squarely in the state's stovepipe, the town claimed about 3,500 residents when Waylon was born there on June 15, 1937. Like many families in West Texas, the Jenningses winced as the Depression drove down cotton prices and dust-bowl conditions swept across the plains. With few factory jobs to be had and cotton farming in decline, they waited for better news. "It's never been easy to make a living in Littlefield, and we had it harder than most," said Waylon in his autobiography. "I don't think anybody had anything in reserve for a rainy day. Even the more well-to-do farmers lived from one harvest to another. When we got up in the morning, all we had was the daily prospect of hitting the cotton patch, or getting in the truck, or going down to the warehouse."

It's almost a cliché in the young lives of country music greats who weren't Rhodes scholars, but Waylon, too, escaped the rigors of poverty through music. He recalled belting out folk and western songs with family and friends and learning to play borrowed guitars. At the movies, he marveled at the romantic blend of crooning and shoot-outs in the Gene Autry and Roy Rogers westerns, and on Saturday nights, the family roasted peanuts and reeled in the *Grand Ole Opry* and the *Louisiana Hayride* on the radio. Waylon, like Kristofferson, idolized Hank Williams, but his father loved Bill Monroe, falling silent whenever the bluegrass king's high tenor sliced through the family's shabby living room.

Years later it was clear how much his father's love of Monroe had rubbed off on Waylon. Monroe's lady friend Hazel Smith was working in the office of Waylon's associate Tompall Glaser in the early 1970s when the aging bluegrass star stopped by for lunch; she suggested they say hello to Waylon, who was recording close by at RCA. The moment she and Monroe peeked into the control room, somebody called out that a "pretty good high-tenor singer" was in the house. "When Waylon walked out and saw Bill, he was visibly shaking," says Smith. "Because it was Bill Monroe. He told me later, 'In my house, in Littlefield, Texas, it was the Bible on the table, the flag on the wall, and Bill Monroe's picture beside it. That's the way I was raised.'"

If the spell of Bill Monroe and Hank Williams hadn't lured Waylon out of Littlefield, something else was bound to. He was a rambunctious teenager, playing football, chasing girls, and tumbling into every sort of juvenile delinquency. At sixteen, his father gave him a Harmony guitar, onto which he promptly emblazoned his name in white paint. He warbled country and western songs at talent shows and on his local radio station, KVOW. Dropping out of high school in the tenth grade, Waylon married in 1955 and soon parlayed his KVOW spot into a regular disc jockeying job on the station. The marriage faltered, but he stuck with radio.

As true then as it is today, radio walked hand in hand with the music industry. From his perch at KVOW and then at other nearby stations, Waylon talked up live performances on the air and spun the latest records. His status on radio made him somebody to know and probably was a big reason that grateful promoters and club owners around West Texas hired him to perform.

Occasionally, he hitchhiked to Lubbock to appear on KDAV's *Sunday Dance Party*, which featured local talent and offered a youthful alternative to the living room atmosphere of *Grand Ole Opry*. Aspiring musicians mostly performed hillbilly music during their few minutes on air, but a lot of them also embraced the wild rockabilly music rushing into West Texas from Memphis, Dallas, and Shreveport. Rising stars Elvis Presley and Carl Perkins had integrated a world that Jim Crow laws couldn't touch, incorporating elements of black rhythm and blues into their beloved hillbilly music.

Waylon was a disciple of Presley, as was a quiet Lubbock native named Buddy Holly, whom Waylon met on the *Sunday Dance Party* in 1954. Waylon and Buddy really got to know each other in 1958 when Waylon went to work for KLLL in Lubbock. Charmed by Waylon's freewheeling on-air banter, KLLL had hired him to trip up the competition at KDAV. And he didn't disappoint: Waylon magnetized area listeners, including Holly, who by then was chasing Elvis with his flashy hits "That'll Be the Day" and "Peggy Sue."

Whenever Holly returned to town, he haunted KLLL, chatting with Waylon about life and Lubbock, and Waylon's career. "He was easy to get along with, easygoing," said Waylon of his friend in 1973, "and he was a monkey in a lot of ways, a real cutup. We sure did have a lot of fun. He was one of the best people I knew in my life." Holly nurtured Waylon, magically arranging a one-shot Brunswick Records session for the twenty-one-year-old disc jockey (with King Curtis on saxophone!), buying him clothes, and, in a final act of generosity, welcoming him to his road band in late 1958 after Holly split with the original Crickets.

Waylon's only biographer, the late R. Serge Denisoff, pegged the inevitability of their relationship. "They were remarkably similar men," he wrote. "Both were highly cautious around people; some called them 'shy.' They shared a desire to succeed in the record business. Waylon was, perhaps, more flamboyant, but there were enough similarities to cement a close friendship."

In early 1959, Waylon famously gave up his seat to J. P. "The Big Bopper" Richardson on the ill-fated airplane that crashed near Mason City, Iowa, and took Richardson's life as well as those of Holly, Richie Valens, and pilot Roger Peterson. As if losing his mentor was not bad enough, the crash saddled Waylon with heavy guilt, for he had teasingly told Holly that he hoped the plane would go down.

Gordon Payne, who played guitar for Waylon in the 1970s, recalls quiet nights on the tour bus when the boss's thoughts drifted back to 1959. "I heard him say, 'Why me? Why wasn't I on that plane?' I said, 'Well, you weren't done yet. It wasn't your time. God had more for you to do than die in the cornfields in Iowa.' [Waylon replied], 'Yeah, but I've always felt guilty. Here was my buddy dead and I was supposed to be on that plane with him. And I wasn't. I didn't want to look at a guitar for a long time.'"

Recklessness and disillusionment plagued Jennings in the immediate years after Holly's death. He retreated to radio, bounced around the club circuit in south-central Arizona, and recorded a dead-end session for a small record label. Then his marriage broke up. He might have limped back to Littlefield but for the promising signals in Phoenix, the last stop on the road to Nashville.

★   ★   ★

THE INTERURBAN ELECTRIC train service, which ran a line north to Dallas from points south, kept a station in the hamlet of Abbott, but the early years of the Depression depleted the town and by the time Willie Nelson was born there on April 29, 1933, residents had to flag down the engineer if they wanted to ride. Abbott, population two hundred, resembled Waylon's Littlefield: bereft of opportunities and reliant on the local cotton crops. When cotton prices shriveled up, residents migrated to Dallas.

Willie's parents drifted away from his older sister, Bobbie, and him early in his childhood. His father, Ira, a musician in some demand, stayed drunk most of the time, and his mother, Myrle, abandoned her children before Willie turned one, choosing a vagabond's life that must have both fascinated and repulsed Willie later in life, for he, too, adopted drifting ways though not always at the expense of his children. Ira's parents, Nancy and Alfred Nelson, whom Willie and Bobbie dubbed Mamma and Daddy, raised them. Mamma taught piano while Daddy farmed and plied his blacksmithing skills.

In 1940, Daddy died from pneumonia, forcing the family to leave its home for a splintered replacement nearby. Mamma found work in Abbott's school cafeteria, and everybody took turns picking cotton, hopping on the farm-worker trucks that trundled out to the fields each morning during harvest time. "I didn't like picking cotton one bit," Willie told biographer Michael Bane. "I used to stand in the fields and watch the cars go by and think, I want to go with *them*."

But the cotton patch's omnipresent labor songs redeemed the back-aching experience. He heard black people moaning the blues, Mexicans crooning in Spanish, and whites humming their church hymns. The radio was no less influential. "I remember when we used to sit around and watch the radio. Because it was new in the house," Nelson told journalist Bill DeYoung in 1994. "There was somethin' there that had some entertainment comin' out of it. The first thing that we tuned in was WSM in Nashville, the *Grand Ole Opry*. That was a regular. . . . I was up late at night a lot, and I'd turn the dial and listen to anything I could really. A lot of boogie and blues, back in the days of Freddie Slack and Ella Mae Morse, and Ray McKinley. And Glenn Miller and those guys."

Nelson, Kristofferson, and Jennings learned from the same *Grand Ole Opry* textbook. But one influence that appears much stronger in Nelson's childhood than in Kris's and Waylon's was the church. Kris rarely attended, and Waylon detested his parents' Church of Christ, whose rejection of instrumental accompaniment rendered the music indigestible.

Willie, on the other hand, waded deep into sacred song. "We went to a very small Methodist church," his sister, Bobbie, told *Texas Monthly* in 2008. "My grandmother was there every time the doors opened. Willie and I were practically born in that church. The first music we learned was from the hymnbooks. Willie had such a beautiful voice. I'd play piano, and he would sing. Then he learned to play guitar, and my grandmother taught us to play together, showing Willie the chords on the guitar and me on the piano and telling us when to change chords. That's the way we learned to play together. 'Great Speckled Bird' was the first one she ever taught us." When church let out, Willie and Bobbie scampered to the county seat of Hillsboro, where gospel singing conventions shook the walls of the town's courtroom, of all places. Hymns such as "I'll Fly Away," "In the Garden," and "Amazing Grace" permeated him.

The eleven-year-old also embraced Frank Sinatra, who modeled the breath control that Mamma talked about when she talked about singing. In years to come, he wielded that breath control to great effect, singing behind the beat and then catching up in a way that surprised and delighted listeners. Indeed, his hard Texas twang would test the uninitiated, but the masses admired how it danced and flirted with the rhythm.

Willie graduated from high school in 1950, and he joined the air force for a stint that he would always dismiss, according to biographer Michael Bane, "with as few words as possible." He didn't last a year, receiving a medical discharge linked to a back problem. Like Waylon Jennings, Willie spent the first years of the new decade negotiating a young marriage, working in radio, and taking practical jobs that paid the bills when radio jobs were scarce. He also wrote songs and lugged his guitar in and out of various bands that melded toe-tapping western swing with the less polished, though more emotionally urgent, hillbilly sounds.

For the rest of the decade, Willie serenaded barroom crowds and sold his songs to any willing buyer, lighting out from his home state from time to time when fields elsewhere appeared greener, but frequently returning to the clubs and the bandleaders and the big Texas skies that were always glad to see him. These were the years in which Willie Nelson created his very own Texas, its borders defined not by rivers and surveyor's lines but by roads between radio stations that invited him to perform on their airwaves and the clubs whose dancers craved rhythm. It would be his refuge in the frustrating Nashville years ahead of him.

*　　*　　*

WILLIE'S FRUSTRATION IN Nashville alternately hinged on his anemic record sales and RCA's tight reins on his recording sessions. However, Waylon's early Nashville years shaped up pleasingly. But only pleasingly. Chet threw plenty of Waylon's records against the wall and more than a few stuck. And if a fan sniffed at Waylon's straight country songs, he could always choose something else among the rockers, folk ballads, and pop-influenced baubles that populated his discography.

In stark contrast to the assertive vocal style that marked his outlaw recordings of the 1970s, Waylon in the mid-1960s was controlled, even gentle, which helped put over the polite sound that defined much of his repertoire, but not his true style. Chet continued to work the contemporary folk angle with Waylon, as he had with RCA's John D. Loudermilk, Bobby Bare, Eddy Arnold, and George Hamilton IV, although the songs shied away from the protest themes of Bob Dylan and Joan Baez, hewing more to the tales of rambling and gambling that cropped up in Gordon Lightfoot's "For Lovin' Me," which Waylon recorded in 1966.

Apparently, Chet also envisioned Jim Reeves as he devised Waylon's path in the studio. Reeves, along with Patsy Cline, who was produced by Owen Bradley, became the embodiment of the Nashville Sound when his sweet-sounding "Four Walls" climbed the country and pop charts in 1957, around the same time that Cline was surging with "Walkin' After Midnight." Reeves and Cline proved that easy-listening music produced in Nashville could compete commercially with Elvis Presley, Pat Boone, and Debbie Reynolds, and both singers enjoyed even bigger hits—Reeves with "He'll Have to Go" in 1960 and Cline with "I Fall to Pieces" in 1961—but they died soon after in separate airplane crashes.

Courtesy of Sony Music Entertainment

Waylon (left) strums a twelve-string guitar
while Chet (right) looks on in the RCA Studio.

When Chet learned of Reeves's death in 1964, he broke down in the RCA offices while session musicians looked on. In time, the realization that he'd lost not only a friend but the goose that laid the golden egg moved him to fill the void. In a conversation in the mid-1990s, Chet refused to speculate about finding a replacement for Jim Reeves, but he may have nominated Waylon Jennings. Of course, the famous country balladeer Eddy Arnold proved to be the heir to Reeves's audience, but at the time of Waylon's first sessions Arnold had yet to score his breakthrough country-politan hits "What's He Doin' in My World" and "Make the World Go Away." So Waylon's early hits found him reaching for distant places in his range on songs such as Harlan Howard's "Another Bridge to Burn," Don Bowman's "Now Everybody Knows," and Waylon's own arrangement of "I'm a Man of Constant Sorrow," all of them drenched in background vocals as if they were Jim Reeves records.

And Waylon clearly enunciated his lyrics, again like Reeves, even on his cover of Johnny Cash's "You Beat All I Ever Saw," a far cry from the boozy delivery first proffered by the Man in Black in 1966. One of the early hit singles, "Anita, You're Dreaming," cowritten by Waylon and Bowman, found Waylon in a serious and cautious vocal mode that remembered Reeves, only this time with traces of Marty Robbins, whose famous Latin sound rose up on Waylon's albums more than a few times in the 1960s.

After two years of emulating Reeves and Robbins, not to mention the likes of Buck Owens and George Jones, Waylon finally showed signs of asserting his own style on 1967's album *Love of the Common People*, which boldly featured Mel Tillis's "Ruby Don't Take Your Love to Town," a rare commentary on the personal toll of war, and Lennon and McCartney's "You've Got to Hide Your Love Away." Waylon's vocals broke out of the safe zone, creating drama or leering playfulness as the lyrics demanded. Waylon hewed particularly toward the title track, "Love of the Common People," another smooth folk-styled ballad, first recorded by the Four Preps in early 1966. "It had it all," wrote Waylon, "the horn stabs that I loved so much, an insistent piano figure that lodged in your brain, and four (count 'em) key modulations upward, so that the song never stopped getting you higher. The lyrics were especially meaningful, for a poor country boy who had worked his way up from 'a dream you could cling to' to a spot in the working world of country music."

Billy Ray Reynolds in a Nashville studio.

It was also meaningful to American Indians, who demanded the song whenever Waylon galloped into the New Mexico reservations to perform. "He was like an idol out there, to the Navajos especially," says guitarist Billy Ray Reynolds, who toured with Waylon. "They'd come in there loaded down in the back of a pickup truck. They wouldn't go in the building until they saw Waylon. We could set up all we wanted to; they wouldn't go in the building and pay the money until they saw Waylon's face. The minute they saw Waylon, you couldn't move in the building." The men would slip outside the side door to drink, says Reynolds, and then circle back to the entrance and pay again for admission. "They'd come in and grab the first girl they could, and they did that strange Indian dance that they did and they'd go right through the crowd, almost knocking people over to get up to the stage. And they'd just slap on the stage and say, 'Waylon, "Love of the Common People."' We'd do that song about twenty times a night."

★   ★   ★

WILLIE NELSON MAY have been a likelier replacement for Jim Reeves. He mastered the intimate delivery like nobody else, including Waylon Jennings. Drawing perhaps from the big-band vocalists who pierced the airwaves of his childhood or his radio jobs that demanded crystal-clear patter, Nelson enunciated everything and projected necessary emotions as if he were turning on a flashlight. He made it sound so easy, so cool, darting in and out of the rhythm as if playing a game of hide-and-seek.

But initially Chet played it strictly country with Willie, pairing him with the genre's beloved standards and Willie's own classic compositions and releasing a live album recorded at Panther Hall in Fort Worth, which caught Willie in his raucous element, the Texas dance emporium. Interestingly, Chet also released a cut from the concert so disturbing that it would surely dispel any possibility of Willie fitting in among the sweet Nashville Sound. "I Just Can't Let You Say Goodbye" recounts a strangling murder in the first-person, in real time, recalling the cruel murder ballads "Knoxville Girl" and "Cocaine Blues"—the likes of which had fallen out of favor in country music by the 1960s. Predictably, Willie's drama receded after two weeks on the singles charts.

Willie onstage in the 1960s.

In 1966, Chet put aside murder ballads and reached for the country-politan sound on the album *Make Way for Willie Nelson*. It featured only one Nelson original, "One in a Row," a dramatic heartbreak ballad that danced easily with the pop standards "Have I Stayed Away Too Long" and "What Now My Love," which also appeared on the album. Willie also sampled from the catalog of Cy Coben, a New Jersey song-writer who'd been coming to Nashville since the 1940s and pitching songs to Steve Sholes and then Chet. His whip-sharp lyrics brought a taste of Tin Pan Alley to Nashville, and when Willie tried on his "Make Way for a Better Man" it left no questions about his versatility: he could breezily deliver swinging pop songs and punch out the country stuff. In future years, Willie would complain that Nashville producers buried his voice in a mix of strings and brass instruments during the 1960s, but on *Make Way for Willie Nelson* nothing could have been further from the truth: Willie's voice pulsed above the mix, very urbane, careering among his lyrics like a Cadillac on a smooth and curving highway.

And yet the album sold little, raising a thousand questions. Why couldn't the golden songwriter with the more than pleasing vocals float to the top? Were the high forehead and the spiderweb wrinkles around his eyes liabilities? Or did his conservative dress, which communicated insurance sales and car dealerships, repulse the audience? Folks in the industry insisted that he deserved the success of Porter Wagoner and Roger Miller but admitted that his lyrics were too complex for the market. Willie complained about lack of promotion. And he resented the handicap of recording without his road band. "I just didn't feel comfortable in that kinda situation. You'd walk into the studio and they'd put six guys behind you who'd never seen your music before, and it's impossible to get the feel of it in a three-hour session. That was true for me, at least."

Willie also charged that he was kept around RCA so his stable mates could pillage his poor-selling albums for material. That may have been true, but the releases suggest that RCA and Chet Atkins respected Willie's artistry. Indeed, his lyrics oozed complexity, standing a sure step above the standard fare churning in the Nashville barrel. However, by hauling in the best of the arrangers—such as conservatory-trained Bill Walker, who embroidered a rich sound, Chet seemed to be giving Willie's gifts their appropriate showcase. Modern lyrics required modern embellishments, so here and there appeared a lonely violin, a moody electric guitar, even a sitar.

But nothing worked commercially. As Chet once said in reference to Willie, "With a record company you can have a whole roomful of people who all put their heads together and grind away at a problem and still come up with the wrong answer."

Songwriter Billy Swan often saw Willie play at the Boar's Nest, a sort of artists' refuge with brown bottles and empty beds that local barmaid

Sue Brewer arranged in her home on Eighteenth Avenue South. Swan often pondered the singer's stagnation. One night, he sat on the floor while Willie towered above him, "like he were a guru, a maharishi or something, and we just listened to him do those wonderful songs in the way only he can do them. Everyone in this town knew that his guy was great. He was not like anybody else."

★　　★　　★

KRISTOFFERSON WOULD HAVE traded his Ranger School tab for Waylon's and Willie's RCA deals, but while those men struggled to find the right sound in the studio, he traipsed the sidewalks of the West End, haunting barrooms and publishing houses, in search of his elusive break. He had signed with Marijohn Wilkin and moved his family into a small house at 3525 Byron Avenue, on the edge of the West End. Eager to pick up where he had left off on his first visit, he worked on economizing his rambling verse and splashed into the Nashville fraternity life. "I suddenly felt like a fish that had gotten back in the right water," says Kris.

One of his best pals was Billy Swan, the Willie Nelson fan who had arrived in Nashville with serious credibility. In 1962, at the tender age of twenty, Swan had watched Clyde McPhatter take his "Lover Please" to number seven on the pop charts. More thrilling to Swan's peers, though, may have been his stint as a gate guard at Elvis Presley's Graceland. Or that he was arrested on his first night in Nashville.

When Swan hit Nashville in 1963, he immediately drove down to Tootsie Bess's honky-tonk bar on lower Broadway, near the Ryman Auditorium. All of the songwriters hung out there, and Swan was anxious to meet them. "At about twelve o'clock it was shoulder to shoulder and I'm drunk and I hear, 'Arrest her,'" says Swan. "And I turned around and they're arresting Tootsie, something about serving a minor. The undercover guys were there. The first thing out of my mouth was 'You can't arrest her.' They said, 'Take him, too.' So they put me and her in a paddy wagon and took us down to jail, and we went before the judge. He didn't even look up when he said, 'Spend the night in jail.' I stayed up all night, afraid to lie down. I didn't even know where in the hell my car was. It was a Sunday morning, however. I found it in the back of the *Opry* parking lot, sitting there all by itself."

Courtesy of Metropolitan Government Archives of Nashville and Davidson County

Lower Broadway in the 1960s. Note the sign for Tootsie's.

Kristofferson joined Swan on future adventures, while both continued to struggle musically: Swan to repeat the magic of "Lover Please," and Kristofferson to win his first hit. It finally happened for Kristofferson when Dave Dudley—known best for paeans to the truck-driving life like "Six Days on the Road"—recorded Kris's "Vietnam Blues" in 1966 and took it to country music's top twenty. But Kristofferson still needed full-time work to pay the bills, so over the next four years, he worked a variety of jobs: ditch digger, carpenter's assistant, and bartender. Billy Swan even got him a job at Columbia Records studio on Sixteenth Avenue South as an engineer's assistant. Swan had worked there after stopping by to pitch songs and play Ping-Pong with studio musicians. But he was leaving for another job right in the middle of Bob Dylan's historic *Blonde on Blonde* sessions in February 1966. The studio manager asked him to keep an eye open for a replacement. "So I walk out of his office," says Swan, "and say bye to Polly the secretary and as I was pushing the door to go out, Kris was pulling it to come in. And the first thing out his mouth was 'Do you know where I can get a job.' I said, 'Yeah, I just quit mine.' And we went back into [the] office and that was it."

Courtesy of Tommy Wayne Burlett

A young Kristofferson, right, with fellow songwriter Vince Matthews.

While he cleaned ashtrays, fetched coffees, and bulk-erased tapes, Kris witnessed the final three days of Dylan's first foray into Nashville. In those days, writers affiliated with reputable publishing companies freely came and went in the middle of sessions around town, so Kris was no stranger to the scene at Columbia. However, Dylan's scene was another sight. Off-duty police officers kept an eye on ambitious fans, while a strange silence enveloped Dylan himself. "He went in, started writing at the piano, and sat there all night long, working on stuff," marvels Kris. "And around seven in the morning, he'd get all the guys in there—they'd been off playing pool and Ping-Pong—and he'd go in and cut some masterpiece. I was in awe."

A romantic telling of this story has the lauded poet mentoring the novice in some small way, but Kris never sought out such a moment. "I talked to his wife—his wife and kid were sitting in the control room. But I never would have talked to him because he was creating. He was out there writing. I couldn't have brought myself to interrupt his thoughts."

In the weeks after Dylan disappeared, Kris slipped demo tapes of his songs to Johnny Cash, still as edgy as the night he first met him. But he doubted that the star ever played them. And he tried to revive his recording prospects, having Marijohn Wilkin produce his composition "The Golden Idol," about a girl who wore too much makeup. But it tanked.

Kris's parents and siblings thought he had lost his mind, wasting his pedigree and impressive educational and military credentials on the songwriting life. His brother flew from California on a futile mission to snap him back to reality, and his father's disappointment was plain. "[They thought] I'd gone down to shit-kicker country and they couldn't imagine that there was anything worth devoting your life to here," says Kristofferson. "I just thought, 'Wow! They don't understand.' Well, looking back, I can understand why they felt that way! Because they didn't even listen to the *Opry*."

Jack Clement remembers a letter from Kris's mother arriving shortly after her son had settled into Nashville. "It was like a two-page, single-spaced letter. His mother was just really putting him down for what he'd done. She was telling him how irresponsible he was and all this shit. At one point, she said, 'When you were thirteen years old and singing Hank Williams songs, we thought that was cute. But now I don't think it's cute at all.' She ended it by saying, it doesn't matter how much money or success he makes in the music business, it'll never make up for what he's doing now."

In comparison with the scene at home in Nashville, his parents' dissatisfaction seemed insignificant. The songwriter's late nights and all-hours job at the studio were splintering his marriage. Frances naturally had grown impatient with the uncertainty that replaced the respectable military career. Money was tight and concerns over the health of their newborn son excruciating. "He was born with his esophagus and trachea attached, a *bad* time," recounted Kristofferson in 1974. "Ran up about a $10,000 hospital bill." To pay the bill, he left Columbia and took a job transporting roughnecks by helicopter to oil rigs in the Gulf of Mexico. He rushed home to his music buddies on days off, and he never stopped writing.

But Frances clung to the upper-middle-class ideals of her childhood in the face of Kris's recklessness. His was the honky-tonk life, ambitious drinking mixed with impromptu jam sessions and casual romantic encounters. And in stark contrast to the image he cut when he married in 1961, he let his hair grow down to his ears and adopted the jeans and vests of his younger Nashville brethren. Often, he fell in with the veterans, like one night when Billy Ray Reynolds, Kris, and Waylon closed the Starlight Club on Dickerson Road.

Seemingly out of options, the gang impulsively headed to Audrey Williams's house. "It was about three o'clock in the morning," says Reynolds, "and we knocked and she came to the door. By then, Audrey had lost a lot of weight and really wasn't in good health. She said, 'Honey, what are you doing out this time of night?' I said, 'We come to hear some Hank Williams stories.'" And the next night Kris might step out with the newcomers, writers such as Mickey Newbury, Donnie Fritts, and Vince Matthews, who measured the pulse of the street for song ideas, and young musicians who pondered not the ghost of Hank Williams but the artistry of Bob Dylan.

The people around Kris would soon help lift him to fame, but for now, he took pleasure in the thrill of his songs appearing as album filler or on a B side, like "No One's Gonna Miss Me," which showed up on a brand-new single by Waylon Jennings and Anita Carter in 1968. He gingerly carried it home. "I was trying to make some impression on my wife, who hated country music," he explains. "I said, 'Look at this. I'm making it.' I was a janitor at the time, so she was pretty depressed. She played it for the people at her bridge club, and she said, 'Well, they don't really like his voice.' And I just thought, 'Well, we are never going to be on the same planet.'"

While friction escalated in the family, Kristofferson also felt squeezed from time to time by Music Row rules that also stifled Waylon and Willie. Only it was Kristofferson's songwriting that sat in the crosshairs. Music publishers demanded snappier scenarios and broadly appealing hooks, but his songs refused to fully conform, like "Best of All Possible Worlds" which again revealed Kristofferson's education by recalling a line from Voltaire's novel *Candide*. "They wouldn't let me demo it the way I wrote it," Kris told writer Peter Cooper. "I wrote it as, 'If that's against the law, tell me why I never saw a man locked in that jail of yours that wasn't either black or poor as me.' They wouldn't let me say 'black.' I changed it to 'low-down poor.'"

I know a lot of times I've read that Newbury and I changed things here. We didn't do it. It was them. It was John and Bob Dylan who changed Nashville from just being a country hick place to all of a sudden being something important that you ought to examine.

—Kris Kristofferson

 Three

Let a Flower
Be a Flower

THE MUSICAL FREEDOM that Waylon, Willie, and Kris yearned for in the late 1960s seemed out of reach in the sterile new office buildings and sagging bungalows that housed the record business on Music Row. The corporate enclave ruled every country artist in town. Except for Johnny Cash, who under the cover of midnight darkness lugged his guitar and his band into the studios of Columbia Records.

Cash followed his own rules in the studio, uncorking classic records that dealt with war, the plight of the American Indian, and other thorny topics—a departure from more traditional subjects of love and heartbreak. Cash's producers let Cash be Cash, which meant throwing away the studio clock, leaving his backing band the Tennessee Three alone, however calcified its boom-chicka-boom rhythm had become, and standing by without complaint while Cash ploddingly chose songs and worked out arrangements—A&R tasks that elsewhere on Music

Row would have been completed days before the session. When Waylon Jennings demanded and got such freedoms from RCA-Nashville in the early 1970s, many proclaimed that he was the first. In truth, as with so many things in that town, Cash—the godfather of Nashville's outlaw movement—had gotten there first.

Bob Dylan came second. He arrived in Music City on February 14, 1966, to record *Blonde on Blonde* and, like Cash, presided over sessions that were the antithesis of Nashville Sound. With the exception of multi-instrumentalist Charlie McCoy, who had traveled to New York in 1965 and unexpectedly played guitar on Dylan's *Highway 61 Revisited*, none of the Nashville musicians on *Blonde and Blonde* had worked big-label sessions that were so free and easy. Throughout six days of recording, interrupted midway by a few live shows, Dylan wandered into Columbia in the evenings, spent hours scribbling down lyrics and a few more on music, then recorded in the morning. Songwriter Billy Swan was in the final days of the engineer's assistant job that he would soon give to Kristofferson during those sessions. He admits that he had only haphazardly followed Dylan's career up to that point, but in between his gofer tasks, he began to see the light. "What was coming back from those speakers was so fucking good: his singing, his performing. That whole album is fantastic."

LIKE DYLAN AND Cash, producers Jack Clement and Fred Foster modeled independence in Nashville. Fixtures in town by the mid-1960s, the two men still lived in the shadow of Owen Bradley and Chet Atkins. But not for long, as their wily hustle and passion for music for music's sake created a thrilling alternative to corporate music making and would attract various freedom-hungry outlaws in the years to come.

Clement stood out in Nashville like a juggler in a funeral parlor. He had established his producing credentials at Sun Records in Memphis, where he worked on Johnny Cash's and Jerry Lee Lewis's recordings.

Plying an impulsive spirit that only Memphis could nurture, he dug feverishly through Nashville's creative world as if it were an old attic chest, and pulled out the old and the unusual, but particularly the unusual. In the 1960s, he dusted off the career of long-forgotten country music father Ernest "Pop" Stoneman, wrote novelty songs for the grim Johnny Cash, and persuaded Chet Atkins to sign the black singer Charley Pride.

"They all wanted to be around Jack," says Jim Casey, who wrote for one of Clement's publishing companies in the 1970s. "Jack would smoke a little dope and do crazy stuff and put them in a chair and spin them around and get them dizzy and play them crazy shit. They'd come to town and that would be the first place they'd go." Toting his ukulele, he was always up for a good sing-along or a night on the town. Waylon's drummer Richie Albright met him for the first time outside Sue Brewer's Boar's Nest: "I got out of the car and just as I was walking up the sidewalk, this guy comes down and I looked up and it was Jack. He walked down the stairs and stopped on the stoop, and I said, 'Jack?' He said, 'Yeah.' I said, 'I'm Richie Albright.' I put my hand out and started shaking hands, and he turned around and threw up. He hung on to my hand. So that was my introduction to Jack Clement."

Cowboy moved to Nashville in 1959 as a freelancer, performing various production chores for Chet Atkins and writing hits such as "Miller's Cave" for Hank Snow and "I Know One" for Jim Reeves. An investment in a studio in Beaumont, Texas, pulled him out of town for a few years, but by 1965, he settled back in Nashville just in time to greet Kristofferson on his first day in town. In addition to producing Charley Pride and Pop Stoneman and the Stoneman Family, he supervised the recordings of the Glaser Brothers (Tompall, Chuck, and Jim), and in 1969 opened Jack Clement Recording Studios at 3102 Belmont Boulevard, a few blocks east of Hillsboro Village.

The stars—Charley Pride and Johnny Cash—turned to him for ideas, but he also attracted writers such as Jerry Foster, Bill Rice, Vince Matthews, Bob McDill, and Townes Van Zandt, all of whom made deep impressions on Nashville in one way or another. "Jack had enough of that Memphis thing in him that he was willing to try anything," observes Casey. "Nashville is very conservative. Nobody wanted to take many chances. Jack was willing to try things and that's a Memphis thing."

It might also be a North Carolina thing. Fred Foster was born there in 1931, the same year Clement was born near Memphis. Like Clement, Foster came to Nashville looking for a poker game, arriving in 1960 and quickly revealing his preternatural knack for building winning hands with unlikely cards.

Roy Orbison had floundered on Sun Records and RCA in the late 1950s before Foster signed him to Monument Records, which he had established in Baltimore in 1958. Orbison enjoyed his greatest days in Foster's care, with hits such as "Only the Lonely (Know How I Feel)," "Crying," and, of course, "Oh Pretty Woman." When Orbison left Monument for MGM Records in 1965, Dolly Parton appeared to steal Foster's gaze. Up to that point, the determined young woman from the Smoky Mountains had failed to break nationally, striking out on two labels. With Foster at the helm, her next two singles climbed the country charts in 1967—"Dumb Blonde" and "Something Fishy." They spent a combined twenty-six weeks on the countdown and attracted Porter Wagoner, who promptly spirited Dolly away to RCA and Chet Atkins.

Photograph by Alan Mayor

Fred Foster.

If Foster had done nothing but cement Roy Orbison's and Dolly Parton's roads to the top, his legacy would be secure, but he had also spied an attractive hand in the black audience that big-label Nashville ignored and left to the tiny black-oriented record companies that dotted the city. Foster's operation stood somewhere between the two: small enough to take risks and big enough to exploit black markets more successfully than the smaller outfits. "Monument had sort of become a pet of radio," recalls Foster. "So I cut an R&B record and shipped it. The phones went wild! And telegrams poured in, letters from radio stations, criticizing me, 'What are you trying to do? We put on a Monument record without auditioning it because it's always good. Here we put on something and there's screaming and hollering in the middle of our program—what in the hell are you doing?' I said, 'Well, I can't do that anymore.' So I started an R&B label."

Like Jack Clement, Foster also housed young writers under the shelter of his publishing company, in his case Combine Music, which he established concurrently with Monument in 1958. The company had given Dolly Parton a contract before she bolted to RCA, and throughout the 1960s attracted such artists as Ray Stevens, Chris Gantry, Billy Swan, Dennis Linde, all of whom wrote songs that bored into Nashville's musicscape and enjoyed Foster's sponsorship without interference. "You've got to let a flower be a flower," declares Foster. "You're going to make a flower bloom differently than it would normally bloom? I don't think so. Just nourish it, give it enough fertilizer, water and let it bloom. It will bloom. Business, hell, I can't stand it. Business has ruined many a good man and woman."

Of course, Combine's biggest acquisition was Kris Kristofferson, who had failed to break through at Buckhorn Music, despite his "Vietnam Blues" and a few others, including "Jody and the Kid" (recorded by Roy Drusky) and "From the Bottle to the Bottom" (recorded by Billy Walker). "Kris always wrote alone," Marijohn Wilkin told interviewer Philip Self, "and so it took him longer without having a cowriter to guide him." Wilkin suggested that Kris's work was often unripe, too close to his recent emotions and experiences. But he had tempered somewhat the epic-poetry style that Jack Clement observed in 1965. However, Marijohn wasn't convinced. "I couldn't carry him any longer," she continued. "He hadn't had a hit."

When Kris left Marijohn in early 1969, Billy Swan probably introduced Kris to Fred Foster. Swan had already signed with Combine and was producing Tony Joe White's first Monument sides, foremost among them the swampy pop hit "Polk Salad Annie." He knew that Foster's publishing company marked the intersection of Nashville's street life and establishment of country music, a perfect place for Kristofferson.

Bob Beckham ran the funky show at Combine. In the 1950s, he appeared as a singer on *Arthur Godfrey's Talent Scouts* and landed a contract with Decca Records, but he abandoned performing soon after to go into publishing, where he proved adept at negotiating the eccentricity of songwriters. "He was a super-likable guy and just drew people," says Swan. "He was a friend, straight-ahead, you never felt like he was above you."

When Beckham joined Combine in 1964, the company had already run through two directors and was operating out in lonely Hendersonville, where Foster also headquartered Monument Records. "I stayed out there for about three weeks," Beckham told writer Michael Kosser, "and I'm thinking, 'Damn, man, if I'm gonna get into the publishing business I gotta leave.'" The new hire persuaded Foster that a healthy Combine belonged among the action on Music Row. Foster agreed, but he made Beckham promise to get his okay if ever he wanted to pay a writer more than the average draw.

After orchestrating the move to 812 Seventeenth Avenue South, Beckham transformed Combine into a good ole boy salon when the workday ended. He opened his bar and office easy chairs to musicians and songwriters from all over town, characters such as Donnie Fritts, a staff writer associated with Arthur Alexander and other soul men;

Felton Jarvis, who produced Elvis Presley; and Texas-born songwriter Mickey Newbury, whose "Just Dropped In (To See What My Condition My Condition Was In)" was about to launch Kenny Rogers's career.

"It was Beckham that changed everything," says Kristofferson. "That office would be, at the end of every day, filled up with songwriters. Good ones. Guys that didn't even write for him, like Mickey, and Shel Silverstein. It was a place where everybody would get at the end of the day, sit and pass the guitar around, try and knock each other out."

The party carried on in the alley behind Combine, where songwriters smoked and gossiped and created mischief. "That was our world right there," declares Swan. "We were throwing knives one time and the knife blade went through the building to the little studio in there. We had to stop for a little while. . . . It was a fun time, really loose. No borders."

★   ★   ★

OUT IN HENDERSONVILLE, a telephone call from Bob Beckham rattled Foster's office. He was touting a new find named Kris Kristofferson, who, he said, had been writing for Buckhorn but needed a bigger draw. Of course, that meant an excursion out to the suburbs for the boss's okay.

In his vest and worn cowboy boots, Kris appeared an unusual sight in Hendersonville, especially next to the dapper Beckham. The sole of Kristofferson's right boot flapped away from the shoe when he walked, so Foster fished a thick rubber band from his desk and wrapped it around his foot. "I don't know what a songwriter was supposed to look like, but he didn't look like one to me, at least not one doing very well. But he was nice enough, and I just put my formula to work: if you came in wanting me to hear your songs, you'd have to sing four. Anyone might luck up and write one. Can't do it four times. Not possible."

Kristofferson recalls singing two songs, but confesses that the beer he had for breakfast may have erased the other two from memory.

"He sang the first song," continues Foster, "which is called 'To Beat the Devil,' which is half recitation. And he's not playing very good guitar! It was a little rough, and I'm listening to this thing. It's like watching a movie. I thought, 'Well that's really a great piece of material. Different.' The next song. I thought, 'Man, I know there's no way this guy can be this good.' Third song. And I thought, 'I must be hallucinating, sure as hell!' Nobody has ever come into my office before or since and laid four classic songs on me. And then he did 'Jody and the Kid.' So I said, 'Well, I'll approve the deal.'"

According to Foster, the other two songs were "Best of All Possible Worlds" and "Duvalier's Dream," which, like "Devil" and "Jody," indulged Kristofferson's passion for the rambling tale. Undoubtedly, the music dwelled on the fringes of Nashville's popular sounds, and featured smart turns of phrase and knowing maturity that Foster rarely heard from songwriters. "He just has such a way of putting it together that it all appeals to me," says Foster. "He's written songs that just tear me up, that may be not commercial, but who cares?"

But there was plenty to indicate that those songs could be commercial. Indeed, nursery-rhyme-simple verse still ruled the day in country music, but conspicuous exceptions marked by complexity of plot and imaginative characterization had already settled on the record charts: John Hartford's "Gentle on My Mind" (1967), Chris Gantry's "Dreams of the Everyday Housewife" (1968), Jimmy Webb's "Wichita Lineman" (1968), and, most recently, Tom T. Hall's "Margie's at the Lincoln Park Inn" (1969).

That day in Hendersonville, though, Foster discerned another dimension in Kristofferson. "I said, 'There is one condition.' His face kind of fell, and he said, 'What's that?' I said, 'If you'll sign with Monument as well, as an artist.' He said, 'What!? You're not serious? Man, I can't sing! I sound like a fucking frog!' I said, 'Perhaps . . . but a frog that can communicate is good enough for me.' So he said, 'Okay, if you're crazy enough to do it, I guess I am, too, then.' And so the next day, he got both contracts."

*   *   *

FOSTER SHARED A small office building with the great songwriters Felice and Boudleaux Bryant and their secretary, Bobby McKee, a woman whom Foster hadn't bothered getting to know. Not long after he signed Kris, he and Boudleaux were in the midst of closing an improbable deal involving a Mexican symphony and steel guitarist Jerry Byrd when Foster scurried down to Boudleaux's office instead of calling. Boudleaux playfully accused him of cooking up an excuse to see his secretary. "I had no idea in the world what he meant," pleads Foster. "I said 'What? Bobby? What're you talking about?' He said. 'Barbara. Bobby. Bobby McKee.' I said, 'Oh *yeah*. . . . Haven't you heard about me and Bobby McKee?'" And I dashed up the steps to my office."

At the same time, in spite of his spectacular audition, Kris had been moaning about a dry spell, so Foster threw him an *On the Road* concept starring "me and Bobby McKee," although Kris thought he heard him say "McGee." Kris hesitated, but agreed to think about it on his next shift in the helicopters over the Gulf of Mexico.

Kris picked up the story in an interview in 2009: "I went down and hid from him for about a month, and then this thing started comin' to me and I remember I was affected by the film *La Strada* that Fellini did. At the time I was flyin' around Baton Rouge and New Orleans. I came back up to Nashville and Billy [Swan] and I went in and put this thing on at this tiny studio at Combine and we stayed up all night doin' it, just the two of us in the studio all night long. He played the organ . . . and we overdubbed our voices many times."

Who before him in Nashville had ever tapped an Italian film for inspiration? Who else but Fred Foster would have accepted the result? "When I showed it to Fred the next day he was just ecstatic—he loved it," continued Kristofferson. "I split it with him. I gave him half. I remember Bob Beckham tellin' me, 'No! You can't do that. You can't split that.' And I said, 'Man, I wouldn'ta written it if he hadn'ta told me to.'"

Beckham knew that Fred would profit handsomely from the publishing alone. Not surprisingly, it was Beckham who made sure he did.

"Beckham was a big, big change," observes Kristofferson. "He pushed my songs in a way that I had not had done by a publisher, really, before that. He had the respect, I think, of the different A&R people on Music Row that if he said something was worth listening to, they listened to it. I hadn't worked with a publisher that was so in tune with the music. He was just totally devoted to finding good songs and pitching them."

"Me and Bobby McGee" finally passed under the nose of Roger Miller, country music's very own urbane wit and inspiration to young songwriters of the Combine set, not to mention the likes of Willie Nelson and Waylon Jennings. Miller glossed up the gritty story, which on paper seemed more inspired by 1969's *Easy Rider* than 1954's *La Strada*, and though it rose to the top twenty in the summer of 1969, Miller was not the vessel to carry an *Easy Rider* ethos. But he was the turning point in Kristofferson's career. Miller had claimed three Kristofferson songs, including "Bobby McGee," and in his wake, artists and producers flocked to the thirty-two-year-old songwriter. And while Nashville buzzed, Kristofferson took all that Roger Miller money and paid off his son's medical bills.

Beyond Miller, down the Nashville street, waited Johnny Cash, who could give Kristofferson a voice like no other.

★　　★　　★

JOHNNY CASH SNEERED at Nashville early in his career. He worshipped its idols—Hank Williams, Hank Snow, and Eddy Arnold—but he despised its institutions, primarily the *Grand Ole Opry*, which he believed scoffed at his Memphis roots. When Cash had gotten too big for Memphis in the late 1950s, he moved his family to California, a sure slap at Nashville, and in 1960, his hit "Smilin' Bill McCall" took aim at every fork-tongued publisher and record man in country music.

However, Cash gravitated toward Nashville in the late 1960s, most-ly because singer June Carter, whom he would marry in 1968, lived there. His headquarters became an apartment in Madison, a Nashville suburb, which he shared with Waylon Jennings, although neither one bunked there very much. "The thing about those two is that even when they were doing pills, they would hide them from each other," says Ha-zel Smith, then an employee in music industry offices and later a well-known columnist. "They would not, either one, ever admit they did pills. I know June would come over and clean up the house. I heard Waylon say that. So that was their way of life there for a while."

Their way of life spilled out onto the streets, too, such as one night outside Sue Brewer's when Billy Ray Reynolds was along for the ride. "Waylon had a brand-new limousine, the first car he bought after he moved to Nashville," says Reynolds. "He always wanted one of the Fleetwood limousines. Johnny Cash thought Waylon's pills were in his glove box and he came through and took a tire iron to pry it open, look-ing for pills. Waylon got sick to his stomach over that one."

Johnny and Waylon occasionally toured on the same package shows and, as Waylon's drummer Richie Albright knew, their pills came along for the ride. One night after a concert, Albright, for some forgotten reason, desperately needed Waylon and was banging on his hotel room door, which was next door to Cash's. The black-clad singer, who was uncharacteristically in his room, stuck his head out the door and offered to help. Albright: "He said, 'I'll tell you what, his bed is right on the other side over here.' He had this big bowie knife. He said, 'There's a picture right over the top of that bed. I bet I can cut the string through this wall.' So he stood back there and threw that damn knife at that wall, taking chunks out of that wall, sometimes it would stick for while. He was going to wake Waylon up by cutting that string."

Cash had joined country music's elite in the late 1950s, but several arrests, including a highly publicized pill bust in El Paso, Texas, not to mention his relentless hotel knife-throwing, jeopardized his career.

Since Hank Williams's tragic flameout in 1953, nobody in country music but Cash had been as popular or as reckless.

But 1968 marked a turning point in his personal life. Buoyed by the critical acceptance and astronomical sales of his surprise hit album *At Folsom Prison* as well as the wedding vows he'd won from June Carter, Cash crafted one of his career's sterling periods. At the core of those good days was ABC-TV's *Johnny Cash Show*. For three seasons (1969 to 1971) it lured national and international talent and cracked open its door just wide enough to let in a handful of unknown local artists looking for a break.

Cash insisted that the show be produced in Nashville, specifically at Ryman Auditorium; he had let go of his disdain for the venerable radio show and the city. Every episode announced to viewers Nashville's connection to one of entertainment's hottest performers and his wildly eclectic list of guests. Joni Mitchell visited, followed by Eric Clapton. Neil Young captivated viewers, and Bob Dylan cast a troubadour spell over them. For the first time in the eyes of the world—for Cash's show boasted an international audience—Nashville emanated cool.

"For a lot of people, Cash had sort of come out of nowhere," recalls Darrell Berger, then a student at Vanderbilt University. "But Cash and Dylan were kind of uncategorizable. And Cash especially was an outlaw before they had outlaws. I remember getting the record *At Folsom Prison*. I thought it was really great. Of course, he wore black and seemed not as slick as those other guys. I listened to him a lot on the jukebox in the bars when I was a little kid. So it was easy for me to take to him as he was going along." To young people like Berger, the Cash show appeared to be a counterculture refuge. But it was that and more: Cash's show staked out neutral ground. Old-timers from Cash's core audience—truck drivers, farmers, housewives—mingled in the Ryman's Confederate Gallery with the long-haired college students who shunned country music and would not have dreamed of visiting the Ryman but for their trust in Cash.

Bob Dylan's visit to Cash's first show stirred America's counterculture, inciting thoughtful reviews in *Rolling Stone* and New York's *Village Voice*. The folk icon had generally avoided public appearances since his motorcycle accident near Woodstock, New York, in July 1966 and even in his busiest days had rarely accepted invitations from network television. But he had emerged from the shadows at Cash's request, nodding to his base on both coasts and empowering his host's show with rock festival credibility.

Soon, a scene sprouted around it. Young songwriters, poets, and musicians haunted the Ryman backstage and hotel rooms and bars where the show's musicians and production staff dwelled, hoping to pitch a song or grab a guest spot or just meet Cash's guests. Kristofferson, who was around so much that he became something of a mascot, camped in the makeup artist's room, strumming his songs for any star who might be interested.

Once Kris figured out that Cash taped two shows a week, he persuaded Bob Beckham to increase his weekly draws and pay for a room at the Ramada Inn, which was the show's headquarters. "So we are having all these jam sessions and having time to pitch songs to people we couldn't ever see other than that," Kris revealed in a 1971 interview with *Rolling Stone*. "So we had just been sort of hanging around the Ramada, and like Buffy Ste.-Marie—we had a great jam with her one time, and she dug all this. In fact she cut [my] 'To Beat the Devil,' but never released it. We had a ball and made some really good friends."

Fellow Combine songwriter Donnie Fritts also appeared when production cranked up. Fritts had been one of the core figures of the Muscle Shoals, Alabama, music engine, with Dan Penn, David Briggs, Rick Hall, Billy Sherrill, and Spooner Oldham. He had cowritten the country-soul classic "Rainbow Road" and more recently the languid "Breakfast in Bed," which appeared on *Dusty in Memphis*, Dusty Springfield's masterpiece. When his friend Tony Joe White performed "Polk Salad Annie" on the Cash show, Fritts finally met the Man in Black. "We went out to his house one day and went fishing with John and his father. I never went fishing, but how're you going to turn that down? I didn't care a thing about fishing, but, God, fishing with Johnny Cash! It was just great."

Fritts would actually take to the stage as Kris Kristofferson's organist later on in the show's run, but in the first year he only played the so-called guitar pulls that sprang up whenever the show's hangers-on and guests sat down to rest at the Ramada Inn. Cash encouraged the jamming, frequently inviting folks to bring their guitars and new songs to his house on Old Hickory Lake after the day's filming had ended. "We'd all sit around in a big circle and show each other what we had," wrote Cash in his second autobiography. "Kris Kristofferson sang 'Me and Bobby McGee' for the first time on one of those nights, and Joni Mitchell 'Both Sides Now.' Graham Nash sang 'Marrakesh Express' and Shel Silverstein 'A Boy Named Sue.'"

In the autumn of 1970, the start of Cash's second season on the air, a reporter for the British tabloid *New Musical Express* found himself in a Spanish restaurant with a crowd of show people, including Joni Mitchell, producer Stan Jacobson, and Dennis Hopper, whose *Easy Rider* gave him white-hot credibility among the counterculture and who earlier in the evening had convincingly recited Rudyard Kipling's poem "If" on the Cash show. Hopper, no singer, had lugged a guitar into the restaurant and between gulps of sangria thrust it into the hands of songwriter Chris Gantry, who sang "Pentagon Bygone," and then he gave it to his current girlfriend, Michelle Phillips of the Mamas and the Papas, who belted out "Me and Bobby McGee." Bucky Wilkin, the son of Kristofferson's early sponsor Marijohn Wilkin, contributed, and Mickey Newbury followed. "It was now three in the morning," observed the reporter. "Hopper stood up and warmly thanked two people not present for bringing us all together—Kris Kristopherson [*sic*] and Johnny Cash."

Indeed, the Cash show was merely one scene in Nashville, but nobody could refute its influence. "It made everybody aware of the serious part of country music," observes Kris. "The part we all believed in."

In effect, Cash and his TV show had joined the civil rights heroes of earlier in the decade in communicating to America that the 1960s lived in Nashville. Yes, visitors would still find a less than sterling nightlife, a local government that enjoyed the status quo, and fundamentalist churches that preached rashly and acted slowly, but Nashville had exported to America the integration of public accommodations . . . and *The Johnny Cash Show*. And that had to be worth something.

★   ★   ★

WHEN THE CASH show debuted in 1969, Kristofferson still carried the dismissive letter from home in his wallet. Its creases turning white from years of folding and unfolding, it must have still sobered him while also sharpening his resolve. Jack Clement had told him to keep the letter in his pocket, that one day they'd run into Johnny Cash, who'd want to see it. "I'll introduce you to him," plotted Clement, "and I want you to whip out that letter and show him."

The day came when Kris found Cash in Clement's office, and, as instructed, he solemnly produced the letter. The son of an Arkansas cotton farmer, who knew something about parental rejection, read the mother's lines, and burst into deep guffaws. "He was laughing his ass off," says Clement. "It was a very intellectual kind of letter, well-chosen words. But just really putting him down." Clement reckons the letter bonded the two artists. From that moment, he recalls, Cash paid attention to Kristofferson and his songs.

Not that Kris wasn't trying on his own to pull at Cash's ear. During his stint changing lightbulbs at Columbia, Kristofferson had slipped demo tapes and lyrics sheets to Cash and June Carter. And according to a story that Cash told, and would have to be dismissed as apocryphal if only Kristofferson himself hadn't confirmed it in later years, the maverick songwriter rented a helicopter, landed it outside Cash's home in Hendersonville, and delivered more demo tapes. Kristofferson collided with the country music veteran at just the right time. As the 1960s came to an end, the star's songwriting productivity had plummeted. Now in constant demand on the road and on television, the man who had given the world "I Walk the Line" and "Five Feet High and Rising" could find neither the time nor the focus to repeat the writing glories of the past, and so he pulled Kristofferson deeper into his fold. "It was a beautiful thing Cash was doing," says songwriter Jim Casey. "It was hopeful especially when he took somebody like Kristofferson under his wing. Kris couldn't sing that well. Couldn't play very well but, God, his songs were just incredible. So that gave everybody hope that you didn't have to be a great singer."

In dramatic fashion so characteristic of Cash, he told Kris and another songwriting buddy Vince Matthews that he was taking them to Rhode Island for the Newport Folk Festival. And he wasn't just taking them; he was giving Kris a spot on his set. It was July 1969, and Roger Miller's "Me and Bobby McGee" was hitting the country charts.

The Newport lineup of 1969 was almost any music fan's dream. Bobby Bland, Muddy Waters, and Big Mama Thornton mingled with Bill Monroe, Mac Wiseman, and Don Reno. The producers even made room for folkies such as Pete Seeger and Ramblin' Jack Elliott, whose prominence at the festival had been reduced over the years to make room for the ticket-selling stars from other genres. The scene was nothing less than bucolic, according to the *New York Times*. "The breezy twang of country strings mingled with the cries of blues singers as audiences strolled from one group to another sampling musical styles or pausing to ask questions," wrote John S. Wilson.

Cash carried a huge revue with him to Newport, including his regulars the Carter Family, Carl Perkins, and Doug Kershaw. Making room for Kristofferson was bound to ruffle feathers among the organizers, but critic Wilson found him magnetic, though his name proved difficult to spell. "The most interesting of Mr. Cash's associates was Chris Christopherson, a lanky, boyish songwriter with an easy, persuasive vocal style, whose observant use of everyday imagery made 'Sunday Morning

Sidewalk' a particularly poignant portrait of loneliness." The correct title was "Sunday Morning Coming Down," and Cash himself would make it his own in 1970.

"If there was one thing that got my performing career started, that was it right there," says Kris. "And Cash was as scared as I was! It was so funny, he wanted me to go out and sing some songs before his set. And they didn't want me to. They said he just had so many minutes himself, so they didn't want me to take away from them. But he let me do two songs. *He made them let me do two songs.* And there was no looking back after that. It went over real well, and they put me on some afternoon shows that had different songwriters, like Joni Mitchell and James Taylor."

Matthews never took the stage, but back home in Nashville, Kris and Vince both trembled with excitement, jogging up Broadway to the rooming house where Billy Swan stayed and slept. "It was six o'clock in the morning," recalls Swan. "And Kris and Vince said, 'Hey Billy.' I had the little side [balcony] door open that faced the street. Kris said, 'John put me on at Newport, and I sang a couple of songs.'"

"He was going to make it," says Fred Foster of his new writer-recording artist. "But what Johnny really contributed to Kris was stability. Like, 'I've already been there and done that, son, don't worry about it. It's going to work out fine. You got a question, just sing it out and I'll holler an answer at you.' That's the way I saw it. They were very close friends."

★ *Four*

Nothing Left to Lose

JOHNNY CASH FORCED change on country music. His live albums recorded at Folsom and San Quentin prisons in the late 1960s became cultural statements like none ever heard in country music, while his television show shepherded rock, folk, and country into one place at the Ryman Auditorium. Country music could not help but pay attention. The industry also eyed Bob Dylan's Nashville session men and welcomed them into every studio around town while acknowledging Kris Kristofferson's mature and slightly elusive poetry, which defined a new style of songwriting in Nashville. Inevitably, the movement they stirred up reached the RCA studios, where Waylon Jennings and Willie Nelson still searched for solid footing.

Waylon's sessions featured alumni from Dylan's recordings and songs by the new writers such as Shel Silverstein (the poet and *Playboy* illustrator from Chicago), Mickey Newbury, and, yes, Kris Kristofferson.

Taking cues from Johnny Cash and Roger Miller, Waylon recorded no fewer than four Kristofferson songs in late 1969 and early 1970, including "To Beat the Devil," about a man's jocular encounter with the forces of darkness. Waylon painted the song with authenticity that could only come from a childhood in poverty and ten years of hard living on the road; indeed, it was one of the first times anybody could sit back and say, "Waylon nailed that one."

For the time being, Chet Atkins had stepped aside on Waylon's sessions, bringing in producers Felton Jarvis, who supervised Elvis, and Danny Davis, a New York veteran who had produced Connie Francis and Nina Simone. The association with Davis, who couldn't ignore the fresh breezes in Nashville, yielded the sterling Kristofferson cuts as well as a flirtatious cover of Chuck Berry's "Brown-Eyed Handsome Man," a top-five country hit in 1969, and a murder ballad titled "Cedartown, Georgia" that wouldn't be released until 1971. Davis also circled back to Chet's old folk strategy, piloting the album *Country-Folk*, which paired Waylon with the Kimberlys, a Las Vegas–based vocal group, on numbers such as Jimmy Webb's "MacArthur Park," which even the birds would agree is neither country nor folk. To say the least, it was an unusual outing that sprouted from Waylon's romance with Verna Gay Kimberly.

Waylon recalled that he'd been attracted to "MacArthur Park," which the Kimberlys regularly performed in their act, and brought it back to Davis. "Danny and I got into it a couple of times over the arrangement," said Waylon. "I knew exactly what I wanted the strings to do; I had to hum the parts. He probably had his own ideas. But the single got into the country Top Twenty Five that fall, and when the Grammys came around, it won for Best Country Performance by a Duo or Group. By then, everybody was more than happy to claim it was their idea." Nothing recorded before or after in Waylon's discography sounded like this album. Monstrous orchestral arrangements alternated with a cheery folk sound that echoed the Seekers, Australia's pop-folk sensation. Think "Georgy Girl." In fact, Jennings and the Kimberlys wheeled out "A World of Our Own," the Seekers' big 1965 hit.

Despite the Grammy, the album soon receded into country music trivia. Only the head-butting between Davis and Jennings lingered in memory. "Waylon liked Danny but the chemistry wasn't there," recalls Billy Ray Reynolds, who was touring with Waylon but not recording with him yet. "He was a good guy but he had a little bit more of a New York attitude than Waylon was accustomed to. They do things differently up there. They don't pull their punches." Over the years, Waylon planted a myth over his relatively minor disagreements with Davis, casting the producer as an antagonist in his own anti-establishment outlaw story. He liked to talk about threatening Danny Davis with a firearm, but Reynolds argues that it flat out never happened. Reynolds had been holding a pair of nickel-plated Colt revolvers for Waylon, and after a year or two, Waylon asked him to bring them to the next session, which Davis happened to be producing. "So I brought them in and gave them to him," says Reynolds. "And all he did was have them out, and he was showing them. That story got so misconstrued, how he pulled the gun." In his autobiography, Waylon wrote that it was Merle Haggard who had returned the guns. But Reynolds knows better.

Funny enough, the music never betrayed Waylon's real or imagined frustrations with Davis. Once they got past the *Country-Folk* album, their marriage produced a gutsy string of honky-tonk favorites and modern ballads that sounded as if the late 1960s had been permitted to enter the RCA studio. Most important, Waylon appeared to have found his voice. Whether Davis had anything to do with that or not, the Davis-produced tracks showcase deeply riveting vocals amid bold instrumentation on starkly realistic songs, many of which appeared on *The Taker/ Tulsa* and *Cedartown, Georgia* albums, both released in 1971. Because RCA-Nashville failed to embrace the idea of the concept album, it happily dropped unreleased scraps from earlier sessions into those collections, spoiling any semblance of cohesion that they might have had.

★   ★   ★

BY THE LATE 1960s, Willie Nelson's recordings also exhibited new maturity, although they, too, were not packaged in concept albums, the new trend sweeping popular music. It's not that RCA was oblivious: Elvis Presley's recent Memphis albums expressed a clear and unified vibe, for example, as did collections by other RCA artists such as Jefferson Airplane and Jose Feliciano. Closer to home, Chet had okayed Bobby Bare's memory trip *A Bird Named Yesterday* (1967) and Porter Wagoner's *Confessions of a Broken Man* (1966) and *Soul of a Convict* (1967), a likely influence on Johnny Cash's *At Folsom Prison* album. But as the 1960s dimmed, the record company neither encouraged nor accepted album-length statements from Waylon and Willie.

In late 1967, Willie, in his bleating, wistful way, had recorded a set of starkly beautiful ballads, including the classic "Sweet Memories," written by Mickey Newbury, but RCA appeared flummoxed in response, slotting them in an album called *Good Times* next to syrupy Nashville Sound material recorded at earlier sessions. Its cover splashed with a comical pose—Willie on a putting green with a cutie in sandals and short skirt—the album hit the stores in late 1968, contrasting sadly with the calculated sophistication of Glen Campbell's smash albums and the danger of Johnny Cash's *At Folsom*. All in all, Willie seemed absurdly out of touch with the market.

Still, the late 1960s and early 1970s hinted at a coming of age in Willie's recordings. Danny Davis and Felton Jarvis, while tinkering with Waylon's recordings, appeared at Willie's sessions with ideas that Chet never had, inserting a tasteful production that owed more to the irresistible modern sounds of a California session than to the Nashville Sound. Dylan alumni—Charlie McCoy, Wayne Moss, and Pete Drake—came over from Waylon's sessions and joined other new hot pickers such as Roy Huskey Jr., David Briggs, and Norbert Putnam. And for the first time in years, Willie's drummer Paul English and steel guitarist Jimmy Day returned to Willie's sessions.

Willie's own songs were as pleasing as ever, at home in a coffeehouse or a honky-tonk, but now they appeared next to his covers of other great songs of the day: Joni Mitchell's "Both Sides Now," Fred Neil's "Everybody's Talkin'," and James Taylor's "Fire and Rain." His interpretation of Kris Kristofferson and Shel Silverstein's "Once More with Feeling" on the *Both Sides Now* album was a perfect alignment of stars in early 1970s Nashville: the seasoned singer and the blossoming songwriters shone brightly.

The Abbott, Texas, native also got caught up in the wave of station-wagon songs that motored into country music. Narratives that dealt with heartbreak and self-doubt in a suburban setting, they proved to be the unintended consequence of Chris Gantry's "Dreams of the Everyday Housewife," not to mention the confessional honesty of Kristofferson's music. This was the stuff of Frank Sinatra's *Watertown* album and Elvis Presley's "Don't Cry Daddy." Even Waylon explored domestic angst with "The House Song," written by Paul Stookey and Robert Bannard, while Eddy Arnold crooned about visitation rights in "Wait for Sunday," by Glenn McGuirt. Willie considered the bittersweetness of raising kids alone in "Little Things," and wandered through an empty tract home in "She's Still Gone," both cowritten with his then-wife, Shirley. The songs must have given pause to husbands and fathers during their commute to work or to the mothers and wives leaving the house for their first job, as so many women had begun to do in the late 1960s and early 1970s. They announced a curious new maturity in country music, but predicted the tug-at-your-family-feelings drivel that deluged the market thirty years later.

Just like Waylon, Willie's vocals nestled into a comfort zone during the Nixon years. They danced with fluidity, unconcerned now with enunciating every edge around the syllables. In 1970, he opened

Both Sides Now with freewheeling arrangements of "Crazy Arms" and "Wabash Cannonball," announcing that the feel of his dance hall days were about to do-si-do into the RCA studios. His newly liberated voice soared on gospel-inspired tracks and classic honky-tonkers "I Gotta Get Drunk" and "Bloody Mary Morning," and would reverberate through all of his future work. In the short term, though, RCA failed to capitalize.

★   ★   ★

IN THE LATE 1960s and early 1970s, Columbia Records plastered Johnny Cash all over the rock-and-roll market while Monument carved out a place for Kristofferson among young buyers in rock *and* country, but RCA continued to think of Waylon and Willie as fodder for the old-line country audience, ignoring younger music fans who snubbed the Nashville Sound. Paul Worley—who would produce the likes of the Nitty Gritty Dirt Band and Lady Antebellum in later decades—was one of those younger fans who might have embraced Waylon's and Willie's cooler tracks had RCA marketed the singers to him. "I didn't know there was a Music Row," he says. "I lived all my life in Nashville, all of it. I went to Vanderbilt and never knew, never heard, had no consciousness of Music Row. I remember going downtown and watching *The Johnny Cash Show* when it was taped down at the Ryman Auditorium, but it was Johnny Cash and he wasn't country, right? He was Johnny Cash. I still shunned country music as far as what was mainstream country, because mainstream was really hillbilly or nasally, in my view, or it was that country-politan kind of pop, really kind of a throwback to the pop out of New York and L.A. of the previous era. So to me that stuff was pretty square. I wanted to rock, or I wanted to soul, or I wanted to acoustify, like Richie Havens. I loved him."

Courtesy of Metropolitan Government Archives of Nashville and Davidson County

Cotten Music Center on Twenty-First Avenue South in Hillsboro Village.

Worley fed his musical hungers in the West End, combing the racks in Sgt. Pepper's record store and the instruments in Cotten Music Center, both located on Twenty-First Avenue South in Hillsboro Village. The music business he knew there rocked like a blues jam compared with the button-down atmosphere two miles away on Music Row. "I started taking guitar lessons [at Cotten] in '65," he recalls. "By '66 I was working there, and by '67 I was teaching there, teaching guitar. We would see everybody from the chitlin' circuit, artists like Freddie Waters and Jimmy Church. These people would come in once a week, and put their money down for their guitar or their bass or their PA or whatever, and they would hang around and play. Sometimes I would have to get in the car with Tom Malone who worked there and go repo. We would have to go to the South Side Lounge over on Nolensville Road and walk in and at least threaten to repo the PA system unless we got our money. I am scared shitless. You walk into a club with a sign on the door that says, 'Leave all guns at the door.' And I am sitting there going, 'Well, I ain't got a gun. I am the only fool around here who doesn't have one. I better bring one so I can leave it at the door.' So I walk in with Tom, and [the proprietor] opens up his briefcase and I am thinking he is going to pull out a gun. . . . He pulls out a wad of money and gave us our money, and on we go.

"Cotten's was a great place because it was where I met John Hiatt; it was where I met Lenny Breau, a great jazz legend. Lenny Breau would come and hang out with Chet Atkins and hang out with Dick Cotten, who was a great jazz guitarist, and they would do gigs around town and Lenny would hang around the music store. . . . Across the street was the Pancake Pantry. Mr. Baldwin, who owned the place, was an older guy and I remember walking in one day and he said, 'You can't come in here.' And I said, 'Mr. Baldwin, it's me. I come in here all the time.' He said, 'Not with that long hair and all that stuff.' So he wouldn't let in hippies anymore. He decided he was not going to let you in if you had long hair."

★   ★   ★

MANY WHITES IN the old town still clung to their segregated neighborhoods and institutions, including the public schools, whose integration had begun with some promise in the 1950s, only to stall in the 1960s. By 1970, a stubborn dividing line marked racial territory in the schools, prompting a federal court to order Nashville to dramatically accelerate desegregation. Mayor Beverly Briley, who had succeeded the pragmatic Ben West in 1962, was defiant. "The courts should stay out of education, and education should stay out of the courts," he railed. But it was no use: Briley and Nashville bowed to the courts and implemented a controversial busing plan.

As if the court's scolding were not enough, corruption and urban decay worthy of a Lincoln Steffens exposé plagued the city. When federal investigators realized that raids on illegal gambling joints coordinated with Nashville police frequently came up dry, they found that many cops on the vice squad were on the take. In addition, news stories about fishy dealings in the sheriff's office and in the chambers of council members furiously rolled off the presses, some of them written by a young *Tennessean* newspaper reporter named Al Gore Jr.

Dilapidation pocked virtually every sector of the city. Lower Broadway near the Ryman Auditorium in downtown became the preserve of winos, prostitutes, and cheap souvenir shops, while white flight hastened the collapse of many once-prosperous neighborhoods. Music Row—a quiet residential area in earlier years—deteriorated, too. Vacant houses wild with overgrowth multiplied as the music industry looked on in horror.

Music Row neighborhood in decline.

The streets in and around Music Row fanned out in a southwesterly direction to the nearby Vanderbilt University neighborhood, where students and hungry musicians taking advantage of cheap rents found creativity, liberation from tired ideals, and hip fashion. While the city buckled under urban decline and Old South rigidity, many of the young people in the West End introduced at street level the ethos of the 1960s, just as the decade was coming to a close. They were outlaws, recalling the spirit of the lunch-counter demonstrators, testing the boundaries that family and society had erected and stirring up a countercultural mood that would soon drift into the beige-painted hallways of Music Row, where people like Waylon Jennings waited.

★   ★   ★

THE VANDERBILT UNIVERSITY community, which had leaned toward the establishment in matters such as the Vietnam War and civil rights, was fast taking up the torch lit by segregation protestors Diane Nash and John Lewis. In 1969, the Vanderbilt chapter of Students for a Democratic Society (SDS) organized peacefully against navy ROTC activities on campus. But the peace wouldn't last and protests sharpened in May 1970 when Ohio National Guardsmen killed four Vietnam War protestors at Kent State University. "The students were morally outraged," says Paul Worley, who had entered Vanderbilt in 1969, "and we were already very much against the war and against the administration that was perpetrating the war. The idea that someone called in the Guard and killed college students who were just protesting blew our minds and instilled in us distrust for authority and fear and paranoia about Big Brother and big government."

By the morning of May 5, 1970, the day after the shootings, the Vanderbilt SDS had blanketed the campus with fliers calling for demonstrations. "They were going to burn a flag on the quad," recounts Lewis Shiner, a sophomore at Vanderbilt at the time of the protest. "And that got pretty hairy. Campus security was there, and they kept it from turning violent, but there was a pretty good shouting match." Within days, hundreds of students abandoned the classrooms to continue protesting, and faculty members voted in a two-week suspension of classes so the Vanderbilt community could get out the vote for local "peace candidates."

"We did a lot of community organizing," says Shiner. "I know a bunch of guys went out to factories and dropped leaflets there. Some kids got beat up. I don't think they were seriously injured, but those factory people did not want to be getting that kind of propaganda.

What I did was cut my hair and put on a tie and went downtown with a bunch of people trying to get petitions signed against the war. No one in my group was physically attacked, but there was a lot of resistance. We weren't getting a bunch of signatures. I remember this one group of guys pulled up in a convertible and asked what I was doing. I told them I was petitioning, so they grabbed the clipboard and drove off. Cops were following us around, like crawling along behind us as we walked. I started out saying, 'Would you care to sign this petition for peace,' and later I was just saying, 'Peace?' And people were shaking their head. 'No peace. No peace. Not interested.'"

Lewis Shiner's pass to the Vanderbilt world.

★   ★   ★

THE MOOD OF Vanderbilt's very own Prague Spring drifted across the West End, creating an appetite among young people for Kris Kristofferson's genre-smashing songs and awakening the consciousness of Waylon Jennings, who began injecting realism into his recordings. Johnny Cash went as far as to film an episode of his television show at Vanderbilt, where he met students who inspired him to write his own protest anthem, "Man in Black."

Denizens of Music Row merely had to walk by the school's grounds to see that change was the order of the day. "The entire campus was painted with psychedelia; some of the most wonderful artwork that I have ever seen existed in the tunnel between Towers One, Two, Three, and Four," explains Paul Worley. "It was like walking through an M. C. Escher painting." The Vanderbilt Student Arts Alliance sponsored art exhibits, poetry readings, and musical performances (including one by a gawky coed named Marshall Chapman and a mellow maverick based in Nashville named Jimmy Buffett). Nationally known musical acts such as Parliament Funkadelic, the Grateful Dead, Poco, the James Gang, Commander Cody, Sun Ra, and the Allman Brothers Band visited the university, replacing Skeeter Davis, the Platters, and bland Motown bands.

Student Michael Minzer encountered jazzman Roland Kirk, who played an open-air concert on Neely Lawn. "Since I had a car, I was enlisted to go pick him up at the airport," says Minzer. "And that was one of the most amazing experiences I had, meeting an artist of that caliber and getting to interact with him for two days, three days. I remember him wandering around with this fantastic spirit cane that he had, with a little caster on the bottom, feathers hanging off of it, and sort of talking to no one in particular. I remember him saying, 'If I was the Allman Brothers, you'd be lined up here for three miles to hear me play.'"

They lined up for home-grown Vanderbilt talent, too. In the campus coffeehouses, on Neely Lawn, at fraternity houses, or under the oak trees at nearby city parks, students gathered to hear the local rock bands, folksingers, and bluegrass pickers. "There were musicians everywhere," observes Minzer. "I can recall walking into music stores and just sitting down and joining in jams with guys that were fantastic players. It was very underground in the sense that no one knew where or how to get to the big time." Minzer, who played bass and sang, and fellow student Lewis Shiner, who drummed, formed a cover band called the Other Side, while Paul Worley pulled together the Vandy-centered band Just Friends.

Courtesy of Vanderbilt University Special Collections and University Archives

Vandy students enjoy a campus concert.

Just Friends sponged up the sound and energy of the Buffalo Springfield and the Who, as well as the big rhythm-and-blues vibe of Wilson Pickett and James Brown, to build an impressive following at Vanderbilt and beyond in the early 1970s. They pulsed with the times, and their superior sound system gave them an edge in the boisterous fraternity houses and bars. By the time Worley graduated in 1973, the band counted audiences of four and five hundred wherever they appeared. "During the summer, things would dry up for us because school would be out," says Worley. "You could go park at a Holiday Inn lounge on West End Avenue, but you had to play top forty and it was just hell. We found a gay bar at the corner of Fifth and Lee. It was called the Other Side, and they loved our music. And by then we were throwing in some jazz and fusion and stuff, Stevie Wonder. They would let us play whatever we wanted to play and then on the break the jukebox would come on and they would get out on the floor and dance to their favorite songs, but they liked us. I remember one night I was playing, and I looked up and out on the dance floor was my mother and her best friend dancing."

The musicians in Just Friends led a small troop of Vanderbilt scholars graduating into Nashville's wider music community. Marshall Chapman, Woody Chrisman, and Doug Green—all of whom would later thrive in the city's music industry—found stages around town, as did Randy Scruggs, who studied at Vanderbilt while emerging as an in-demand session artist (appearing on many of Waylon's records) and a more-than-worthy heir to his father Earl's musical tradition. Pennsylvania native Dick Bay, a 1970 graduate in philosophy, failed to rise as high as Scruggs and Chapman, but the bands he joined embodied the town-grown pollination that nourished Nashville's underground music scene and drifted to the edges of Music Row.

Courtesy of Vanderbilt University Special Collections and University Archives

An antiwar protestor at Vanderbilt.

Bay played piano with his group Dick Bay and the Bay Area Bombers, which also featured songwriter John Hiatt on bass. Proffering a country-blues sound with a heavy dependence on original numbers by Hiatt, the band played Vanderbilt's Graduate Student Pub and a black joint called Rufus Carter's Place in Mount Juliet, east of the city, where it found a reverse image of black R&B band performances at Vandy frats. Tracy Nelson's Mother Earth—which was based in Nashville at the time—played there, too.

Dick Bay of the Babushka Brothers.

Courtesy of Dick Bay

"It was pretty much local-locals," recalls Bay. "The clientele was pretty much all black. So we and whatever entourage we brought with us from Vanderbilt were the only white folks there. And it was very much out in the country. The only heat was a potbelly stove. It had pool tables in one area and then the bandstand, such as it was. At least once a night Rufus Carter managed to grab hold of the microphone and he'd go off on some long tangent, which usually started with 'This band gon' play tonight!' And then he'd go off talking about God knows what. Usually somewhere in there he'd sing 'You Are My Sunshine.'"

Finally, the band disintegrated over creative differences, sending Hiatt off to a prosperous singer-songwriting career. "I remember him as a very nice and humble fellow," says Darrell Berger, a Vandy student who hung with the band, "yet someone who was very aware of how talented he was, and he fully expected to make it big, though he didn't know how or when back then."

The Bay Area Bombers morphed into a gypsy-rock jug band called the Babushka Brothers, which replaced Rufus Carter's Place with the Exit/In on its itinerary. The Exit/In had opened in the fall of 1971, pasting inaugural ads in the *Vanderbilt Hustler* that earnestly pledged to offer "really good music" in a quiet setting with plenty of Budweiser and Michelob on tap and, with a subversive wink, "a whole bunch of munchies." Nestled on Elliston Place, which was a short dash across West End Avenue from campus, the club's first advertisement in the *Hustler* touted Lana Chapel, a singer-songwriter on staff at Combine Music, and David Allan Coe, a menacing character whom many students saw cruising the streets in a black hearse and jamming in nearby Centennial Park. In time, Kris, Willie, and Waylon took turns on the club's stage.

The Babushka Brothers reached their pinnacle as part of a two-day festival at the Nashville War Memorial Auditorium in the summer of 1972. "We were playing with a whole bunch of other people, a lot of whom were names at the time within that singer-songwriter circle," says Bay. "The headliners were Mac Gayden's Nameless Band, Dianne Davidson and Friends, Chris Gantry's Turkey Farm Surprise, Jay Bolotin, John Hyatt, and Rich Mountain Tower." When the festival closed, the band disintegrated. Few people remembered the Babushka Brothers after their demise, but they forged another link—as did Just Friends—between the rock-and-folk–influenced creative spirit that had taken root at Vanderbilt and the musical revolution slowly permeating the rest of Nashville.

Courtesy of author's collection

Advertisement for the Exit/In, 1971.

Handbill plugging a Nashville music festival.

★ ★ ★

KRIS KRISTOFFERSON EMBODIED the independence and the happy mingling of various styles that marked Nashville's musical scene. Among the more ambitious young musicians, Kris was proof that money and fame could accompany artistic freedom. Unlike any Nashville-based artist, he climbed to prominence in long hair and corduroy pants, recording his own songs without any particular allegiance to a set of country music standards. "He was my milepost," says singer-songwriter Guy Clark, who hit town in 1971. "He wrote in a way that no one had ever heard before. Or you thought you'd heard it, but it was the first time you heard it. Kris has a real respect for the language, a student of poetry and a poet himself."

Kristofferson's unscheduled debut at the Newport Folk Festival in 1969 heralded the coming of his recording career. "Suddenly, I was a performer," says Kris. "It amazes me that I wasn't more amazed at the time. But that's the way my life was going. I fell out of grace with the helicopter company, and all of a sudden great things were happening. Ray Price got my 'For the Good Times.' We had a studio full of musicians [at his session]! Violins and everything! Nobody had ever paid that much attention to anything of mine before."

In 1970, Fred Foster released Kris's eponymously titled debut album. Produced with session musicians outside A-list circles, it communicated eclecticism and spontaneity: talking blues appeared next to tender ballads next to unhinged jams. His vocals, though unspectacular, recalled the purring swagger of Jim Morrison and the hijinks of Roger Miller while the arrangements tapped the jug-band styling of the Mamas and the Papas and the Bob Dylan of *Highway 61 Revisited*. On top of everything, the songwriter's wordplay sparkled, like on "Duvalier's Dream," which spun repartee between the words "woman" and "man" and to great effect repeatedly invoked the idea of believing:

> *It's hard to keep believing when you know you've been deceived / To face a lie and dare to try again / But there's nothing like a woman with a spell of make-believe / To make a new believer of a man.*

"*Kristofferson* is a superb album," cheered *Rolling Stone*. "Kris shows plenty of versatility—from a rousing gospel chant, 'Blame It on the Rolling Stones' . . . to tender mellow things like 'Casey's Last Ride' and 'For the Good Times' to rockin' country stuff like 'Best of All Possible Worlds.' His lyrics are always right; he can be bitter, cynical when he has to be, then turn around and be poetically pretty without being saccharine."

The album hit the streets in June 1970, coinciding with an excit-

ing engagement at the Troubadour nightclub in Los Angeles, where he
would open for Linda Ronstadt. A staffer on *The Johnny Cash Show*—
on which Kris had appeared in April—knew folks who booked the chic
spot and had sent them the Cash protégé's music on audiotape. Kris
hastily mined the Combine world for a band: Donnie Fritts on organ,
Dennis Linde on guitar, and Billy Swan on bass. "One day Kris came
in the office at Combine, stomping and saying, 'Somebody backed out
of playing guitar at the Troubadour,'" says Swan. "I was the only one in
the office and I knew that Dennis Linde was going and playing bass, so
I said, 'Kris, look, I'll play bass. It's only the top four strings of a guitar.
We'll get Dennis to play guitar.' And he said, 'Great.'"

Courtesy of Sony Music Entertainment

Kristofferson onstage.

The fabled West Hollywood club showcased the cream of California's country-rock pioneers as well as singer-songwriter travelers from
the East Coast. In addition to Ronstadt, artists like the Byrds, Buffalo
Springfield, Neil Young, and James Taylor basked in the acclaim of

Troubadour gigs. "That was the place to go in L.A. at the time," says Donnie Fritts.

After a few nights, says Fritts, the crowds swarmed to Kris. "The lines were around the building, just trying to get in to see Kris. And Kris was the opening act, you know! But all these movie people were there. Word got around fast that there was somebody very special there in town. People wanted to be a part of it one way or another." Barbra Streisand showed up after reading an ecstatic review of Kristofferson's performance, but the newcomer wasn't around to greet her. "I had been out with [Dennis] Hopper the night before," confessed Kristofferson in 1997, "and I fell asleep in the parking lot. When I woke, it was dark, and I was supposed to be onstage." Streisand returned two nights later and she found him where he was supposed to be. By the second week, according to Billy Swan, Ronstadt opened for Kristofferson.

The Troubadour vibrations opened the doors to more club dates in cities around the country and made a place for Kris on bills with country rockers on the West Coast. In California, Kris also met Janis Joplin, with whom he had a brief affair before shoving off with the band—which by now included former Lovin' Spoonful guitarist Zal Yanovsky—to play the Isle of Wight festival and the Bitter End in New York. Kris also played Carnegie Hall to rapturous reviews and collected the Country Music Association's Song of the Year award for "Sunday Morning Coming Down." A *New York Times Magazine* feature story in December 1970 proclaimed that Kris was the "New Nashville Sound."

"We weren't prepared for what happened with Kris, and Kris was not prepared," says Fritts. "We started performing in June of 1970; by August we were playing in front of six hundred thousand people at the Isle of Wight festival. We in no way were really prepared for that. If we had to fill out something that [asked about our profession], everyone of us would have said, 'songwriter,' even Kris. That's what he is, he's a songwriter. Everything happened because he was a songwriter.

"I loved the way he sang," admires Fritts. "I loved the honesty of his singing. You know, you get 'Sunday Morning Coming Down': hell, the best record you're going to hear on that is Kris Kristofferson because he's so honest and true. So no matter how bad the band sounded—and believe me, we were not that good—it didn't matter because Kris Kristofferson was singing 'Sunday Morning Coming Down' and all these absolutely brilliant songs. . . . Sometimes, if you get a hot band, people start listening to that shit more than they do the songs, but they weren't listening to licks with us, because we couldn't play any! We could play the melody, the chords."

In October, Kris and the band had landed back in California and were playing a show in Carmel when word came down that Janis Joplin had died in Los Angeles at the Landmark Hotel after a night of hard partying. Either Joplin's producer, Paul Rothchild, or her friend Bobby Neuwirth also told Kris that Janis had recorded "Me and Bobby McGee" shortly before she died. He was devastated. "I lived with her, slept with her, but it wasn't a love affair," he told an interviewer in 1997. "I loved her like a friend. She was very soulful, a passionate person but very childlike to me, a little girl in dress-up clothes. She was an unhappy person. Even though she was fun to be around, she felt that the only thing that made her attractive to the world was her art, her talent, her stardom. And she was intelligent enough to know that it was temporary."

A few weeks later, he arrived back in Nashville from the road to find Joplin's posthumously released *Pearl* album in his mailbox at Combine. It was night, and he had not yet heard her roof-raising treatment of "Me and Bobby McGee," so he and Donnie Fritts found an empty turntable. "He listened to it over and over again," says Fritts, "because he felt like this was going to be a real big record, you know. He was going to be hearing it, and he wanted to get used to hearing it just by himself. Well, we wrote a song with her in mind that night. 'Why was she born so black and blue' is how we started. Of course, 'Epitaph' is the name of the song. When we wrote the song, I did it with just very simple chord changes. But when I got home, I added all these R&B passing chords.

It would not change the melody, but it would just put it a little bit somewhere else.

"The next morning we were in the studio, and I got Kris over to this piano. I'll never forget, it was a Wurlitzer. And I showed him what I had done. Well, I didn't know Fred Foster was in the control room. He said, 'That is what I want to hear on this record, exactly the way you did it. I don't want anything else on the record. I just want you two.' Later on, I think they put strings on the last verse."

The tribute to Joplin ended up on Kristofferson's second album, *The Silver Tongued Devil and I*, which hit the country charts in October 1971. "There has never been, and probably never will be a better song-writer album," raved the critic Dave Hickey in *Country Music* magazine. "I don't see how Kristofferson is ever gonna write a better batch of songs; the material here will create such demands on him that he will never have the peace or the time again."

Kristofferson turned country music on its ear: "That Silver Haired Daddy of Mine" of yore giving way to the Silver Tongued Devil, a Nashville jumping jack flash. Young fans of the album connected tracks such as "The Pilgrim-Chapter 33" and "Breakdown (A Long Way from Home)" with a general theme about the border between conformity and outlaw life. But Kristofferson doubts that he was building a concept album. "I can't really remember," he admits. "I know at the time, I was just trying to put together my best songs in a way that all made sense." He suggests that life was moving too fast at the time to even contemplate a concept album. "It was like I had stepped onto a train or something, and it was going. And I was just going along, trying to stay ahead of it! Trying to do what I'd been doing for four years or whatever, trying to put together music that made sense and just keep doing what I was doing. I'm really kind of amazed by it all, looking back. I was doing things instinctually, and I'm glad it turned out as good as it did. It was like all of a sudden being treated like someone! It could have been easy for me to fall off of whatever wagon I was on there. Things kept breaking my way, getting in films—and all that happened when I was working at the Troubadour. Any one of those things would have been enough, but then it just kept going on and kept working."

At the Troubadour—as Kris indicates—he encountered Hollywood, and met the actors Harry Dean Stanton and Dennis Hopper as well as the young director Bill Norton. Hopper engaged him to appear briefly in his film *The Last Movie*, while Norton immediately pegged his star potential, tallying up the singer's rugged sensitivity, intelligence, and quarterback good looks.

Norton gave Kristofferson the title role in *Cisco Pike*, a movie about an ex-rock musician just out of prison who's lured back into the underworld by a corrupt narcotics agent. His costars—Gene Hackman, Stanton, and the ubiquitous Karen Black—came highly recommended, but even so, the movie failed to capture the audiences who'd been attracted to such films as *Easy Rider* or *Midnight Cowboy*. *Rolling Stone*'s Ralph J. Gleason was a lonely voice in its corner. "Kris Kristofferson surprised me by turning out to be as good an actor as he is a singer, at least in this role. . . . Kristofferson has just the right touch of beat to him to play the role of Cisco, driving and driven inexorably to what we know from the moment we see him on screen to be a tragic end."

Cisco Pike's quick fade from theaters was of no consequence to Kristofferson, for soon film offers rained down. Over the next three years, he starred in three major productions: *Pat Garrett and Billy the Kid*, *Blume in Love*, and *Alice Doesn't Live Here Anymore*. And he appeared as a biker in the 1974 thriller *Bring Me the Head of Alfredo Garcia*. What's even more amazing is that these films were made by the leaders of the new director-centered Hollywood. Iconoclastic filmmakers Sam Peckinpah (*Pat Garrett* and *Alfredo Garcia*) and Martin Scorsese (*Alice Doesn't Live Here Anymore*) apparently saw in Kristofferson the naturalism and intensity that their styles demanded.

Young musicians in Nashville could pick up the godhead pop music journal *Rolling Stone* and read about their hometown hero recruiting Bob Dylan to act in Peckinpah's *Pat Garrett and Billy the Kid* and then chiding Dylan in a Mexican studio as the folksinger haphazardly recorded the soundtrack music. Who recruited Dylan to do anything? And then chide him? It was too cool for words.

Kris was Nashville's very own Dylan, a quiet balladeer whose quick connection with the hip big-city nightclubs and Hollywood directors somehow—like the Cash TV show—endorsed the city. Youth culture was afoot in the Western world, and Kris symbolized Nashville's contribution to it. The city seemed poised to move past the Lefty Frizzells, Eddy Arnolds, and Porter Wagoners of the old guard and embrace a younger man with shoulder-length hair who wrote like a poet and charmed the northeastern media elite. "I'll never forget seeing *Look* magazine," says Donnie Fritts. "That's when *Look* magazine was real big. And he was on the cover. Things really had changed. You don't see Hank Snow and those other cats that've been there for years [in magazines]. You know what I mean? Ain't nothing against them, but here was a new guy, young guy. Here was the new thing coming out of Nashville, and Kris was the head of it."

Fred Foster had bet on Kristofferson pushing Monument to the vanguard of Nashville creativity, filling the void that Orbison had left five years earlier, and energizing his cash flow. It also gave him the satisfaction of rebuking his two partners in Monument—minority shareholders—who had protested the company's deal with Kris. One partner, speaking for both, had argued that the helicopter pilot would crash to the ground. "And it just dawned on me," says Foster, "this is never going to work. I said, 'I want to make you all a proposition. We'll get a third party in and decide a fair market value of your stock, and I'll buy you out. Or I will dissolve the company this afternoon and re-form it tomorrow without you in it. And you get nothing. But you no longer work here.' They laughed and said, 'Okay, fine. You'll see. He'll break your ass.'" Foster allowed that Kris might just do that, but he promptly bought out the partners anyway.

"And so the day rolled around when the *Billboard* story came out that Kristofferson was the first songwriter to have four Million-Air performance awards from BMI in one year. I clipped it out and photocopied it and sent it to them."

*As my country no longer requires my services, I have made
up my mind to go to Texas.*

—Davy Crockett

 Five

With Purpose
Down There

DESPITE WINNING THE Grammy for "MacArthur Park" in 1969, Waylon continued to grouse about RCA's control over his recording activities. "Chet knew I wanted to make my own records," complained Waylon in his autobiography. "He opposed that mainly because RCA had several producers, and if he started letting artists like myself and Bobby Bare produce themselves, he'd lose some people he was very fond of, like [producers] Bob Ferguson and Ray Pennington."

In 1970, Chet actually lost producer Danny Davis, who left RCA to focus on his profitable Nashville Brass ensemble, which turned country songs into fodder for beautiful-music radio stations. At the same time, Felton Jarvis edged closer to an exclusive production arrangement with Elvis, which would pull him away from RCA-Nashville's daily routine. Their replacements—Jerry Bradley and Ronny Light—would deeply alter Waylon's course at the label. Bradley, particularly, would cook up the Grammy-winning *Wanted!—The Outlaws* album in 1976, which galvanized Waylon's career and fueled the outlaw marketing machine.

When Chet hired Bradley, he tapped into Nashville's royal family, choosing tradition over the new maverick impulse embodied by producers Fred Foster and Jack Clement. Jerry was the son of Owen Bradley and the nephew of session guitarist Harold Bradley. After attending Peabody College in the West End, he spent much of the 1960s running his father's publishing company and mixing recordings at his studio, dashing away on weekends to race cars around the South. "I'd mix his sessions and I would hear him and the artist and the important people—his bosses and managers—get into discussions about business," says Bradley. "I was always interested in the conclusions to what they were talking about, whether it was about a contract or a song. I could hear both sides of it."

Anxious to stake out his own place among the A&R elite in Nashville, Jerry mentioned his availability to Chet one night in Printer's Alley, where they'd gone to dinner with Harry Warner, a Peabody classmate of Jerry's who worked at BMI. Chet just looked at the portly young man and dragged ponderously on his cigar. "About twelve o'clock at night," says Bradley, "coming back, they let me out of the car and I thought, 'I'm going to make one more pitch.' I said, 'Don't forget about that now. If you ever get an opportunity, give me a call.' He said, 'You might make a good executive, Jerry.'

"About a month later, he called me, and I looked at the message. I picked up the phone and called my daddy and I said, 'Chet Atkins is calling me.' He said, 'Well, call him back!' I said, 'I think he might be calling me about a job.' He said, 'Hell, son, you've got a damn job. If he's got a damn opportunity, take it!'"

In the short term, Jerry assumed Danny Davis's role, but Chet also served up a bigger opportunity than Jerry could have imagined. "The minute he came into the company, he was designated as the one who would become the heir apparent," says Ronny Light, whom Chet had already hired. "Whether it was spoken or not, everybody knew. Chet didn't want the day-to-day operations. He wanted somebody else to do it."

It's no wonder. Blustery managers, grumpy artists, and meddling RCA executives from New York burdened Atkins. Over drinks with friends, he mused about flying off to Mexico with his guitar. And he was also battling cancer.

"Chet used to have Monday morning meetings," says Bradley. "I'll never forget it. He was sitting behind the desk, and we were all in his office and he had a set of encyclopedias over on the table. I guess he wasn't feeling well. We were discussing product, and he got up, went over to the encyclopedia, and took it back over to his desk. Looked up something, shut the encyclopedia, and put it back up and left. After the meeting, he left and went to his doctor. Next thing you know, he's diagnosed with colon cancer."

After surgery a few weeks later, Chet asked Ronny Light if he'd read an article about cancer in the new issue of *Esquire*. "I was hoping he didn't see it," says Light. "It was an article about different cancers and life expectancy for each cancer. I said, 'Yeah, I read that.' He said, 'Do you see how long I got to live?' I said, 'No. I don't think it said how long *you* got to live.' It was about a year and a half. I knew that his health was bothering him. He told a bunch of people, 'I guess if I ever get it, I'll get it from smoking cigars.'"

His battles with Waylon couldn't have helped, either. He burned hours lecturing him about his drug use, but Waylon ignored him, always steering the conversation back to his complaints about producers. Chet worried over an advance he'd given the singer for a new bus, which revenues weren't justifying, and winced when promotion men complained that Waylon refused to make courtesy calls to radio disc jockeys and record distributors.

In the wake of Davis's departure, Chet naturally was in no mood to reassume his studio work with Waylon, so he handed the singer's production chores to Ronny Light, who came to producing from the performing world. He and his brother Larry appeared regularly on a music television show in Nashville during the 1960s and, with Eddy Arnold as their sponsor, recorded a single for Canadian American Records. Ronny also played guitar for Arnold on the road, wrote lead sheets for some of the big publishing houses in Nashville, and coproduced with Felton Jarvis RCA's girl duo the Lonesome Rhodes. With Jarvis turning most of his attention to Elvis, Chet directed the twenty-four-year-old Light to cover for Jarvis.

Light's deep Nashville pedigree appealed to Chet's conservative bent, but, ironically, Light's work, particularly with Waylon, pushed RCA up to the gates of the forward-thinking, Kristofferson-influenced Nashville. The Harlan Howard songs and covers of pop and folk songs in Waylon's repertoire that had begun to fall away under Danny Davis's reign continued to recede in favor of rock flavor and mature themes. "He had tons of cuts [in the can]," says Light, "so as his producer I listened to all the old cuts and found things we could release, including 'Cedartown, Georgia.' That was not in my best interests, but it was in Waylon's best interests." That song, produced by Davis, became the title track of Waylon's first album with Light and won an unexpected write-up in *Rolling Stone*. "It's this album that Waylon goes after everybody (including your mother) and intends to bring everybody over to his side. It's all *Dynamite stuff*, as they say at Tower Records. Word is that if Waylon Jennings isn't already a country superstar, he soon will be."

Light and Jennings liberally tapped the young songwriting community and recorded the work of Lee Clayton, Mickey Newbury, and Billy Joe Shaver, which was reminiscent of Johnny Cash's consumption of Kris Kristofferson, Vince Matthews, and Larry Gatlin. Jennings also sampled Matthews and continued to explore Kristofferson. And, some years after meeting Willie Nelson for the first time in Phoenix, he tried out Nelson's "It Should Be Easier Now" and "Pretend I Never Happened." The men's relationship was cemented in 1971 when their names appeared together as songwriters on "Good Hearted Woman," a hit for Waylon in 1972.

Despite the shared writing credit, "Good Hearted Woman" was Waylon's song from the start, claims Billy Ray Reynolds. He had actually asked Billy Ray to add some verses for a half share of the credit; however, the guitarist had refused, arguing that the song needed nothing but to be recorded. "The next day or so," explains Reynolds, "he got into a poker game and he did the same thing to Willie. And Waylon even suggested the line that Willie is supposed to have written. It was Waylon's line and Willie said, 'Hey, I like that.' So Willie wound up with half the song and half the publishing. I don't want to make Willie mad at me, but Waylon already had that song written."

On record, the rollicking Waylon-and-Willie number featured an unusual snare pattern on the choruses, mingled with a bold bass drum, a percussive style that marked Waylon's sound on the road. Nashville producers could be squeamish about a heavy drum presence—no fewer than three drummers contributed parts on the "Good Hearted Woman" session—but Light approved.

Waylon and the young producer's harmony in song selection notwithstanding, Waylon confessed in his autobiography that he badgered Light to distraction. "Ronny was young, one of the nicest people in the world, and didn't deserve the misery I put him through. I got more freedom with him as a producer, although I was still using musicians who didn't know what I was about."

Light doesn't remember Waylon's concerns about musicians. Such conflict, he says, took root between Waylon and the top guys at RCA-Nashville. "When I produced Waylon, he never once asked to use one of his band members, except for [steel guitarist] Ralph Mooney, and we used Mooney. The issue never came up." Bradley, who was taking more administrative responsibilities with each new day on the job, claims that he, too, never argued with Waylon about session musicians, that it was Chet who clung to the older ways.

However, that's not to say that Bradley and Waylon lived peacefully. To the contrary, they rammed heads almost from the start. "I was in an office with [artist relations director] Wally Cochran and Waylon," recalls Bradley, "and they were having an argument and they were cussing each other. And Waylon and I started cussing each other. And I said, 'Hell, I'm not going to stay down here and let you cuss my ass out.' And I just walked out and walked on up to my office. He was all doped up. He was cussing out Wally and if you knew Wally, he was full of shit anyhow. It was a conversation about nonsense. And I didn't let him run over me."

In the spring of 1971, recalls Billy Ray Reynolds, conflict sparked between Jennings and Bradley over music. Reynolds had written a Civil War concept album, and Waylon was recording a few tracks at RCA. Ronny was producing, but Bradley was teasing Waylon about the project, reminding him that the war was over. Angered, Reynolds urged Waylon to go elsewhere to work on the tracks. The singer only shook his head and pointed out that his contract required he record at RCA. The album died right there.

Another conflict illustrated not only Waylon's beef with RCA but the bigger wall between establishment Nashville and the emerging youth movement in country music. In December 1970, Waylon and his band had settled into a residency at the Troubadour in Los Angeles while Kristofferson shot his first scenes for *Cisco Pike*. Inevitably, Waylon's people and Kris's people crossed paths, leading to a wondrous jam session in Billy Ray Reynolds's hotel room, which included Kris, Joan Baez, Tommy Smothers, Mickey Newbury, Dottie West, Neil Diamond, and comedic actor Larry Storch.

"Somebody sent out for some hamburgers," says Reynolds. "But they were cold when they got there. Everybody left and I was about trashed out and laid down on my bed. And Kris was on the other side with his feet on the floor; he laid back on the bed with the cheeseburger in the air. And the last thing I remember him saying was, 'I got to be on the set at six o'clock.' It was three-something then. I woke up about nine-thirty or ten the next morning and Kris was still lying there in the same position with the cheeseburger up in the air, just like he'd been when I went to sleep. I woke him up and he went on. He was late for work that day."

Waylon missed the hotel party, but he had seen Kristofferson sing "Lovin' Her Was Easier" during his L.A. stand and immediately wanted to record it. He asked RCA-Nashville to arrange studio time in Los Angeles with Ricky Nelson's band. "At the time," wrote Waylon, "he had a good bunch of guys with him, including Sonny Curtis." Initially, RCA refused, but Waylon persisted, calling Harry Jenkins, who had become Chet's boss in New York after Steve Sholes's death, and winning his permission.

As Waylon later wrote, "It was a great record, up-tempo, with a guitar riff that was like a clarion call to arms every chorus." Back in Nashville, RCA released the song, but only as album filler. Waylon believed it was a sure hit single and blamed Chet's old objection to recording anywhere but 806 Seventeenth Avenue South; however, RCA's promotion head, Elroy Kahanek, disagrees: "It wasn't the normal Waylon Jennings kick-ass-type song. I just felt like, that's just not Waylon. To me, it was just such a beautiful love ballad that it just didn't fit what radio wanted to hear from Waylon." On August 7, 1971, Roger Miller took "Lovin' Her Was Easier" to the country charts; two weeks later, Kristofferson himself introduced it to the pop side.

Even if RCA had released the recording as a single, the company might have struggled to keep up with demand. From producer Ronny Light's perch in the studio, he could see that it was RCA's Achilles' heel. When a record caught fire on radio, he says, the company's manufacturing plants often lacked the capacity to quickly turn out more copies. "They would press ten thousand on an artist whose last record sold fifty thousand singles," complains Light. "I went to them and said, 'Why do we do this? How much do we think we're going to sell?' And we knew immediately when we had a good record. All the producers knew, everybody knew. Radio knew immediately. We're sitting there with ten thousand pressed and I said, 'If we're going to sell fifty thousand records let's press fifty thousand records on the front end and get rid of them.'"

The fickle pressing habits also popped up on the list of grievances Waylon frequently took to Wally Cochran, Nashville's head of artist relations. Recalls Kahanek, "Waylon walked into Wally's office, and he said, 'Cochran, why in the hell can't I get my promo copies.' Wally says, 'They're selling so fast we're pressing them as fast as we can, Waylon.' He'd do that with the bluegrass acts, which you couldn't give away back then. He told Lester Flatt one time, 'It's hot. It's selling like crazy.' I said, 'Wally, why did you tell him that? You know it's not true.' He said, 'It made him feel good, didn't it?'" In any case, argues Kahanek, nobody at RCA worried about sales as long as its artists shone on the trade-magazine charts, which reacted to a combination of sales, radio airplay, and good old-fashioned backslapping. "You'd bullshit about sales," explains Kahanek. "You'd be on the phone talking with the head of *Billboard* and say, 'Well, Charley Pride sold twenty-six thousand singles this week.' We might have sold twenty thousand. You had to keep a record of all this stuff, so it wouldn't catch you and bite you in the ass." The dubious sales reports moved Pride up the charts, which pleased RCA brass in New York, who boasted about "chart share" to stockholders.

Coy about specific methods, Kahanek further claims that he could dictate chart positions. "One day in my office this artist called me from another major label and said, 'Elroy, good God, will you slack up? I've got a record right now that could be our first number one, and we know we're not going to get there because you've got that damn top five sewed up.' I said, 'Well, that's my job.' He said, 'Man I tell you what.' I said, 'What?' 'I'll give you two thousand dollars if you'll just back off a little bit.' I said, 'Look, you're a good friend. I'm going to let you go to number one.' So I called *Billboard* magazine and I said, 'Hey, do me a favor. Keep so-and-so at number two. Go ahead and take so-and-so to number one.' They did. It wasn't two months later another artist called me and said, 'Elroy please . . .' I did the same thing for them. They were friends. Back then, it wasn't so cutthroat; you helped other artists even if they were on another label."

If Waylon understood that the record companies, not the record buyers, anointed number-one artists, he may have dropped his pressing plant petitions, but with outlaw attitude he railed on about manufacturing and promotion and production and instrumentation. And he was mostly rebuffed. Until an accountant from New York interceded. And then RCA had to listen.

★　　★　　★

THE BIG RECORD sales that Chet envisioned for Waylon back in 1965 had obviously failed to materialize, which made him heavily reliant on touring, mostly as part of country music package shows assembled by veteran agent Lucky Moeller. During Moeller's long career in booking and promotion, he established contacts at every fair and cow palace in the country, assuring that his artists were never at a loss for work. In time, Waylon became one of his most popular offerings, which was a double-edged sword. Indeed, Waylon's concert circuit was long and profitable, but Moeller often booked shows at dingy and dangerous clubs that country music troubadours called "the skull orchards."

"One tour would be a nice chain of hotels," recalls Billy Ray Reynolds. "But some of them were just pure knife-and-gun-type clubs. We'd even have people shot in front of us, when we'd be on the stage playing. Jealous husbands and people like that fighting. They were just strange places.

"[One shooting] happened in Kentucky, near Louisville. Waylon was between sets. We'd do four sets a night at that time. This particular night he ordered a salad [during the break] and this lady was loose in the crowd and was flirting, especially with him. She came over to the table and was sitting on his leg. She started reaching over into his salad bowl and pulling the lettuce out of his bowl. He just quit eating and said, 'Billy, do about three songs and call me up.' So she kept messing with him. And I did my three songs and introduced him and he came on up. She was dancing with other guys, and this guy just walked up and shot the guy she was dancing with right in front of us. We all started trying to figure out how to get behind the PA speakers. It was some little old joint."

As the exhausting dates piled up, Richie Albright took a long sabbatical from Waylon's band. He was run-down by work and too many pills taken to stay awake on the road. "This town ran on amphetamines," says Albright. "There were a couple of doctors in town; all you had to do is walk in and tell them, 'I'm on the road,' and they'd pull out their prescription book and say, 'What do you want?' Everybody walked around with their pockets sounding like a drugstore." Albright also had a healthy taste for weed, in contrast to Waylon who preferred only his pills. "When we came to town in the sixties," continues Albright, "I remember I was at a party one night and everybody was drinking, everybody had a handful of pills, and I lit a joint and everybody freaked out and said, 'What are you trying to do, get us busted?' Hardly anybody did it."

Perhaps Albright should have used more discretion. In 1969, he was busted twice, which may have spooked Waylon and hastened Albright's departure from the Waylors. For the next three years, his strong hand kept the beat in a variety of bands before he finally returned in April 1972, only to find Waylon sadly diminished. Suffering from hepatitis that he contracted while playing an Indian reservation in New Mexico, Waylon threatened to either go back to Phoenix for good or sharpen his guitar playing for session work. "He was just fed up," explains Albright. "He was making the same money he was in '69. Things weren't really going good. He was just tired and fed up."

Waylon's RCA contract was about to expire when he summoned the drummer to discuss it. "He looked like a chameleon, he was so yellow from the jaundice," recalls Albright. "He called me in and said RCA had offered him five thousand dollars. That's the moment when I said,

'Bullshit. This ain't going to get it. We got to do something.' So that's when I went into action. I didn't do things before Waylon said to do things, but at that moment, I said, 'Let me do this and I'll see.' I just made a few phone calls."

During his hiatus, Albright had played with the country-rock band Goose Creek Symphony, whose manager, George Laibe, introduced him to a character named Neil Reshen. Reshen, who was a business manager at the rock magazine *Creem* and steered the career of jazz legend Miles Davis, indeed knew how to squeeze the dollars from a record company and could help Waylon deal with RCA. "Neil and I talked and he came down to Nashville," says Albright. "I told Waylon, 'There's a guy that you need to talk to. You're probably not going to like him but you need to hear what he has to say. Don't let RCA pull you in.' So Neil came down and spent a few hours with Waylon that afternoon. We were taking Neil to the airport, and we called Willie, and Willie came and met Neil at the airport. Those two got hooked up in that one little weekend. There was frustration especially when they were getting ready to shaft Waylon, and I couldn't stand for that."

★   ★   ★

LIKE WAYLON, WILLIE could find neither rhyme nor reason at RCA. But while Waylon's recent albums showed signs of life on the charts, Willie's fizzled. In 1971 and 1972, only two of his four album releases dented the charts and then only for a total of six weeks. Nineteen seventy-one's *Yesterday's Wine* showcased two of Willie's finest songs to date, "Yesterday's Wine" and "Goin' Home," which could make you cry, but the album opened with a strange existential dialogue between Willie and a host of angels who sound like church elders reading aloud a church supper menu. It tried to be a concept album, but it lacked a clear thread, despite Willie's claims to the contrary. "I think it's one of my best albums," he lamented, "but *Yesterday's Wine* was regarded by RCA as way too spooky and far out to waste promotion money on."

Courtesy of Maryland Room, University of Maryland

Willie fields autograph seekers.

One last album on RCA—*The Willie Way*—enchanted *Rolling Stone*'s Chet Flippo, who noted that Willie sang "with a freshness drawn from his own blues-tinged country style," but it arrived in stores packaged in the most unimaginative album sleeve ever to come out of Nashville. To nobody's surprise, the record faltered, and Willie, his outlaw attitude pricked, continued to blame his dismal sales on RCA's marketing engine. "Chet liked me," said Willie in a 2008 biography. "He liked my writing, my singing. He didn't care much for my guitar playing, but at that point, I didn't either. But whatever happened in Nashville, no matter how much I liked it, no matter how much Chet liked it, if it got to New York, when it would come time to promote and spend money, if it came out of Nashville, it didn't get the budget."

The RCA men still around who remember Willie's tenure at the label disagree. Ronny Light argues that the company did everything it could to help Willie sell, while Jerry Bradley blamed a public that hadn't yet warmed to Willie's sound. Elroy Kahanek had struggled to sell Willie's records to radio stations when he started as a regional representative in 1969, and he still struggled when he took over national promotion in Nashville in 1971. "They were just off-the-wall," he says. "They weren't mainstream country. Back then country radio wasn't going to play anything that was different. His music was the same as it always was and he wasn't going to change it, and country radio wasn't going to accept it at that time."

Evidently, Willie needed the aggressive management that Reshen provided. However, by the time Willie signed with him, RCA-Nashville had already decided to cut loose its resident cosmic cowboy. "I was in sort of the same situation I had been in ten years earlier," reflected Willie. "My band would fill a Texas dance hall. We were stars in Texas. But in Nashville, I was looked upon as a loser singer. They wouldn't let me record with my own band. They would cover me up with horns and strings. It was depressing."

Nashville's rejection might have stung a bit more but Willie had already left town, mentally and physically. Billy Ray Reynolds, who as part of Waylon's band frequently toured with Willie, had seen the frustration building in 1970 while they played dates in Buffalo and Toronto. "Lynn Anderson was on that tour with us," says Reynolds, "and they loved Lynn Anderson and they hated Waylon and Willie. They called us hippies." After the tour, says Reynolds, he and Willie tramped across Willie's farm outside Nashville, where the Texan still had Toronto on his mind. "There were fields back by a little old pond near Willie's house. Willie said, 'Let's sit down here and listen to the orchestra.' There were thousands of frogs, and we were sitting there on the dirt listening to them. There were just unbelievable sounds." In the darkness, Willie noted the altos, sopranos, and basses. "It was kind of strange having somebody like Willie Nelson talking about the orchestrations of a frog pond. He and I sat on the embankment, and he started talking about, 'I just don't know what I'm going to do. It seems like nothing I do works.'"

His uncertain commercial prospects weighed on him, but they were briefly overshadowed by the untenable situation at the farm, where his new girlfriend, Connie Koepke, lived under the same roof with Willie's first wife, while second wife, Shirley, fumed nearby in Nashville. Something was about to blow. And it did. On December 23, 1970.

"I was at a Christmas party downtown in Nashville," said Willie, "and my nephew called and said, 'Come home, your house is on fire.' When I got there it was in flames and there were firemen everywhere. So I run and get my stash bag and run out. I had a pound of good Colombian in there and I knew I was gonna need to get high." According to legend, before Willie left the party, he instructed his nephew to pull a damaged car into the garage, so he could claim it later on his insurance.

When the smoke cleared, Willie and Connie and his children rolled out of Ridgetop and headed to Bandera, Texas, an old sheep-raising town northwest of San Antonio. He rebuilt the home in Ridgetop and held on to his acreage, but he never returned to live. "I knew I only had a few years left to do what I was going to do, and I had to make a move," said Willie in 1976. "I wasn't going down there to quit. I was going down there with purpose."

Over the years, he returned to Music City time and time again whenever work demanded it, but Texas was his home, and in 1970 it represented more than just a string of one-nighters. Its music scene, like the Dallas Cowboys of the NFL, was fast gaining a national audience.

★　★　★

FROM HIS NEW stage in Bandera, Willie Nelson could see the state's hard-core conservative white working class giving up floor space to the white hippies who poured out of urban centers such as Dallas and

Austin. Indeed, the Texas brand of country music traditionally blended honky-tonk, western swing, and the blues, and was now adding rock elements and ethos in a way that recalled favorite son Lyndon B. Johnson's pragmatic negotiations with black America's inevitable push for civil rights.

Willie reckoned that he first saw the unexpected combination of patrons at the club Big G's, in Round Rock, Texas. It "was a highly redneck place back then," Willie told country music historian Robert K. Oermann. "But there was a few little long-haired cowboys that were coming in there, and of course they got the shit kicked out of 'em a couple of times. But they kept comin' back. They kept showing up."

It must be said that the crowd Willie saw in front of him mirrored that of Johnny Cash, drawn in thanks to the Man in Black's prison albums and popular television show. But in Texas, this curious mingling was largely confined to the bars, particularly a reimagined gas station that was Kenneth Threadgill's, the spiritual home of eclecticism in Austin. A fiddler and folk music lover, Threadgill gave over his space to pickers filtering in and out of the progressive culture around the University of Texas. "Threadgill's was the first place in Austin where I saw the rednecks and hippies packing into one place together," said Mary Egan, who fiddled for Greezy Wheels, one of the staple bands playing around Austin in the early 1970s. "They'd pack in there on Wednesday nights to jam. Threadgill would be selling long-neck [bottled beer] as fast as he could pass them out, and everybody'd get up and try to play." During the 1960s, blues spots and rock clubs sprouted up all over Austin, but Threadgill's was common ground. It might even have been a place where whites and blacks mixed, if Texans had done that sort of thing.

In 1970, the main stage for this country-rock movement moved to the Armadillo World Headquarters, housed in an old National Guard armory in Austin. A magnet for hippies, truck drivers, and state office workers, the Armadillo hosted an enticing mix of national and local acts. John Sebastian, John Prine, Bette Midler, and Jerry Garcia rubbed shoulders with Texas-based acts such as Doug Sahm, Commander Cody and His Lost Planet Airmen, Jerry Jeff Walker, Leon Russell, and Asleep at the Wheel. "But the obvious plus was the crowd: mobile, shouting, native-costumed young people with beer, music, and the thought of being Texans," wrote Jan Reid in his classic history, *The Improbable Rise of Redneck Rock*. "The dress wasn't exotic like in San Francisco; the style ran to boots, jeans, T-shirts, long hair, and cowboy hats. The bellowing mobs scared the daylights out of Bette Midler, exacted smiles of karmic delight from John McLaughlin and the Mahavishnu Orchestra, enticed Billy Joe Shaver to play several times for free, and subjected John Prine to the stifling early-summer heat of Armadillo."

In the summer of 1972, Willie and his family left Bandera for the suburbs of Austin. He'd been playing Austin clubs such as Big G's and the Broken Spoke, and the scene around town seemed infinitely cooler than Houston's or San Antonio's. Naturally, Willie sought out the Armadillo World Headquarters, where he personally arranged a gig with Greezy Wheels opening. "The manager was real optimistic about it," Willie continued with Robert Oermann, "and sure enough, there was a whole lot of people who showed up. A whole lot of young people. Plus, there were a few of the cowboys from Big G's who had ventured in there, just to see, because they'd never been around the hippies and the long hairs. Anyway they came in there and mixed around. They looked around, and they wound up not disliking each other at all. They found out that it's not hard to like Hank Williams and Ernest Tubb. They found a common ground."

In the wake of the Armadillo gig, Willie dialed his friend Waylon in Nashville and urged him to get his band down there as soon as possible. When Waylon finally paid a visit, the audience who paid to see him erupted. "There was hippies and cowboys and everybody together and they were screaming and really getting off on it," says drummer Albright. "Waylon turned around and said, 'Go get that little red-headed son of a bitch. What's he got me into?' We hadn't been in a situation with hippies and cowboys side by side. It was quite the rush. When the crowd gets almost louder than the band, you know you're doing something right."

Although Willie wasn't the first artist with national credentials to move to Texas—Michael Martin Murphey, Jerry Jeff Walker, and B. W. Stevenson had preceded him—he embodied like nobody else the union of hippie and hillbilly, where the boundaries between rock, country, and folk suddenly blurred. He channeled the spirit of Threadgill's on bigger stages all around Texas and became the patron saint of an ethos and style of music that was alternately called redneck rock or progressive country or outlaw.

"Going back to Texas has sure been good for Willie Nelson," wrote Fort Worth native Dave Hickey in *Country Music*. "You get the impression that when he was living in Nashville he was sending out his songs like a stranded man sends out messages in bottles, and that when he moved to Austin, he suddenly discovered that all those bottles had floated to shore among friends."

Willie delighted his Texas fans by donning his own outlaw attire. He replaced the ties and turtlenecks, the blue blazers and brown slacks of Nashville's past with the loose-fitting jeans, bandanas, tennis shoes, and cozy cotton shirts of the so-called cosmic cowboys: Murphey, Walker, and Sahm. He often wore a cowboy hat, and with every passing week after landing in Austin, his hair dropped lower and the whiskers on his face multiplied. The contrast was startling. He had gone from looking like a singing insurance peddler to the spiritual leader of a back-to-nature pod.

The new Willie and the Austin movement that swirled around him magnetized the national press. Reporters from big newspapers and magazines parachuted into Texas to taste a slice of Austin life and give Willie a lot of honey press. The attention, more than he had ever known, polished his reputation in the eyes of concert promoters around the country. He fell back on the national circuit, making the proverbial grueling string of one-nighters from Buffalo to Boise.

A stop in Nashville gave him his next recording contract, this time with the legendary rhythm-and-blues label Atlantic, which by the early 1970s was also collecting an impressive array of rock acts and seeking a niche in the country music world. In 1972, Jerry Wexler, Atlantic's legendary producer, and label boss Rick Sanjek had stopped by a songwriters' jam in Nashville just in time to catch Willie in the spotlight. The singer unfurled a collection of mostly unrecorded songs that presented male and female perspectives on a relationship gone sour. "He got on the stool late at night when the party had thinned out," said Harlan Howard, who hosted the party, "and he sang like a total album with a gut string and a stool. He just went from one song to the other and then [Jerry Wexler] from New York . . . flipped out." Afterward, Wexler shuffled up to Willie and offered him a contract. Willie welcomed the invitation and pointed him to Neil Reshen, who negotiated a healthy advance and lots of artistic control.

In February 1973, Wexler reserved five days at Atlantic's storied recording space near Columbus Circle in Manhattan and tapped the Turkish-born staff producer and arranger Arif Mardin to lead the proceedings. Mardin, who could pass for Peter Sellers's Inspector Clouseau, loved jazz and had studied to be an arranger at Berklee School of Music in Boston, before he joined Atlantic in the early 1960s. At first he did little more than deal with administrative tasks, but he soon joined Wexler and Tom Dowd on Aretha Franklin's production team and, in 1969, contributed arrangements to Dusty Springfield's *Dusty in Memphis*. More recently, he had produced Austin kingpin Jerry Jeff Walker and coproduced and played piano on the *Doug Sahm and Band* album, the Texas guitar slinger's first outing after dissolving the Sir Douglas Quintet. Accordingly, the studio that Mardin oversaw when Willie hit town could not have differed more from RCA's if it had been located in the Cathedral of St. John the Divine.

Mardin opened the door to Willie's band, freed him from the glare of the studio clock, and let the boys smoke their pot, a no-no at RCA-Nashville, where the session musicians who partied did so in their cars on break. In Nashville, artists punched the clock. In New York, Wexler and Mardin orchestrated an event. Journalists from *Creem* and *Rolling Stone* visited the studio while rumors flew around town that Bob Dylan, Leon Russell, and Doug Sahm might show up to accompany Willie. Of the three, only Sahm appeared, to add licks to the Bob Wills classic "Stay All Night (Stay a Little Longer)" and Willie's own "Devil in a Sleeping Bag." An army of Willie's friends, including B. W. Stevenson, David Bromberg, Sammi Smith, Larry Gatlin, and Waylon, visited, too, chiming in on the rollicking "Stay All Night." Even Willie's wife, Connie, and *Creem* journalist Ed Ward joined the chorus during a deluge of gospel recordings on the session's last day.

On the first day, Ward feared that Willie and his musicians might not measure up to New York standards. "Happily," he confessed later, "I'd underestimated the professionalism of all concerned, not to mention the core ensemble of musicians themselves, who decided to test the sound of the studio with a spirited version of 'Under the Double Eagle,' which left me awestruck: Willie wasn't only a great songwriter, he was a goddamn virtuoso on that battered Martin guitar of his!"

In five days, Willie cut thirty-three songs, twelve of which appeared on the first album, *Shotgun Willie*. And when the last inch of tape slipped through the machine, Mardin popped open a bottle of expensive French wine and toasted the room. It was early in the morning when Willie stepped out onto Broadway. "Gotta get back to Texas," he told *Rolling Stone*'s Chet Flippo. "We play in Round Rock tomorrow."

★   ★   ★

SIX MONTHS LATER, *Rolling Stone* continued the story of *Shotgun Willie* in a sterling review: "With this flawless album, Willie Nelson finally demonstrates why he has for so long been regarded as a C&W singer-songwriter's singer-songwriter." Atlantic released only one more Willie Nelson album, the Muscle Shoals–recorded *Phases and Stages*, before its country division folded, but, like *Shotgun Willie*, it woke up the critics and endorsed Willie's creative vision.

Nashville's a great place to be right now—like Paris in the twenties—a place where you can get together with people and rap.

—Mickey Newbury

 Six

The West End Watershed

AFTER THE NEW York sessions, Willie ambled back to outlaw country. The very mention of Round Rock, Texas—that small town that prepared to receive Willie's caravan—suggested a magical destination where folk-rock mingled with native dance hall and honky-tonk creations meant to accompany wildly changing attitudes and lifestyles. It was as if the elusive Summer of Love had floated to Texas after fleeing the grungy Haight-Ashbury district of San Francisco.

Elements of that spirit had also traveled to Nashville, where musical and intellectual cross-pollination, experimentation, and promise of freedom had awakened in the city's West End. The streets running across and along Division, Broadway, and West End between Music Row and Hillsboro Village delineated Nashville's very own Austin or Greenwich Village, where young musicians and other searchers gathered to play, parade, party, and talk politics. Like those sister neighborhoods, the West

End watershed encompassed a major city park, a university, cheap rentals, diners, and the all-important nightclubs and taverns that embraced struggling musicians who played for young people newly licensed by a reduction in the legal drinking age from twenty-one to eighteen.

The lucky musicians arrived and quickly found sponsorship on Music Row: Jimmy Buffett, who worked at *Billboard* and wrote for a small publishing company; John Hiatt, who wrote for Tree Publishing; Dan Fogelberg, who turned up with a Columbia contract; Dave Loggins, who was signed to MCA Music Publishing; and Dianne Davidson, who recorded for the independent label Janus and got session work as a background vocalist. "We were all hippies," says Davidson. "We tried to scrape up enough money to pay the rent, buy some smoking dope, and a jug of cheap wine and guitar strings. Most of us had connections in the business that helped take care of us in that way. We had publishing deals. We had production deals. We did sessions. That was how you made some money. Then your gigs—if you made money great, if you didn't that was okay."

Dan Beck, from Pittsburgh, was unsponsored, but he smelled the unusual fires burning in Nashville and came anyway. Later he would play a brief but key role in Willie Nelson's career, but in 1971 he was a college student itching for a songwriting deal in Nashville. He knew that Dylan had recorded there, heard about Kristofferson, and read in *Rolling Stone, Creem,* and *Circus* about the artists streaming into the city to record or appear on *The Johnny Cash Show* or both. The list of artists working in independent studios such as Quadrafonic, Woodland, Music City Recorders, and Cinderella astonished him: the Steve Miller Band, Gordon Lightfoot, Lonnie Mack, and Neil Young, just to name a few. During the school year, the Earl Scruggs Revue stopped in Pittsburgh, which only supercharged his imagination. "This was post Flatt-Scruggs," explains Beck. "His sons were my age, and it was electrifying. They were putting elements of rock with their dad's banjo."

Beck wrote songs and played in a rock band that had periodically traveled from Pittsburgh to New York looking for a break. "We could afford to hang out about two days, then we'd have to go home. And we'd come back six months later and knock on doors." Nashville seemed more promising, fewer closed doors, and cheaper accommodations. "So I talked to my band: 'Hey, let's all go to Nashville,'" says Beck. "Well, I was the only one in college, and for that reason, I was the only one who was broke. The rest of the guys worked in the steel mills; they're all nineteen or twenty years old, driving Corvettes. Everybody's like, 'Yeah, let's go to Nashville.' Well, when it came time to go, everybody backed out because they had these lifelong union jobs."

So Beck flew into town by himself and asked a cabbie to take him where college kids lived and people made records; he planned on staying for the summer. That night, he wandered into the Red Dog Saloon, on Division, where David Allan Coe was playing and a musician and writer named Willie Fong Young was watching him. Beck fell into conversation with Young who offered him a place to sleep. A job busing tables at the House, a club on Twenty-First Avenue South, soon followed. He couldn't have picked a livelier spot to work: Marshall Chapman had gotten her first paying gig there a few months before Beck arrived, and by the fall she was a magnetic regular. "The girl, all six foot two of her, had beautiful eyes surrounded by a waterfall of blonde curls and a hole in her white jeans that ran from her knee all the way up," swooned a fan who watched her take charge of the club.

Beck, too, marveled at Chapman's act and returned to the Red Dog Saloon to see the spectacle of George and Arizona Star, a female duo whose Dada-ish musical play, *The Lobotomy*, featured songs like "We're Off to See the Gizzard." "They used to live in a carriage house over by Belmont [College] that I don't think had a bathroom in it," recalls Beck. "So they used to come over and use our shower, bathtub, change there, and go out and busk. And they were notorious down there. Star was a beautiful lady who had this Marilyn Monroe persona, so that every hillbilly guitar player in Nashville was chasing her. George was sword-wielding; she wore these Edwardian velvet suits and looked very dykish. It was just a scene."

Courtesy of Dan Beck collection

From left to right: Kinky Friedman and Dan Beck hanging with pop-country singer B. J. Thomas.

While Beck pondered his future in Nashville, Young hired on another new roommate, aspiring songwriter Kinky Friedman, who came from Texas by way of a Peace Corps stint on the island of Borneo in the South China Sea. They bunked at 1909 Broadway, the same building where Billy Swan heard Kristofferson yelling the news of his Newport gig through his open window. Many a night, Beck, Young, and Friedman haunted the Red Dog and the sleazy, greasy Burger Boy joint, just steps up the street from their apartment. Or they slipped into Music Row studios to watch sessions and then stretched out the night at the Exit/In. Invariably, they ended up at the Pancake Man in the Holiday Inn on West End. "All the session guys would come in for a late-night breakfast and tell stories," adds Beck. "And we were game. This was a nightly thing. Eddie Rabbitt was hanging out there then. It was a real street thing."

Friedman concentrated on writing a country music opera while he and his Texas Jewboys band jammed into Glaser Sound Studios on Nineteenth Avenue South, working on his outrageous musical commentary on the Jewish condition that would become the *Sold American* album of 1973. Anyone who saw the cigar-chomping, western-clad bard sing "Ride 'Em Jewboy" or "We Reserve the Right to Refuse Service to You" did not soon forget him. On the street, he was just as outlandish, snorting and growling at the proselytizing so common in Nashville and ridiculing the town's political conservatism.

Each and every evening, says Beck, the Jewish outlaw rose from his chair and approached the French doors of their apartment, which looked down on Broadway. "It was like the pope's window. It was just before we'd head to the Pancake Man every night, and he would open those doors and take a drag on his cigar and shout out in his gravelly voice, 'Assassinate Your President.' And he did this every night at the same time. I thought for sure one night they [the police] were going to show up and drag him off to jail."

Photograph by Michael Streissguth

The apartment building on Broadway where Billy Swan, Dan Beck, Kinky Friedman, and Willie Fong Young lived.

Characters such as Friedman and Arizona Star enlivened Nashville in Beck's eyes, but he also saw the city's hard edge, like when the Nashville police spied his Pennsylvania license plates and virtually disassembled his car looking for drugs. While still searching for a day job to support his writing and his Pancake Man habit, Beck got an appointment with RCA executive Wally Cochran. "I sat down in this airport-lounge-size office that was nothing but golf clubs because that's probably what he did all day," says Beck. "I remember giving him my little pitch, and I'm from the North, my hair's long, and he listened to my little thing and paused and said, 'You know, I think you ought to go home.'"

★   ★   ★

A SIMPLE STROLL along quiet West End streets, some of them canopied by lush magnolia, dogwood, and ash, could lead to unexpected and exhilarating encounters. "I remember when I lived on Sixteenth or Seventeenth Avenues South when I was in graduate school," recounts former Vanderbilt student Darrell Berger. "About ten o'clock at night, I'm walking in front of one of the recording studios. There was this guy sitting there strumming this guitar. We talked for a while, and he was really nice. Later I realized it was Billy Joe Shaver, just sitting there because that's where he was." The Texas singer-songwriter might have been taking a break from recording his *Old Five and Dimers Like Me*, which Kristofferson produced, financed, and sold to Monument.

On a different night, Berger heard what he calls "this ungodly hot banjo" coming through the walls of his apartment. Later, he spied the virtuoso in the hallway. "He was about my age but looked younger," continues Berger. "He said, 'Gee, I hope my music doesn't disturb you.' I said, 'Are you kidding? Leave the doors open!' It was a guy named Larry McNeely, who replaced the banjo player [John Hartford] on the *Glen Campbell Goodtime Hour*."

Later he encountered Allen Ginsberg who had shown up for a jam session at McNeely's house. "Somebody must've got the idea to get the best musicians around together. This was Larry McNeely on his banjo, and Allen Ginsberg on his finger cymbals and squeeze box! So if you think Johnny Cash and Bob Dylan were coming together over a great chasm, you should have seen Larry McNeely and Allen Ginsberg! It was one of those great, undocumented evenings in Nashville."

Berger's classmate Michael Minzer ran across Ginsberg in Centennial Park, where he was sitting under a tree, chanting while his lover and fellow poet Peter Orlovsky played the harmonium. Established in conjunction with the hundredth anniversary of Nashville's founding, the hundred-acre park attracted people of all stripes. A girl simply known as "Roxy" routinely planted herself on the steps of the park's replica of the Parthenon, singing and playing her accordion, and a dancer named Rico swayed nearby. Young people from all over the West End lazed in the grass, counted the clouds, and kept one drowsy eye peeled for Lieutenant Charles Stoner, the police's deliciously named vice-squad chief. "There's a wonderful little concrete shell out in the middle of the park," says Minzer. "We used to climb down into that. I remember a friend of mine from Kentucky brought back four or five garbage bags of some kind of wild pot that had grown by the side of the road. So we hunkered down in that shell and smoked so much pot we probably floated out of there." Then it might have been an illusion when Minzer saw the tattooed former prison inmate from Ohio, David Allan Coe, jamming in the park, his old black Cadillac hearse parked in front of the Parthenon, his name spelled out in masking tape on the car door. "He was standing out there with a little battery-powered amplifier," recalls Minzer, "just singing to anybody who would listen."

At night, waifs of the West End marched in the direction of the clubs. Young musicians and songwriters no longer sought out the Professional Club or Tootsie's, which had served a previous generation; they were headed to the House and Bishop's American Pub. Of all the newly popular dens, the Exit/In was the rage. Since it opened on Elliston Place, a street where Nashville's elite once dwelled, the club had drawn a loyal audience looking for rock and folk and hip country music. "The Exit/In was the main thing when it opened," declares Darrell Berger. "It was a real watershed because all sorts of people came to Nashville to record, but they oftentimes didn't perform; they were just kind of in and out. The Exit/In gave them a chance to perform, pick up a few bucks, try out some new songs. It was also a chance for people who were not going to fill up a regular auditorium or a big venue. I remember [saxophonist] Charles Lloyd came to the Exit/In. I remember Jimmy Buffett was there before his first album came out. Jerry Jeff Walker, people like that." Barefoot Jerry, Nashville's answer to the country-rock band phenomena, often played the Exit/In to enthusiastic crowds. Led by session man, songwriter, and producer Wayne Moss, the band boasted A-list virtuosity with hippie attitude as well as a Monument Records contract. Dozens of unsigned bands knocking around Nashville attempted to emulate them.

Billy Swan, sporting a beard and mustache, sitting with the band Barefoot Jerry. Leader Wayne Moss is standing second from the left.

Outside the Exit/In at night, Elliston Place bustled. George and Arizona Star posed on the sidewalk while clubbers dashed into the Gold

Rush for another drink and hungry college students invaded the Elliston Place Soda Shop, whose carrots and cottage cheese plate passed for vegetarian fare in early 1970s Nashville. After the music faded on Elliston Place, nighthawks hustled across West End Avenue to the Burger Boy or the Pancake Man, where they might find drunks fumbling with a slice of pie, country stars slamming the pinball machines, or Kinky Friedman holding forth on Richard Nixon.

Photograph by Alan Mayor

Bobby Bare (left) and Shel Silverstein at the Exit/In.

★   ★   ★

THE YOUTHFUL ENERGY in the West End inevitably rejuvenated the creative spirits of musicians and songwriters who had arrived in the years just prior to the neighborhood's awakening. Kristofferson, of course, rose in the new tide and then fueled its momentum. He was joined by Vince Matthews and Jim Casey, songwriters who—like Kristofferson—bridged the old Professional Club and new Exit/In worlds. Vince had arrived in town from Chicago in the mid-1960s and eventually signed a publishing deal with Jack Clement, while Jim Casey followed three years later when recording artist Dickey Lee invited him to write for a publishing company he owned with Jack Clement and his protégé Allen Reynolds, who decades later produced Garth Brooks.

Courtesy of Jim Casey

Songwriters Jim Casey (left)
and Vince Matthews, at Casey's
wedding in Kingston Springs,
Tennessee.

According to Casey, Clement encouraged his writers to stretch their
artistic abilities into other fields, like record producing and filmmaking,
so Casey produced Matthews, who sang flatter than Johnny Cash and
looked as handsome as a lifeguard. "Vince was the guy who idolized
Elvis when he was a kid," says Casey. "In his class when everybody was
supposed to show up for his graduation picture with a black coat on and
a tie, Vince went and rented a white tuxedo. And they made him go
change it. He was always different."

By 1969, Matthews was making important connections. Johnny
Cash recorded his "Wrinkled, Crinkled, Wadded Dollar Bill" and invited him to sing "Melva's Wine" on his television show; Cash himself
would cover the song in 1971. Unfortunately, Matthews rarely capitalized on such opportunities, which people around him attributed to his
unusual appetite for pills and alcohol, although most everybody was
using in Matthews's world.

"There was a doctor over in East Nashville," recalls Casey, who lived
near Centennial Park. "Vince and John Harris [of Barefoot Jerry] were

both skinnier guys, and I was the fattest one of some of those guys, so they would have me go in for the checkup. And you'd pay twenty-five dollars for a checkup and he'd take your blood pressure and listen to your heart and then he'd say, 'What do you want.' And then you told him what you wanted. The big one back then was [the amphetamine] Obedrin-LA, that's an 'LA turnaround' and the little brother of that was called the yeller. It was a smaller dose of Obedrin. People did all of that in private, but believe me you could tell when somebody was on an amphetamine because they'd be all livened up and sweating and their hair is greasy. They'd be talking a mile a minute and making big huge plans, always making a big plan for something."

Vince's big plan was the *Kingston Springs Suite*, which dealt with the clash between new ways and tradition, viewed through the old railroad men and blacksmiths who lived in his adopted hometown, some twenty-five miles west of Nashville. His enthusiasm drew a team of supporters. Johnny Cash offered his Hendersonville recording studios, Kris Kristofferson invested thousands of dollars, songwriter Shel Silverstein chipped in and consulted, and Jim Casey held Vince's hand in the studio and everywhere else. The notion of a concept album was at home in the times. "Nobody knew what the future was going to hold," says Casey. "We all thought, 'This is really cool. Look at these great albums that people are cutting.' And one album that really made us think that was [the Nitty Gritty Dirt Band's] *Will the Circle Be Unbroken*. It was a concept album that was so wide-ranging but really about the music. We all thought, 'Wow. This is going to expand. There's going to be more concept albums and these great writers. It's going to become easier and easier.'"

Soon, the town of Kingston Springs became West End West as Vince's friends retreated to his home on Saturday afternoons. "I used to take my daughter out there to go fishing," says Kristofferson. "It was very small. But there was a group of us who'd just sit around, and all we thought was important was music."

In 1972, Matthews invited his benefactors down to Kingston Springs for a presentation of his suite in the grammar school's gymnasium. Johnny Cash, his wife, June, and their son John Carter sat in folding aluminum chairs while the townspeople took seats around them. Coal-oil lamps flickered, and a local chorus warmed up the audience. "This time, I came to be entertained," bellowed Cash to nobody in particular.

Matthews—with his halting vocals—reeled off the songs in twenty-five minutes, and then invited the audience back to his house for chili, where Cash obliged a request to sing "I Still Miss Someone" and then got in line for food. "The Cashes sat up there and it was the neatest thing because they really felt like down-home folks," says Jim Casey. "All the town folks were there but nobody bugged him. It was at night and they were all sitting in different places around the yard and in the house. They just genuinely had a great time. Relaxed. Like they really belonged."

But Cash as well as Vince's other supporters had other projects of their own. Left in Vince's hands alone, the future of *Kingston Springs Suite* seemed questionable. "By this time I was working on the road some, and finally making some money," says Kristofferson. "I gave him a bunch to pay off a bunch of bills he had, and he went right over and bought a [studded] Elvis suit."

Jim Casey remembers that it was actually a cape: "This was just like Vince. Kris said he saw Vince come down the street and say, 'You won't believe what I bought. I bought this cape.' And he put this cape around him." He told Kris that it would be perfect for the performances of his masterpiece, that when the last song, "God Save Kingston Springs," faded, he'd spread the cape around himself as the stage lights dimmed. "Vince was never supposed to be a [performer]," concludes Kristofferson. "But that's where all the money went."

In the fall of 1974, Vince's wife, Melva, hired a film crew to shoot a vignette in Kingston Springs to accompany the music. The sketch called for villagers to march up the main street singing behind Vince and his guitar while the camera cut away to shots of the old blacksmith's wagon and other images of small-town life. About a hundred locals flowed into town on a Saturday morning while the crew parked a cherry picker on the railroad tracks, the highest point around, to get the best shots. "All of a sudden," says Jim Casey, "I noticed everybody pause and just look around and I thought, 'That's a funny look on their face.' And then I realized they were listening to the train coming up around the curve. The train was highballing through there from Memphis to Nashville, not slowing down a bit. They had tried to get the cherry picker off, but it had its hooks down in the asphalt. The cameraman and the driver dove out of there. That train came around and hit that cherry picker and completely blew it up into a million pieces. Unbelievable. It derailed the whole train, shut down the tracks for a day. The whole thing blew apart."

Later, Vince reshot the scene, but the townspeople—none of whom was hurt in the catastrophe—had tired of the visionary in their midst. "That signaled the end," says Casey. "It really did." To this day, no *Kingston Springs* music or film has ever been officially released. Vince wrote two hits in 1975—"This Is My Year for Mexico" for Crystal Gayle and "Love in the Hot Afternoon" for Gene Watson—before moving to New York City. He eventually returned to Tennessee, where he died, alone, at his home in Waverly, forty miles west of Kingston Springs.

IRONICALLY, MANY OF the new artists flooding the West End hailed from Texas, choosing Nashville at the same time Willie Nelson was rejecting it. Nashville, of course, already had its share of Texas influence, from Ernest Tubb to Waylon Jennings. But Texas-born singer-songwriters who arrived in the 1960s such as Kris Kristofferson, Mickey Newbury, and Townes Van Zandt (who was in and out of town playing clubs and making records for Jack Clement) were giving a slightly younger generation of Texas singers and songwriters cause to rethink Nashville, even as Austin was blossoming. Guy Clark, from West Texas, hit town in 1971; Marcia Ball, from western Louisiana by way of Austin, followed in 1972; Fort Worth–born Hugh Moffatt arrived in 1973; and Steve Earle, raised near San Antonio, followed him in 1974.

Houston-born Rodney Crowell drove to town in 1972 and proved to be one of the most influential new arrivals from the Lone Star State. Crowell's parents grew up sharecropping in west Tennessee, met at a Roy Acuff show in 1942, and moved to the oil refineries of Houston shortly after they married. "In that east-side Houston common labor culture, the music was out of Nashville," explains Crowell. "Hank Williams was a hero in our household and, later, Johnny Cash." Because the Nashville kings defined country music, he never considered going to New York, Austin, or Los Angeles. Besides, you could drive to middle Tennessee in one day, if you got up early in the morning.

In what became one of Nashville's great hungry-artist stories, Crowell slept in his car amid the musty aroma of sumac trees, bathed in lakes outside town until the weather turned cold, and poked around the West End meeting songwriters. Finally, he found a house to rent on Acklen Street in Hillsboro Village, with fellow Texas songwriter Richard Dobson and bass player Skinny Dennis Sanchez. "Every night there was songwriters and the hard drinking all night long, and song swapping," says Crowell.

Courtesy of author's collection

Rodney Crowell.

"Most everybody wrote creatively by themselves somewhere and would come together and show their wares," says Crowell. "And it was never about collaborating or writing on the spot. It was like, 'Hey, here's something I'm working on.' It was a shared experience of like, 'How's it coming? Where you getting with this as an artist?' And it was great for me to be around that because I could sense growth in other artists and sort of measure that in myself. It'd be three a.m. and David Olney pulls out 'Saturday Night and Sunday Morning,' and he'd just written it. And we'd go, 'Oh fuck.' The bar just got higher."

Early on, Crowell met Guy Clark, who had come to Nashville from Los Angeles after eight months there writing for RCA's Sunbury Music. One of those writers with the all-important sponsorship, he'd been given the chance to move to New York but chose Nashville because of Kristofferson's reputation and the brotherly songwriting community. He wasn't long making his mark: In 1972, Jerry Jeff Walker—one of the big names of the Austin movement—cut "L.A. Freeway," which Clark had written about his short stay in California. The song's commercial sizzle turned heads in Nashville, placing him directly in the center of the new songwriting community that had pulled him there in the first place. His brooding good looks and expansive songwriting style put him in the same category as Kristofferson. "We were all young," growls Clark. "We were all on fire. We were writing songs. Most everybody I knew was more than happy to play [their] new songs anytime [they] wanted to do it, and you could do the same. It wasn't a competitive sport. It was kind of a movable community. It was far-out."

Clark and his wife, Susanna, mentored many of the unsponsored musicians in town. They did the same for the troubled Townes Van Zandt, first when they crossed paths in California and now in Nashville. Songwriters gathered at a large table in the Clarks' East Nashville home, carving their names in the wooden surface, swapping songs, inhaling Guy's thoughts about music, and then, just inhaling.

Backstage at the Exit/In (left to right): Jerry Jeff Walker, Donnie
Fritts, John Prine, Guy Clark, and Billy Swan.

With that "L.A. Freeway" money, Guy had bought a house on Old
Hickory Lake in Hendersonville and often invited Rodney out to visit.
One night, they chugged around the lake's perimeter in Guy's boat until Guy found the place he wanted to stop. And then he cut the engine.
The water slapping the sides of the boat, Clark pointed to Johnny Cash's
house. Crowell marveled at the glowing windows of the massive struc-
ture, unaware that the tall man inside would figure dramatically in his
career and personal life.

Back in town, Guy dominated the Exit/In stage and Rodney played
singer-songwriter nights at Bishop's American Pub on West End Avenue, where the owners fortified the players with free hamburgers and
beer, and patrons filed in and out all evening. "Basically, it's busking
indoors," quips Crowell. "You play, and you pass a hat. And six or eight
people would go on each night, and I'd pick up six dollars. [Back then],
it was a dollar for gas, sixty-nine cents for breakfast, and a little money
left over."

Advertisement for Bishop's American
Pub, 1971.

Soon Crowell caught the attention of guitarist and RCA recording
star Jerry Reed, who along with Harry Warner and Chet Atkins owned
the publishing company Vector Music. "They just heard a couple songs
that I wrote that they thought were good. So you invest a hundred dollars a week in this guy. I was dead broke and they pay me a hundred
dollars a week to write songs. Man, I could eat! Keep a roof! And not
have to work at anything other than writing. It was good. And I think
that it probably was just that Kristofferson had made it, so that Harry
Warner and Jerry Reed *and* Chet Atkins recognized that 'this kid, he's
got some of that.' I was free. They were from a different school. I was
from a new school. I had a hippie girlfriend and drove a Volkswagen

and had long hair and smoked dope. They scratched their chins and were like, 'Oh, okay. I don't get it, but keep the songs coming. Show up every once in a while.'"

When Reed recorded Crowell's "You Can't Keep Me Here in Tennessee," the young outlaw edged away from the seedy West End world and toward the Old Hickory Lake possibilities that Guy Clark enjoyed. New chances and golden opportunities abounded for Crowell. Like when he visited the Palomino Club in North Hollywood, California, to see his new Texas friend Mickey Raphael playing harmonica with Willie Nelson. "Unbeknownst to me," recalls Crowell, "Willie says, 'There's a songwriter in the audience, and I'd like him to come up. I'm going to sing a song of his.' So I went up onstage and sang 'Till I Gain Control Again' with Willie. And I remember floating up there and going, 'Oh, I've just been knighted by Willie Nelson.' It was a pivotal moment for me because I felt like I was really in. I felt like I was really an artist."

Paris of the thirties, my ass, it was one big con.

—**Kinky Friedman**

★ *Seven*

Hillbilly Central

SINGER AND SONGWRITER Miriam Eddy caught Waylon's eye in Arizona in the early 1960s, when she was married to the wizard guitarist Duane Eddy. Her wild dark hair and eyes like a doe's could rivet any man, so, naturally, when Waylon met her again in 1968, he hadn't forgotten her. "She had separated from Duane," wrote Waylon, "but they weren't divorced yet. Her sister, Sharon, brought her to a show, and I got her up on the stage to sing with me. . . . I looked at her and said, 'Hey, little girl . . . want to run off with me?' She gave me the eye back. 'Call me in six months' was all she said."

Within a year, they married and forged a musical partnership that became central to the outlaw music legacy. He helped her sign with RCA and coproduced her first sessions. Working as Jessi Colter, an old family name with outlaw resonance, she played keyboards for Waylon on the road, and, shortly after their marriage, appeared on *The Johnny Cash Show* in a stunning red dress while Waylon sang his 1969 hit version of Chuck Berry's "Brown-Eyed Handsome Man." In 1970, their duet cover of Elvis Presley's "Suspicious Minds"—produced by Ronny Light—tore up the country charts. Like Tammy Wynette at George Jones's side, Jessi polished Waylon's image, and their marriage set the stage for Jessi's run of hits in the mid-1970s. Waylon's run of big hits, however, got rolling independent of Jessi. For that, he had manager Neil Reshen to thank.

From the very start, Reshen took up the Waylon banner and refused to let it touch the ground. "He was a typical go-get-'em kind of guy," says Billy Ray Reynolds. "We played Max's Kansas City in New York and when you stepped on the subway, there was a big poster of Waylon and it said, 'Waylon: His Music Ain't All That Sweet.' He had them plastered everywhere. We did a week there. It was just phenomenal. Anybody who was in New York at the time, they all came to see us. . . . From there it was just kind of a mushroom that exploded."

In 1972, Waylon unhooked Reshen's muzzle. The new manager charged that RCA had let Waylon's contract lapse by failing to pick up its option, and demanded a host of concessions from Chet and company. The two parties clashed for months, while Reshen let rumors fly that Atlantic coveted Waylon just as it had Willie Nelson. In May, Waylon recorded four songs with Ronny Light at the helm, and then, in what amounted to a strike, disappeared from the RCA studios for six months. Among that last quartet of songs that Waylon recorded that day was one from Willie's pen: the appropriately titled "Pretend I Never Happened."

Waylon wanted the moon: control over advertising budgets and artwork, a big advance, and the right to produce his own records. No doubt, he had taken note of the artistic freedom everywhere around him—on the streets of the West End, in Austin, in the songwriting career of Kristofferson—but his demands also echoed those of young directors and movie stars in Hollywood who were extracting big budgets from the big studios to make movies without interference. The old lions out west conceded that youthful autonomy paid dividends; however, the big labels in Nashville weren't so sure. Not even Kristofferson produced his own records.

According to Waylon's biographer R. Serge Denisoff, Atkins and his heir apparent Jerry Bradley tried to deal with only Waylon, without Reshen, but the singer rebuffed them, forcing the executives to joust with the prickly New Yorker, whose chinstrap beard misleadingly gave him the look of a cherubic Mennonite. Angry phone calls and threats dragged on for months, until an autumn meeting of the parties at RCA-Nashville during which Reshen restated his demands and the executives finally listened. By the end of the day, RCA green-lighted Waylon's request to produce his own records, as well as an advance that hovered around seventy-five thousand dollars and an 8 percent royalty rate.

In a statement to the press on November 27, 1972, RCA trumpeted its continued relationship with Waylon, and less than a month later, Waylon returned to the studio, recording tracks slated for the album *Lonesome, On'ry & Mean*. He brought his own band and turned first to Vince Matthews and Jim Casey's "Laid Back Country Picker," which failed to make the final album cut and remained unreleased for thirty-one years. The finished album smelled a little like his previous RCA outings because it mixed old and new tracks, but Waylon's deep and easy vocals and the churning country-rock sound unleashed by the Waylors on the title track charted a new course for Waylon. "While Steve Young, the terminal country and folk music outsider, may have penned ["Lonesome, On'ry & Mean"]," wrote critic Thom Jurek, "it is Waylon's delivery as an anthem that bears in it all of the years of frustration at not being able to make the music he wanted to that is heard in the grain of its lyrics."

★　　★　　★

WHEN THE TENSE negotiations over Waylon's contract subsided, the singer is said to have looked the weary Chet Atkins in the eye and assured him that his quarrel had been with the company, not him.

Obviously, Waylon sensed that the negotiations had drained Atkins. And he was right. Within days of Waylon's return to the studio, the producer-guitarist abandoned the helm.

"It was after five o'clock one afternoon, and I was in my office," says Jerry Bradley. "Chet was in a meeting with Waylon. And Chet was behind his desk, and Waylon was sitting on a couch. Chet called me in, and said, 'Jerry, I need you to come in for a minute.' And I came in and Chet and Waylon were in a very heated discussion about drugs. They were going at it pretty good and Chet said, 'Well, that isn't going to matter, because I'm quitting tomorrow.' I didn't say anything. Waylon said, 'Well, who's going to take your place?' Chet turned [to me] and said, 'He is.' And Waylon said, 'Well, hell, I want off the label.' I just kind of shrugged my shoulders and didn't say nothing." RCA rushed out another press release announcing that Chet would still be working with roster artists but wanted more time to perform and record. Jerry Bradley was now in charge, although insiders knew that he'd been essentially running the office since 1970.

News of Chet's departure overshadowed Waylon's revolutionary contract, but in time the country music industry got the point. For the first time in anybody's memory an RCA artist based in Nashville would determine his own path in the studio. But most in the business never knew that the tempestuous negotiations to win that freedom had driven Chet Atkins from top management.

★   ★   ★

IN MARCH 1972, as Waylon and Neil's quarrel with RCA had taken shape, Willie Nelson made plans for the Dripping Springs Reunion, plainly intended to be the Austin area's very own Woodstock. Promoters envisioned selling almost two hundred thousand tickets for the three-day festival, which featured towering Nashville stars such as Roger Miller, Bill Monroe, Earl Scruggs, Loretta Lynn, Roy Acuff, and Hank Snow as well as their younger counterparts in the songwriting world, most notably Kris Kristofferson and Lee Clayton. Performances by Waylon and Willie and Kris were slated to close the extravaganza on Sunday, March 19. Strangely, few Austin-based performers joined the bill. At the very least, however, the combination of Snow, Kristofferson, Acuff, and Clayton announced the old guard's step to the side for youth culture, whether in Austin or Nashville.

Willie's name drew the stars, but Willie controlled neither promotion nor the weather nor the venue. Staged at a ranch outside Austin, the planners had tried to plant grass to create lush seating in the farm-yard amphitheater, but the seeds never sprouted and concertgoers pitched their camps on hard dirt. They also endured unusual heat, dusty wind, and emcee Tex Ritter's bad jokes. Still, the Texas working folk with their beer and the hippie contingent with their pot carried on without a care, taking in a rich array of performances.

"You'd look out there and it'd be hillbillies, cowboy guys, and then you have the hippies, all having fun together," says Donnie Fritts, who went with Kristofferson. "I think that was a big part of what was developing there in the seventies. And then you got on the stage with Willie and his family and Waylon and whoever was there. It was one of the most important gatherings of the seventies, bringing all the different acts and people together in one place. And it happened through Willie Nelson."

From a money standpoint, the festival flopped. But various reporters lured by the hillbilly Woodstock hook memorialized Willie's big dance on the dry plains. Rock-and-roll photographer Jim Marshall showed up with cameras dangling around his neck, along with *Rolling Stone*'s writer Grover Lewis and photographer Annie Leibovitz. They found all of the egos, groupies, drugs, backstage drama, and audience foolishness of one of those big-time rock-and-roll shows. "Everywhere now there are spiraling cairns of empty Pearl and Jax and Lone Star beer cans," observed Lewis. "A rawboned high-school kid in a wide-brimmed straw hat, a white shirt with pearl snaps, a Texas belt buckle, and those kind

of Wrangler jeans that drape down across the boots, covering all but
the toes, trips over one of the piles on his way back from a Porta-Can
and goes sprawling, ass over teakettle. He lurches to his feet and grins
vacantly. . . ."

Onstage, Tex Ritter barred Tom T. Hall from answering his loud en-
cores, and Loretta Lynn sashayed through a set of saucy hits. Backstage,
the stars and promoters argued over money and allotted stage time.
Earl Scruggs generously stuck around to fill in for acts such as the Light
Crust Doughboys and Merle Haggard, who didn't show, and Waylon
Jennings revealed his wide streak of magnanimity, according to Dave
Hickey, who was hired by the festival to coordinate talent and later
contributed regular meditations on Texas warbling to *Country Music*
magazine. Hickey observed that Waylon and the Waylors had finished
their segment and pocketed their money when they learned that one of
country music's stalwart names—whom Hickey did not identify—was
refusing to play until his cash appeared. "Then, without it being asked
or implied," he wrote, "Waylon reached into his pocket, pulled out the
roll of bills he had been paid, and handed it back to the promoter. 'Here
you go,' he said. 'Give the old fart his money. . . .' The promoter nearly
burst into tears, and when he tried to thank Waylon, Waylon grabbed
him by the shoulders and pointed him off toward the 'country music
star's' bus."

When the last tones blared from the stage, *Rolling Stone*'s Lewis approached Willie and asked if the whole three-day spectacle was worth
repeating. Nelson's pensive eyes dropped down. "You mean if the same
people was runnin' it, or somebody else was?" he replied. "I don't know
about the same people." Indeed, Willie returned. The following year,
this time on Independence Day, Dripping Springs let the nation know
once again about the growing multi-striped cult of Willie, instigating
a string of annual July Fourth picnics elsewhere around the state that
would be far better attended, more profitable, and just as circus-like.

Amid the Dripping Springs hullabaloo, Waylon Jennings encountered Billy Joe Shaver's songwriting. Shaver, whose "Good Christian Soldier" had made Kristofferson's *Silver Tongued Devil* album, was Texas-born but like Kinky Friedman and Rodney Crowell and others he had brought his goods to the Nashville marketplace and remained. Waylon's guitarist Billy Ray Reynolds had first encountered the songwriter in the late 1960s, when Reynolds was screening submitted demos for a publishing company owned by steel guitarist Pete Drake. "I was just worn-out, just completely worn-out and the boxes were just full [of demos]," says Reynolds. "There must have been a couple thousand reel-to-reel tapes in there. So one day, kind of like drawing in a raffle, I was going to find something at the bottom and pull it. I stuck my arm down there and got a tape and came out with it. I put it on the reel-to-reel. It was the worst singer I ever heard and terrible guitar playing rhythm. But I listened to the song. It was almost like listening to Shakespeare. It was well written and just knocked me out. I called this boy, and I said, 'I don't know who you are and you don't know me and there's nothing I can do for you. But I just want you to know that I just heard one of your songs and it just knocked me out.' He thanked me and about two weeks later I came in one morning to work and I looked up and there was the ugliest, meanest-looking human being that you ever saw. Standing in the door way. It was Billy Joe Shaver."

Down in Dripping Springs, Shaver had ridden to the festival with fellow songwriter Lee Clayton and *Rolling Stone* journalist Lewis, who made Shaver a main character in his story. Lewis followed Shaver as he performed as part of a songwriters' set, critiqued the armed security, and chatted with a hippie chick. By the end of the article, Shaver was smiling silly over Waylon's interest in two of his songs: "Black Rose," about interracial romance, and "Willie the Wandering Gypsy and Me," about you know who.

In his autobiography, Shaver recalled Waylon tumbling out of his Dripping Springs trailer cum dressing room when he heard the songwriter playing "Willie" backstage. "He asked me if I had any more cowboy songs," wrote Shaver. "I said I had a whole stack of them. He said he wanted to do an entire album of those songs, and told me to come to Nashville so we could record it. (He didn't know I already lived in Nashville or that I'd already written a song for Kris. . . .) The whole conversation didn't last ten minutes, and nobody signed anything."

★   ★   ★

BACK IN NASHVILLE, hairstyles may have remained above the ear around the offices of RCA, but elsewhere in the industry Waylon and more than a few men and women in their thirties began to look like young people strolling on the West End sidewalks. Nowhere was this more apparent than on 916 Nineteenth Avenue South, where Tompall, Jim, and Chuck Glaser ran a studio that married country music's Brylcreem past with its long-locks present. Its doors propped open to let in the young breezes sweeping through the West End, the so-called Hillbilly Central offices became an outlaw safe haven. Former employees recalled Willie Nelson lazing on the front lawn, and Waylon haunting the offices at three in the morning.

The Glaser Brothers had come to Nashville in the late 1950s after performing as a teen vocal group in their home state of Nebraska. In prairie theaters, the trio sat on stools and harmonized while their father, Louis, hid behind the stage curtain and announced songs. Later, they rated an appearance on the popular *Arthur Godfrey's Talent Scouts* and then latched on to Marty Robbins, whose 1957 do-wah hit "A White Sport Coat (and a Pink Carnation)" demanded that crooning singers appear behind him onstage.

The Robbins gig brought the brothers to Nashville, where they parlayed their act and association with the golden hitmaker into a small empire. When Robbins wasn't on the road, they joined other package shows, including Johnny Cash's. And they formed a publishing company that signed, among others, John Hartford, who laid the company's golden egg: "Gentle on My Mind."

Jim Glaser recorded on Starday and then RCA while writing several hits for the family publishing company, and Tompall played guitar on sessions, including Johnny Cash's, and collaborated with Harlan Howard to write "The Streets of Baltimore," a big hit for Bobby Bare in 1966. That same year, the brothers teamed with Jack Clement, who produced their string of moderately successful albums on MGM. In one big way, the brothers were a lot like Clement: they spent the spoils of their latest successes on developing their business presence in the music industry.

Although Chuck was said to have the business eye, Tompall emerged as the strongest personality among the brothers and the face on their business endeavors. He also proved to be the most difficult. The singer often butted heads with Marty Robbins when the brothers worked for him, and he once came to blows with Jack Clement, according to Jim Casey, who saw it all. Says Billy Ray Reynolds, "Tompall was pretty much an alcoholic and just arrogant. He looked over at me [one time] and he was drunk and his eyes were all watery and he said, 'You'd probably knock the hell out of me if I got smart with you.' I said, 'Let's just don't go there, Tom. Let's be friends.'"

Photograph by Alan Mayor

Tompall Glaser.

Around the music business, Tompall's tirade against the folk-rock Byrds was legendary. On March 15, 1968, the folk-rock band had somehow wrangled a guest spot on the *Grand Ole Opry*, and Tompall was hosting its segment. He introduced the songs, and the band performed the scheduled "Sing Me Back Home," but then Gram Parsons veered off the set list and sang "Hickory Wind," which he dedicated to his grandmother. "You could see Glaser turn red from the neck up," Byrds road manager Jimmi Seiter told Parsons's biographer, David N. Meyer. "He was fucking livid. He thought we told him the wrong songs on purpose." Backstage, Tompall stormed at Parsons.

By 1972, Tompall demanded that people accept in him the independence Parsons had asserted on the *Opry*. Though still under contract to MGM, he had become another independent producer, although not just another independent producer: he produced himself in his own setting, the Glaser Sound Studios. It was exactly the model Waylon had set his eyes upon when he and Reshen renegotiated with RCA.

The studio hosted a fraternity of singers, songwriters, and Nashville dropouts living the verse of a strumming and bumming honky-tonk song. "It was just people hanging around, getting a little groove on, having fun," says Donnie Fritts, sounding as if he were describing a barroom in Austin. "We threw knives in the back of that place for hours at a time. We got really good at it, too." Former disc jockey Roger Schutt, known to all of Nashville by his old WKDA radio moniker "Captain Midnight," slept in the office at night and took care of little jobs for Tompall during the day, when he wasn't throwing knives. Struggling songwriter Peck Chandler, from Oklahoma, camped out in an outbuilding devoid of electricity, screening songs for the brothers' publishing company to earn his lodging. "They had an extension cord from the studio running over the property and into his room, and he slept on a mattress on the floor there," says Even Stevens, who briefly wrote for the Glasers and later produced Eddie Rabbitt and others. Occasionally, adds Stevens, Chandler's screening of songs involved nothing more than holding to his ear a tape submitted by a starving writer, grunting dismissively, and tossing it across the room.

In the Glasers' prairie box house, which was large by Music Row standards, business carried on with a semblance of normalcy, but at night the studio and offices awoke like a junkie in need of a fix. Sessions burned into the small hours until Tompall and his entourage peeled out into the streets in search of pinball machines, drinks, and greasy food. It was the bohemian-outlaw spirit of the West End run amok. In 1973, Dave Hickey ventured out with Tompall and his guys, who this night included Billy Joe Shaver and Roger "Captain Midnight" Schutt. "I discovered two principles of Glaser nightlife," wrote Hickey. "First, no pinball machine is passed by unplayed, and, secondly, any establishment which possesses a pinball machine hasn't much luck in trying to close while Tompall is playing the machine." Cruising like pimps in Tompall's 1972 Lincoln Mark IV, the gang stayed out until the edge of dawn, finishing up back at the studio with a few hangers-on from the Burger Boy. "The Jack Daniel's goes around again," observed Hickey. " 'Midnight' goes out on the couch, Shaver goes to sleep on the floor. Tompall picks up his guitar and starts playing the spiritual medley from [his new] album, and suddenly all the energy is back."

Tompall had encountered Waylon over the years, first in Phoenix, when the Glasers were touring and Waylon was disc jockeying, and then in Nashville, when Tompall tried to pitch him songs from the brothers' publishing company, but their relationship took hold in the early 1970s, when Waylon's relationship with RCA soured. According to Billy Ray Reynolds, Waylon had never really liked Tompall, but while the two were on tour in Europe, they found common ground. "We wound up in England at the same hotel. We just so happened to be in the lobby and Tompall came through and I said, 'You all got to get together and talk about the studio thing. We ought to do some demos over there.' They sat down on the couch, and I was gone about two hours or more and I came back and they were still sitting on the couch, right in each other's face, the biggest buddies you ever saw."

Waylon needed a place to house his publishing company, in addition to a studio where he could work out of RCA's reach. So he married his publishing interests to Tompall's and then set up his physical office at Hillbilly Central. The union of two independent spirits began. "You know, before Waylon and Tompall got together, they didn't know there was anybody else like them," said Hazel Smith, who worked for the Glasers at Hillbilly Central. "I think both of them secretly thought they might be crazy. They'd both been going their own way alone for so long, it never even entered their minds that someone else might feel the same way about country music and Nashville. They were both full-grown men, but still you like to know you're not alone."

★   ★   ★

PUTTING ON HOLD for the moment the transfer of his recording activities from RCA to the Glasers, Waylon returned to RCA's studios after *Lonesome, On'ry & Mean* to make the album that many consider his artistic zenith and the outlaw movement's first album: *Honky Tonk Heroes*. Recorded in the late winter and early spring of 1973, the record's roots coiled down to Dripping Springs and Billy Joe Shaver. In his autobiography, Shaver claimed that he returned to town after Dripping Springs assuming that Waylon had agreed to record a whole album of his work, but, of course, the *Rolling Stone* article that had so prominently featured the young writer only mentioned *two* songs.

According to Waylon's drummer Richie Albright, the idea for an entire album of Shaver's material sprang from a discussion with Bobby Bare, who published Shaver's songs and had invited Waylon over to listen to a whole clutch of them. The sparse stories of about highways lost and found appealed to the singer, despite the writer's skimpy track record, so he plucked a few more to go with the two from Dripping Springs. "If Waylon liked the song, that's what we did," says Albright.

"He could find a good song in the worst demo that you ever heard in your life. I wouldn't listen to it past the first verse, and he'd put it out. He'd start playing something and see the expression on my face and he'd say, 'Just listen.' So I'd give it a good listen and sure enough, he knew a good song. He had this Cadillac Deville and in the backseat there'd be cassettes stacked high. He'd say, 'Boy I got a good song the other day.'"

In the months after Dripping Springs, while Waylon battled with RCA and then completed *Lonesome, On'ry & Mean*, Shaver badgered him. "I'd leave messages at his office and he wouldn't call back," said Shaver, "or I'd call and they'd say he was on another line—I knew damn well he only had one line." Finally, he burst in on one of Waylon's sessions at RCA. "The walls were lined with girls and bikers and all kinds of hangers-on," remembered Shaver. Waylon sent Captain Midnight out of the studio with a hundred-dollar bill for Shaver if he'd just get lost. "That just pissed me off even more—I told Midnight to tell Waylon he could stick it up his ass. Midnight wasn't about to do that, and I'm pretty sure he just stuck that hundred-dollar bill in his pocket."

On February 19, 1973, Waylon pulled Tompall into the RCA studio as he finally turned to the Billy Joe Shaver songs, only they soon discovered that Shaver remained an annoyance. "We were doing the album and Billy Joe was around," says Albright, "and we [began] 'Honky Tonk Heroes,' so we cut the first part of the song and we stopped, and Waylon said, 'This is the way we're going to do it.' And Billy Joe had been sitting in the back and he come walking up, saying, 'What are you doing? You're fucking up my song. That ain't the way it goes.' Pretty soon Waylon and Billy Joe are just hollering at one another. Billy Joe didn't understand the way we were putting it together. Finally Waylon said, 'You just sit back. When we get finished, you can tell me if it's right or wrong.' So he finally agreed with that and then we put it together and he said, 'Yeah. That's good. That's the way it goes.'"

Photograph by Alan Mayor

Billy Joe Shaver (right) proved taller
than Willie Nelson.

When it came time to pick a single to release from the Shaver sessions, RCA promotion man Elroy Kahanek says, the company didn't
see one, so it asked Waylon to tack on to the album one more song from
his sessions. There were no leftover Shaver songs, but there were a few
others, including Steve Young's "Seven Bridges Road," Jimmie Rodg-
ers's "T for Texas," and Shel Silverstein's "The Leaving Coming On."
Finally, Waylon chose "We Had It All," written by Donnie Fritts and
Troy Seals. "That was really weird," observes Fritts. He recalls cruising around one night in Waylon's Cadillac with Waylon, Shaver, and
Captain Midnight when Waylon vaguely announced that somebody
else was getting writing credit on the album. "Whose song is it?" asked
Fritts, worried about Shaver's temper. Waylon mentioned "We Had It
All" and, to Fritts's relief, Shaver just shrugged. "It was a blessing to be
on that album, obviously. It was also very strange, having one song not
by Billy Joe. It seemed like a lot of people didn't like it."

Laden with dubbed-in strings and lots of echo on Waylon's vocals, "We Had It All" departed sonically from the balance of the album, not surprising in light of RCA-Nashville's checkered history with the album format. On the charts, the single proved one of Waylon's worst showings in years, discouraging the company from investing much more promotional effort in the album. "Their attitude then was that's not going to work," says Kahanek. "Let's go on and concentrate on something else."

Nonetheless, critics celebrated the album. "After many years of overproduction on record," applauded *Rolling Stone*, "Waylon Jennings' new album offers an opportunity to hear the crisp, robust no-nonsense sound which has been his trademark since his early days with Buddy Holly's Crickets." The review and others like it sensed his newfound freedom to make records the way he liked to make them. The theme carried over to the album cover, which snubbed the dreamy portraits and stilted scenarios that graced most country music albums in favor of the just-hangin'-out portraiture of the Beach Boys' *Sunflower* (1970), Tracy Nelson's *Mother Earth* (1972), and the Allman Brothers Band's *At Fillmore East* (1971), to name a few. On *Honky Tonk Heroes*, Waylon and his unkempt friends clutch drinks and guffaw at some unknown remark. Perhaps they've just poked fun at Jerry Bradley or Chet Atkins, or repeated a ribald joke told last night at the Burger Boy. In any case, the picture symbolized a renegade spirit that clashed with corporate ethos and linked with rock-and-roll cool. The album itself christened country music's outlaw era. Indeed, it was quintessentially outlaw, co-produced by Tompall, who kept one foot on the West End streets, recorded generally without RCA's influence, connected to Texas through Billy Joe Shaver and, of course, Waylon's origins, and bathed in risk, having gambled on the work of an untested songwriter.

★　　★　　★

WHILE *HONKY TONK HEROES* staggered on the charts, Waylon continued to spar with RCA. In September 1973, manager Neil

Reshen announced again that Waylon was splitting from the company, claiming breach of contract and trumpeting an imminent deal with a new label. In an interview with the *Tennessean*, he pointed to disagreements over Waylon's creative direction. The following day, RCA tersely replied that its artist was bound by the contract negotiated the previous November. "He tried to get out of the contract," said Wally Cochran, head of artist relations, "but there's nothing he or anybody else can do about it."

Reshen's appearance in the paper was more than just a ploy to boost albums sales with a dash of real outlaw rebellion. Instead, he was probably reacting to RCA's objection to Waylon's plans to record his next album at Glaser Sound Studios. During the *Honky Tonk Heroes* sessions, Waylon had blanched under the watchful eye of the RCA staff, which he claimed reported his studio drug use to Jerry Bradley.

One of the impediments to Waylon's dashing off to another studio was the recording engineers' union, whose contract demanded that RCA-employed engineers run the board on all company sessions. Waylon's move to the Glasers would leave the engineers in the cold, handing Jerry Bradley his first big Waylon problem since rising to Chet's old perch. "I'm in the middle because I loved the artists, but I'm management," pleads Bradley. "I have thirteen, fourteen engineers down here, and I'm trying to figure out how to do sessions. We had to coordinate that. It was a ridiculous situation to mix the freedom of making a session with a union, and we gave the union fair warning that it wasn't going to last."

During this latest round of negotiations with Reshen, New York–based vice president Mel Ilberman stepped into a hallway and asked Bradley if he really wanted to keep Jennings. "The answer was yes," declares Bradley, who remembers Ilberman's response. " 'Well, we got to get through this union problem.' It wasn't whether we wanted to keep Waylon or not keep Waylon: it was the union problem. Waylon wasn't going to let us keep sending the damn union guy everywhere he went. Ultimately, they just shut the studios up."

RCA sent an engineer to Waylon's first sessions at Glaser, but that never happened again. As Bradley points out, after a few years RCA and other labels merely divested themselves of studios and let artists record anywhere they wanted. It was a second blow in Waylon's favor: he'd brought down Chet Atkins and then toppled the engineers' union.

NO CEREMONY ANNOUNCED Waylon's first session at Hillbilly Central. Tompall just marched in one morning and told everybody to make way for the nighttime arrival of Waylon. He'd be with his producer . . . Willie Nelson. Who was no more a record producer than he was a duck trapper.

Photograph by Michael Streissguth

The building that housed Glaser Sound Studios as it appears today.

Glaser engineer Kyle Lehning scratched his head at the sight of Willie, but bolted upright when he spied Waylon. "I was in the studio playing a Wurlitzer electric piano through a wah-wah pedal into a guitar amplifier, just kind of farting around with it," says Lehning, who would go on to have a highly successful producing career. "And when Waylon walked in the door, he didn't say, 'How are you?' He didn't say, 'Hey, I'm Waylon.' He said, 'I hate those things.' I turned it off and said, 'Yep, you're the artist, go in.' And the band set up, put up all the gear, bass player came in. Within a half hour, tape was rolling. And Willie was in the control room with me. The very first thing they recorded was J. J. Cale's 'Louisiana Women.' And they kicked into it, and I was young and I thought, 'This is pretty cool, Waylon's pretty cool, I like this whole thing.' But this is how arrogant I was: While we were doing the playback of the first take, I hit play and went back out in the studio and turned the Wurlitzer back on and just started playing the Wurlitzer through the wah-wah player to the sound of the take coming through the door. And Waylon comes storming in there and said, 'Hey, hoss, show me how to run this tape machine and put that on this record!' And I thought, 'I'm gonna like this guy!' "

Waylon's first number-one song, "This Time," came out of his first re-cordings at Glaser, not to mention the top-five album of the same name. And Lehning's Wurlitzer indeed made it to the final master, as well as his keyboards, which he played when Jessi Colter wasn't around; unex-pectedly, he even contributed a trumpet part on the album's "Heaven and Hell." Such unscripted seasoning defined the studio and fueled the search for the right feel rather than sonic perfection.

Like Lehning, Music Row photographer Alan Mayor witnessed the uninhibited collaborative spirit at Hillbilly Central. "I was at a Shel Silverstein show at the Exit/In and was invited back over to Tompall Glaser's studio. Tompall and Shel were working on an album and they were trying to pick a single and they were playing their material for us and at the same time a very wired Waylon kept running to the door, sticking his head in and saying, 'Shel, I'm stuck. I'm trying to write this song, and I can't think of the lyric to go with it.' And he would give the line and Shel would just pop out the line and Waylon would say thanks and disappear for a few minutes. Then he'd come back in and say, 'I'm stuck again.' And Shel would toss him that follow up to the couplet and Waylon would disappear."

If Lehning was delightfully shocked that so many of his fingerprints appeared on *This Time*, he was mystified when Waylon collared him and took him on the road for a few months. "Jessi was opening for Waylon, and Waylon said, 'Why don't you come out and play second keyboard to Jessi on the road?' Jessi was playing grand piano and she had that kind of great gospel feel and style, and I played a Fender Rhodes with this crappy-sounding string ensemble through a Fender amp. Imagine how awful that sounded. So I learned her show, which was about thirty minutes. We were in Sacramento, California, and I played her set—and Waylon's band backed her up on the road. And Waylon was just standing in the wings with that leather Telecaster of his on his body. And Jessi got up and started to walk off the stage, and I got up and started to walk behind her. And Waylon said, 'Where're you going?' I said, 'Well, she's done with her set.' And he said, 'Oh no, you're going to play with us now.' I said, 'God, Waylon, I don't know your set!' And he looked at me and said, 'Hoss, there's only three chords!' I loved him for that. And he knew I played guitar and he would not let me see his hands! He never called the song title or anything. He'd just end one song and start the next. So I was always looking around and trying to figure out [the key]. It was funny. Finally, by osmosis I figured out the show."

It was more difficult to figure out how to react to the Hells Angels, who rushed to see Waylon whenever he played San Francisco venues like the Boarding House. "It started with a couple or a few and the next thing I knew, every place we'd play, it would look like a biker convention," says Billy Ray Reynolds. Waylon was like an accessible Sonny Barger to the gang members, out there on the road where bikes could follow, his dress accenting the up-yours rhetoric that appeared in magazines and newspapers across the country. "I refuse to be two different people," he would say. "I'm my own man. I'm as good as the best and as bad as the worst." When the bikers showed no signs of disappearing,

Waylon allowed them to provide security at shows, provided they left their stripes and guns at home.

But Hells Angels—who smelled like Altamont—unnerved Waylon. "Waylon had this tough-guy image, with the black hat, Mr. Outlaw and all this stuff," says Lehning. "But he was anything-but in those kinds of situations. We'd pull up to a venue and he'd be looking out the window [and say], 'Here they are, here are the motorcycles.' And he'd be like, 'Oh, God.' He was just afraid somebody would get hurt. It was not fun. But these guys loved him. And I remember him sitting on the bus going, 'Okay, I guess I got to walk out here.' And there would be this one particular Hells Angels guy named Deakon. And he'd walk off the bus and go, 'Deakon! Brother! Good to see you. Yeah!' And I could just see him going, 'I hope he doesn't pull a gun!'"

With no guns in sight, Deakon was only too glad to flash some muscle on behalf of Waylon and his band. "Every time we played Santa Monica Civic Auditorium, they had this one big [security] guy and he was just a pain in the neck," explains Reynolds. "He was a big weight-lifter-type guy and he'd give us stickers and badges to wear. Well, I didn't like to stick them on my clothes and I'd have them in my pocket and show it when I came to the backstage. He insisted that we have them sticking to our clothes, and anytime I went there, he'd give me a hard time.

"When we got off the bus, I always took my guitar and Waylon's guitar and our amps. So I was pretty loaded, so Deakon said, 'Let me get the door for you.' So here's this guy, and he remembers me from the last time. Deakon walked in front of him, and Deakon takes his arm and puts it under his throat and shoved this guy. You would have thought it was a D9 bulldozer pushing him up against the wall. And he said, 'Do you see this guy here. Don't you ever fool with him again.' This guy went and turned to jelly. I didn't have any more trouble out of him. But that's the guy Deakon was: he was as gentle as a lamb, but he was a tornado when he wasn't happy."

You walk down the crummy street, where practically
nobody is out now, for it is after dark and the pawnshops
and groceries and clothing stores are closed, and the
dummies wearing the new suits with the big red price
markers carrying the slashed price have been carried
in off the pavement and only the drugstore and the
delicatessen show lights in the block. . . . The wind drives
a sheet of newspaper over the cement with a dry, rustling
sound which reminds you of leaves rustling at night, when
you would be walking along a path in the woods,
at night, by yourself.

—**Robert Penn Warren**

★ *Eight*

Burger Boy Outlaws

THE AURA OF the outlaw, in the Old West sense of the word, had followed Waylon around country music since the late 1960s, when the news media began reporting the antics of his band members—drug busts, car crashes, lawsuits, and a shoot-out in Atlanta that left Paul Gray, one of the Waylors, dead. Although most of the public trouble went down out of Waylon's sight—including the shooting—his name was attached to it. And coupled with whispers about his three divorces, voracious pill-popping, and that session at RCA where he supposedly brandished a gun in front of Danny Davis, it made for the ultimate outlaw recipe. It's no wonder that the Hells Angels swarmed around him: he was the white Bumpy Jonas, a bad mother battling the John Shaft of his imagination.

Publicity photographs framed Waylon in leather vests or coats, blue jeans, and a black cowboy hat; and, in deference to the hippies, whimsical embroidery appeared on his shirts and beaded hemp hugged his neck. He dressed as a gunfighter on the cover of 1972's *Ladies Love*

Outlaws album and by 1974's *This Time* his hair and mustache had grown shaggy.

His folk-country efforts and Carl Smith look of the 1960s a dim memory, Waylon's recordings of jagged ballads such as Kristofferson's "Sunday Morning Coming Down," Steve Young's "Lonesome, On'ry & Mean," and Billy Joe Shaver's "Ain't No God in Mexico" only fueled an evolving bad-boy image that the U.S. consumer—raised on the legend of the outlaw—was inclined to gobble up.

In America, romantic bandits such as Jesse James, Billy the Kid, and Pretty Boy Floyd galloped through the national imagination with a zeal that had faded little since that dirty Robert Ford plugged James in the back of the head at St. Joseph, Missouri, in 1882. Yellow journalists and pulp historians exaggerated their criminal exploits and dubiously assigned them noble intentions until the myths overran the facts. Repeated tellings—in verse, the penny press, and family lore—transformed the rogue characters into Robin Hoods who plundered usurious banks, burning mortgages and spreading the loot among families in need. And always some calamitous event earlier in life justified their deeds. Indeed, they became archetypal outlaws, mostly western, who honored what Thoreau called "the right," whether it was legal or not. The American citizenry—bold marchers toward frontiers and champions of the little guy—identified with the outlaw ethos and over the decades promoted new men and women to the ranks: Belle Starr, Emmett Dalton, Ma Barker, John Wesley Hardin.

In the 1960s and 1970s, popular films such as *Bonnie and Clyde, Easy Rider*, and *Butch Cassidy and the Sundance Kid* served up an array of sympathetic lawbreakers, while outlaw-colored albums like Bob Dylan's *John Wesley Harding* and Johnny Cash's *At Folsom Prison* sold like a getaway car. FM radio, too, echoed the trend, broadcasting the Eagles' "Outlaw Man," the Steve Miller Band's "Take the Money and Run," and Eric Clapton's and Bob Marley's recordings of "I Shot the Sheriff."

While popular culture celebrated the outlaw mythos, a new breed of outlaw rooted authentically in social justice emerged. They included Diane Nash and John Lewis of the Nashville integration demonstrations, athletes Tommie Smith and John Carlos, whose black power gestures stirred the Mexico City Olympics in 1968, and Daniel Ellsberg, who leaked the Pentagon Papers, revealing governmental secrets about the Vietnam War. Indeed, even the workaday college student, as portrayed in weekly magazines and network news programs, communicated outlaw ethos. "They are serious people who take questions of war and peace, wealth and poverty, racism and emancipation personally and passionately," noted the *Washington Post*. "They do not agree with the way their universities deal with these questions. As a practical matter, they cannot leave the universities, so they are fighting for a part in the decision-making process."

★　　★　　★

IN 1973, A NORTH CAROLINA disc jockey who was promoting a Waylon-Tompall concert called Glaser Brothers staffer Hazel Smith and asked her how the men described their music. "I reached under my desk," says Smith, "and pulled out *Webster's Collegiate Dictionary*, and I started looking up words, like *mustang*. That wasn't it. I decided to look up the word *outlaw*. I don't know why I did. I'd never looked it up before, and there was a definition there, but the very last line said these words: 'Living on the outside of the written law.' And I thought to myself, 'You can't say how a song is supposed to be written, nor can you say how a singer is supposed to sing a song.' But what these guys were doing, the music, was certainly different from what had ever been done in this hillbilly town. And they were just beginning to feel their roots, and they were mature enough that they wanted their [records to sound] the same way it was when they did their concerts. I'm telling you, that's all they wanted. They wanted their music to be as good as it was when they were doing their live shows." Over the ensuing years, Hazel's creation slowly engulfed the various labels for that country music with rock attitude coming out of Nashville and Austin—such as "progressive country" and "redneck rock," and "redneck hip."

"You know, living on the outside of the written law, that is not something that somebody'd been put in jail for," Smith continues. "That's somebody that don't agree with what's going on. That's what I felt like it was, and to me it had everything to do with music. Nobody wanted to shoot nobody! It wasn't that. I just thought that they had something. I mean, you got to have a title."

Whenever Waylon, Tompall, Billy Joe, and others appeared together in concerts, the Glaser booking agency—doing business as Nova Productions—packaged them as "outlaws," and soon journalists, particularly those at *Country Music*, wielded the term like a salt shaker. In January 1974, *Country Music* ran a Dave Hickey essay headlined "In Defense of the Telecaster Cowboy Outlaws," which listed Waylon and Willie atop a roll call of deviants that included Kris Kristofferson, Billy Joe Shaver, Tompall Glaser, Kinky Friedman, Lee Clayton, Mickey Newbury, and Townes Van Zandt.

Waylon (right) with Willie.

"Just by watching and listening," wrote Hickey, "I can tell you they're just about the only folks in Nashville who will walk into a room where there's a guitar and a *Wall Street Journal* and pick up the guitar." He also poked fun at journalists bent on categorizing artists, but, ironically, his article immortalized the core group of outlaws as if they were signers of the Declaration of Independence, effectively establishing a genre, if not a marketing label. He only forgot one name: David Allan Coe, the tattooed guy with the black hearse who had graduated from the Red Dog Saloon and Centennial Park to the Exit/In.

Only by early 1974 Coe had written Tanya Tucker's hit "Would You Lay with Me (in a Field of Stone)" and moved up to urban clubs such as Max's Kansas City in New York. He remained based in Nashville, though, and to most in the West End circle, his behavior screamed "outlaw" a little too loudly. With an eye on Johnny Cash's prison myths, the thirty-four-year-old told everybody he'd done a stretch on death row for killing a fellow jailbird who tried to rape him. For a while, major publications like the *New York Times*, *Rolling Stone*, *Penthouse*, and *Country Music* swallowed his dangerous-man story, but then a Texas documentarian discovered the lie: Coe had served time for possessing burglary tools and indecent materials, never for murder.

After serving out parole in Ohio, Coe had persuaded Shelby Singleton's Plantation Records to jump on the Cash prison-album juggernaut and record two albums with him, both of which tanked. "According to people who knew him then," wrote *Country Music*'s Marshall Fallwell in 1974, "he was cocky, maybe a little scary, demanding that people stop what they were doing and listen to his songs at Linebaugh's or Tootsie's Orchid Lounge. It was during that period that he developed his flamboyant personal style, sporting sequined suits and wide belts with his name burnt into them."

The Tanya Tucker hit inspired Columbia Records to sign Coe in 1974. Dan Beck, who had left behind songwriting and jobs at music trade papers to become Columbia's first Nashville-based publicist, saw just enough interest in Coe's persona to think he might make it. "You'd have a beginning-of-the-year convention," says Beck. "David played one of those and tore the place down with 'If I Could Climb the Walls of the Bottle.' I remember that night, that was a smash." And then the *New York Times* reviewed Coe on a bill with Orleans and Jimmy Buffett: "Now he seems to be on his way, and on the strength of his performance . . . , it would be impossible to stop him."

The praise buoyed Columbia, but its faith in Coe never returned many dividends. He produced a twelve-year string of moderate hits and titillated audiences with an all-girl band that backed him for a time, but Nashville kept its distance, particularly after the death-row lie surfaced. "In a way, we didn't necessarily take David that seriously," says Beck. "I remember songwriters used to go see him play someplace, and he'd play somebody else's songs and say he wrote it! People used to laugh."

David Allan Coe.

According to Richie Albright, Coe irritated Waylon, always trying to ride his coattails and frequently misleading him. "A great, great songwriter," says Albright. "A great singer. But he could not tell the truth if it was better than the lie he'd made up. Waylon didn't make him comfortable enough to hang around. But Willie [did]. I was around Willie quite a bit and David Allan was with him eighty percent of the time. Willie allowed him to hang around."

Coe wrote and recorded a song called "Waylon, Willie and Me," exploiting his relationship with his fellow outlaws. "Waylon was nice enough to play guitar on [it]," says Albright, "and he walked out of there and said, 'Shit, I don't know why I did that.'"

In the end, the menacing cloud around Coe—the tattoos, mysterious prison past, black sedans, and black tour bus—made some people think that this outlaw bit might be real. "His need to be looked upon as that jail mate to me was a little ridiculous," observes photographer Alan Mayor. "But he took it seriously and therefore you had to. And he had people around who would be willing to beat you up for him."

Those people around Coe were the Outlaws motorcycle gang, who flocked to him as steadfastly as the Hells Angels descended upon Waylon. Hugh Bennett, a bouncer and sound man at the Exit/In, saw up close the gang's dedication. "We were loading David out at the Exit/In one night, and I bet a guy fifty bucks that he couldn't get out in a certain amount of time. We were tired of them. We wanted them to go. He'd taped up the thermostats, and it smelled bad. It was just a grunge kind of night. It was not a nice night. The Outlaws were his security. And one of them grabbed me and hit me in the head and the fight was on. I lost. I wound up in the hospital with a broken head and broken ribs."

★   ★   ★

WAYLON NEVER CULTIVATED the ex-prisoner image. He was content to let his clothing, big-boss songs, and battles with RCA define his outlaw persona. Privately, he was more reckless, abusing drugs, chasing women, and staying up all night with his buddies as they roamed the streets like a posse. "He wouldn't go to bed," remarks Richie Albright. "Like so many guys back in that time, I think they had to reach that point before their creativity started kicking in, before their mind would let go to write." Fueled by amphetamines, he was more likely to lope into J.J.'s Market on Broadway or the Burger Boy than to write songs; there he could indulge his childlike obsession with pinball machines, but he would also hold court with Tompall, greet songwriters, discuss business, and select his next romantic conquest.

"They'd play [pinball] one place a while and then they'd play another. I mean, these places would stay open all night," declares Hazel Smith. "A lot of times, you'd go in and you'd never know who'd be in there with them. And they'd be playing pinball. It was something they enjoyed doing. I don't know why in the world anybody would enjoy playing pinball.

"One night, [the journalist] Martha Hume was in town; she'd come down from New York. We knew they was at the Burger Boy playing pinball. And when we walked in the Burger Boy, Tompall had moved [the machine] through the hall, down into the dining area in the restaurant, [damaging the floor]. I said, 'What in the world did you move the pinball machine for, Tompall?' And he said, 'Because I wanted to play pinball in here with Waylon.' And that's what they were doing. They were in there playing pinball. And he had to pay for that. He just wrote them a check. He was making a lot of money back then. A lot of money."

In the panorama of country music hobbies, Johnny Cash fished, Willie Nelson golfed, Marty Robbins raced cars, Loretta Lynn tended a vegetable garden, and Bill Monroe raised cattle. Waylon Jennings and Tompall Glaser played pinball but not the pinball wizard's flippers-and-bells game. It was, as a *Vanderbilt Hustler* reporter observed, like a slot machine with some skill involved. "They are all-business pinball machines with nothing but numbers and colors, and a player may alter the ball's direction only by pushing, striking or twisting the machine firmly but gently with his bare hands. If the player can use his eyes and hands well enough to guide the five steel balls into a jackpot combination of colors or numbers, he wins money." Five hundred winning games paid

$125 and on up the line. It was illegal for proprietors to pay out on the wins, but the vice squad ignored it.

Waylon and Tompall spent thousands watching steel balls scatter across the table, and when they did collect, they pumped the quarters back into the machines. The manager of the Burger Boy, Terry George, once stood by while Waylon spent three thousand dollars in sixteen hours. "It was an addiction," says George. Waylon chose to call it "mental masturbation," adds Richie Albright. Whatever it was, Waylon frequently hit up George to keep the balls rolling. "Sometimes he'd get into me for two, three, or four thousand dollars," claims George. "And I'd go to him and say, 'Waylon, I need to get a check. This is my operating money.' One day I went to him and asked for a check and he didn't have his checkbook, [but] there was a white paper sack for to-go orders and he wrote me a check on a paper sack. Well, I thought, 'This fool is giving me a white paper bag as a four-thousand-dollar check. I didn't want to offend him because he was messed up or he appeared to be. I thought, 'I'll just wait until he's in a better frame of mind.' Well, he didn't get into a better frame of mind anytime soon, so I went to the bank, and I said, 'You all are going to think I'm a nut. . . .' And I handed it to them and they cashed a paper bag. This actually happened."

The pinball machines and sticky booths of the Burger Boy attracted stray Vanderbilt students and a nightly parade of drug dealers, pimps, and prostitutes. During the day, Music Row office workers and songwriters stopped for lunch, but students at Belmont College near Hillsboro Village stayed away from the eatery on orders from the dean. "The atmosphere in the restaurant was not bright, not clean," says George. "It was a greasy-spoon-like atmosphere."

George says he ignored the restaurant part of the business as Waylon and his crew spent more and more time filling his six pinball machines and drawing burger-buying curiosity seekers and song pluggers. "You had people who would stay there all night long. I didn't stay there. I left. I was out doing what I did. But [songwriter] Barbara Cummings, her and her brother Bobby would sit there all night long trying to get Waylon or somebody to notice them, to get a record deal or something. You had certain people who would just stay there like them. It was their life, it's what they did."

George catered to the stars, finally moving three pinball machines into a back room to which only Waylon and Tompall had access. It became another office or a second home. "Next to the pinball," says George, "[Waylon] had a leather pouch and he had a hook on the wall where he'd hang [it], and he'd keep his whiskey in his leather pouch. I never saw him take a swallow of that whiskey." Of course, Waylon preferred pills, which kept him trained on the silver balls all night, until he crashed. "I came in one morning and found them on the floor singing religious songs," continues George. "They were all messed up. I never knew what to expect when I came in, in the morning."

Once, George found the pinball machine near the door where they had tried to take it out of the restaurant, but usually he just found the machine in its place and Waylon standing at it. "One morning I came in and [Waylon] said, 'You think I'm a damn fool, don't you?' I thought to myself, 'Yeah, I do, putting your money in these machines.' And he told me he wrote 'Good Hearted Woman' playing a pinball machine. I said, 'You're no fool then if that makes you write songs, inspires you to do that; it's kind of like an investment.'

"He played pinball all day all night, all day all night, all day and the next night [perform] a concert," explains George. "And he was all messed up, but he walked out on that stage and the man was Waylon Jennings. It was pretty amazing. During these three days and three nights he didn't as much go home and take a bath or nothing. He just stayed at the restaurant."

Like George, Albright routinely saw Waylon parlay three days' roaring into a credible show. "Amphetamines were a problem," he observes. "Some of those people have an addictive personality and some don't. Waylon would just push it to a certain limit. Sometimes it was a problem. He always did his shows. Maybe he wasn't in the best shape or he had been up too long and lost his voice. That was the biggest problem, just staying up too long. Other than that, he always took care of everything else."

Back at the Burger Boy, Waylon could buy his pills from dealers who hung around nightly and choose from the girls who stopped in when they saw the big cars out front. If the stars were looking for women, they manned the three pinball machines in the dining area. "Waylon one day was playing pinball and this guy came in there with his wife or his girlfriend," says George. "His dream was to have Waylon record a song; he called himself a songwriter and as far as I know he never got anything recorded. He was asking Waylon to come up to his apartment and listen to a demo tape and Waylon said he would go, so Waylon went over there. After about twenty or thirty minutes, this guy came back and had three or four rolls of quarters. I said, 'Where's Waylon?' He said, 'He gave me these quarters and told me to come down here and play pinball.' I thought, 'This is a little odd.' This guy's wife or girlfriend came in later in the day and she was talking to me and she said, 'Waylon wanted to get rid of him, so we could be alone.' He sold his wife for a roll of quarters is what happened."

The most wretched Burger Boy sight may have been a woman named Helen who was obsessed with Waylon and had followed him back to Nashville after she met him on tour. Terry George remembers her as "Hurricane Helen," but Waylon called her "Crazy Helen." She haunted the street behind Hillbilly Central, he wrote in his autobiography, always trying to slip in the door: "We tried to bar her from the building, but occasionally she'd slip through and lock herself in the bathroom. I didn't know what to do with her. I tried to give her money to get back home, but after two or three days, she was back."

George, too, recalls her persistence. "I came in the Burger Boy one morning, and I saw this girl sitting here. It was early in the morning, and she'd obviously been there all night. We were open twenty-four hours a day. A beautiful, pretty, pretty girl. She attracted my attention. Well, it turned out she followed [Waylon] down there. She told me this. She was just extremely infatuated with him. The next thing I know this girl was just into all kinds of drugs and seeing things underneath the table. It just kept getting worse and worse. She ended up losing all her teeth and ended up just horrible-looking. Basically, they just used her. Nicknamed her 'Hurricane Helen' and you understand why they did that. She would sleep at RCA under an air conditioner out back, and when they wanted to use her they'd use her and then chase her off."

Waylon wrote later that Jessi gently persuaded Helen to go back home.

★ ★ ★

AROUND THE BURGER BOY and Hillbilly Central, there was one true criminal outlaw who ran with Waylon and the rest. He matched the musical outlaws quarter for quarter in pinball, and he had been a recording artist, although by the early 1970s he rarely sang anymore. He lurked on the fringes of the Hillbilly Central fraternity, appearing at sessions and then disappearing, lumbering bloodied into the Burger Boy after a scuffle in some back alley. He served hard time, shot a man, abused drugs with manic abandon, and was known to attack rivals with a bicycle chain, like one of those killers depicted in Truman Capote's *In Cold Blood*.

His name was Lee Emerson Bellamy, although everyone knew him as Lee Emerson. That's how his name appeared on his Columbia Records singles released in the 1950s and on the dozens of songs he wrote for other artists. His own records never charted, but he made a lot of money with "I Thought I Heard You Calling My Name," a hit for Porter Wagoner in 1957, and "Ruby Ann," a number-one smash for Marty Robbins in 1963. In the early 1970s, he was signed to Fred Foster's Combine Music, although his mind was often too clouded to do much writing. "He was doing a lot of pills," says Richie Albright, who frequently saw him at the Burger Boy. "He just stayed up and stayed high, and I think he felt that was the way he had to be to write. Maybe that's where he got all his good ideas. He was respected as a songwriter, but he was always so out of it that people didn't open their doors to him. And it really got frustrating for him."

Emerson hit Nashville in the mid-1950s, recording rockabilly-influenced sides for Columbia and sidling up to Marty Robbins, with whom he toured and recorded duets such as "I'll Know You're Gone" and "Where D'ja Go." Emerson looked out for Marty's song publishing interests and co-owned a booking agency with him. Memorably, though, the lean, muscular ex-marine took care of Marty's messy business on the road.

"When Lee smiled sometimes, it was sort of an evil smile," says Cowboy Joe Babcock, who cowrote with Emerson and sang behind Marty on the road from 1959 to 1965. "He had a big smile but his eyes would sort of bug out. He was a nice-looking man, but he was rough enough that if he held you up in a bank or something, you'd give him everything you had because he had the look that he'd shoot you. You'd know that Lee wasn't bluffing."

Emerson the bodyguard hovered close to Robbins, slipping into the audience to find loudmouths or pranksters throwing quarters. "One time we were playing a dance and a drunk was out in the audience heckling Marty, saying he wanted to fight him," recalls Babcock. "Marty said from the stage, very courteously, 'Well, sir, I would love to do that, but I have a man who does that for me.'" The fellow hollered that Marty should send that man out into the ballroom. "In the meantime," says Babcock, "Lee had seen what was going on, and he approached from the back, six foot two with a trench coat on and all kinds of weapons all over him. He tapped him on the shoulder and with that big smile said, 'I'm that guy. I'm the guy that does Marty's fighting for him.' He hit that guy on the elbow with his billy club, popped him on the elbow. You know how that can hurt. The guy dropped to the ground and disappeared under the crowd on his hands and knees."

Drugs proved to be Emerson's undoing, breaking up his marriage, fraying his relationship with Robbins, and hampering his songwriting. Babcock recalls Emerson overdosing and his fights becoming more frequent and savage. "One time when Lee went down to Printer's Alley, he came back to the office all beat up. Somebody had gotten that bicycle chain away from him and worked him over in the face with it. Busted his nose all up. He had his wild and woolly ways. . . . He could have been so much more if he hadn't gotten into pills, or had found the Lord."

Donnie Fritts befriended Emerson at Raleigh Publishing, where they both were signed, and then at Combine Music when they landed there. He saw sadness with the danger and recalls Emerson's grief when a woman left him to become a prostitute in Birmingham, Alabama. Sure, says Fritts, his friend set out to pummel the man who lured her away, but while she turned tricks, he checked into the hotel room next to hers just to be close by. And she never knew.

In 1965, Robbins and Emerson parted ways. Robbins sold the Emerson songs in his publishing company and left him at home when he went on the road. Three years later, Emerson shot a man in Memphis named Willie Joyner. The bullet only injured its target, but Emerson ran from the police as if it were murder, says son Rodney Bellamy. He jumped bail and fled to Florida, where the police finally hunted him down. Back in Memphis, he received a three-year sentence, and in 1971 he resurfaced on the streets of Nashville. He signed a writing contract at Combine, which proved a direct conduit to the world of Hillbilly Central, where he ran with Fritts and tagged along from time to time with Waylon and Tompall. "I know that he hung with Johnny Cash some," adds Hazel Smith, "and it might have been because he was a pusher or something. He probably was. No doubt. I don't know how the hell he made a living if he wasn't."

Emerson relied on forged prescriptions, according to Jim Casey. He explains that John Harris with the band Barefoot Jerry had gotten his medical license and gone into practice to make sorely needed money after a divorce. "John was not writing scripts [for uppers and downers] all over the place. He did not do that. That wasn't the deal. But I think Lee Emerson knew he had the ability to, and Lee Emerson stole a pad of John's scripts with his name and numbers and all of that stuff. Eventually the state got on John Harris about it. They came after John, and John was fearful for his career."

Courtesy of Rodney Bellamy collection

Lee Emerson (right) in the 1950s with Opry legend Roy Acuff.

Fritts warned Emerson that people all around Nashville wouldn't mind to see him dead, and if he ever got badly shot or stabbed, not even the police would care. "If somebody kills you, they'll give him a medal," Fritts told him.

Waylon and Tompall may have wished for so dark a life outside the law to go along with their white-man Super Fly pose, but they could live vicariously through Lee Emerson, Music Row's criminal outlaw.

We in Nashville were, of course, provincial innocents.

—Ralph McGill

 Nine

Between Worlds

DESPITE WILLIE'S AND Waylon's newly gained freedom in the recording industry and the rising youth culture embodied by Kris and the city's college students and aspiring musicians, the old order would not release its grip on Nashville. A few judges still barred women from wearing pants in their courtrooms, the city banned ads for birth control, and private clubs that excluded racial minorities were happily tolerated. Indeed, the heavy smell of frying chicken frequently obscured the earthy aroma of patchouli.

Nixon had smelled the hot grease burning and brought his southern strategy to Tennessee in 1970, when he backed Republican William E. Brock III of Chattanooga against incumbent Democrat Albert Gore Sr. for a seat in the U.S. Senate. Brock outpolled Gore by almost fifty thousand votes in an election that also saw the rise of a Republican governor and the defection of many Nashville-area Democrats to the other side. Democratic mayor Beverly Briley had led that dash to the GOP, endorsing Nixon in 1968 and setting the stage for a Republican presidential candidate to carry Davidson County, Nashville's home, for the first time since Reconstruction.

In the wake of city-county consolidation in the early 1960s, which created what is known as Metro government, Nashville's conservative voting base had moved to the suburbs and then beyond to outlying counties such as Sumner and Williamson.

Rosanne Cash with father Johnny Cash.

Rosanne Cash—whose lone outlaw star may be her cover of Kristofferson's "Broken Freedom Song," which she contributed to one of her dad's 1974 albums—didn't need a political map to tell her about conservatism in the Nashville area. In 1973, at the age of eighteen, she moved away from her mother in California to her father's home in Hendersonville, in Sumner County, about eighteen miles northeast of Nashville. It was far away from the verdant West End, and stuck in the pre-Woodstock era. "The counterculture was really visible in L.A., obviously, and it spilled over into Ventura [County, California, where I grew up]," she says. "You know, we'd go to the beaches in Los Angeles and Malibu and Santa Monica and just hang with all of the kids. So the counterculture was what I identified with. And then I got to Nashville and it was like it never happened. I mean, girls were still curling their hair and wearing pretty, frilly blouses, and things were really slow. And it was just very different. I think I actually tried to change myself at first. Like, I'm going to fit into this and slow down a bit, kind of narrow down a bit. But I couldn't. It was too hard.

"In my dad's house there were elements of the Old South. He had the black staff. Not totally. He had half and half. But Miss Leatha, this elderly black woman who cooked for him, it was as if she was still Civil War era: the way she thought, the way she acted with this great deference and kindness. So those Old South divisions were still really palpable."

Old South divisions aside, there were days when Nashville's authentic hillbilly culture echoed throughout the city like a rebel yell. Newspapers reported about the bride kidnapped the night before her wedding by a jilted lover, the shoplifter caught with six packages of country ham stuffed in his shirt, and the man shot over one dollar in a game of craps.

A far more serious story that nonetheless cast something of a rural prewar patina over Nashville was the brutal murders of *Grand Ole Opry* star David "Stringbean" Akeman and his wife, Estelle. Cousins John Brown and Douglas Brown stalked and killed the banjoist and rube comedian at his rural home north of Nashville late on November 10, 1973, after the weekly *Opry* broadcast. The city was thrust into the national headlines, becoming part of a tragic 1970s American narrative whose murdering characters also included Ted Bundy, John Wayne Gacy, and Gary Gilmore.

The couple's deaths also illustrated the dramatic convergence of old and new in Nashville. In life, Stringbean attracted network television producers and concert dates at folk-crazy colleges and universities, yet his personal life seemed more nineteenth century than 1973. News coverage of the murders and the subsequent investigation revealed a couple who lived in rusticity, leery of the modern world, preferring quaint hiding places for their money over banks and letting checks pile up as if they were junk mail. Furthermore, Stringbean relied on Estelle to drive him everywhere, suggesting a certain rejection of new technology, not to mention an old-world view of the role of women.

★　　★　　★

WHILE NASHVILLE WRESTLED with Stringbean's murder, another institution forced the city to contemplate its past and its inflexibility. Since 1943, the Ryman Auditorium had played host to the *Grand Ole Opry*, but in 1970 its owners, the National Life and Accident Insurance Company, broke ground on the venerable radio show's future home: Opryland USA, Nashville's Disneyland on the Cumberland River. Moving the symbol of Nashville's country music heritage up the river and out of town to the middle of an amusement park offended many, but performers unanimously welcomed it. Consensus inside the music business was that the Ryman was old, rickety, and ill-suited to host the growing number of country-themed television shoots invading the city. "Why, I've stood on that stage down there doing a matinee and looked up and could see the sky," complained Roy Acuff, who was the Ryman's leading critic. "It's definitely a fire hazard and even the bricks are falling off the walls." The plush new Opry House, its bricks firmly mortared together, would be state-of-the-art when it opened in the spring of 1974, akin to any venue in New York or Los Angeles.

But the transition was hardly quiet. When the last note from Acuff's fiddle disappeared into the ether on the *Opry*'s final broadcast from the Ryman, National Life was planning to raze the old tabernacle and use some of the debris to build a new chapel at Opryland. But preservationists, led by Ada Louise Huxtable at the *New York Times*, howled: "That probably takes first prize for the pious misuse of a landmark and the total misunderstanding of the principles of preservation. This travesty has convinced a lot of people that demolition is an O.K. thing. Among them are Billy Graham and Tennessee Ernie Ford, who is reputed to be waiting to sing the first hymn."

National Life blinked, agreeing to study the matter for a year. But then more bad press climbed into the church pews of the *Opry*. A stand-off between the show's management and longtime cast member Skeeter Davis demonstrated that intolerance and double standards still lived in Nashville. The city seemed determined to make people forget that Diane Nash and John Lewis had ever lived there.

The Davis debacle began to take shape on Saturday, December 8, 1973, as Metro police fanned out across the hills and dells north of Nashville looking for Stringbean's killers and National Life fended off barbs from the Ryman's protectors. Skeeter Davis, known for her earnest religious convictions as much as for her sublime 1960s pop hit "The End of the World," kicked off her segment on the *Opry* that night by criticizing the arrest of several traveling Christians who were proselytizing at an area shopping mall. By the following Saturday night, *Opry* manager Bud Wendell had indefinitely suspended her from the broadcast.

Artists who appeared on the *Opry* knew of no official policy banning them from making political or religious statements, but they obediently adhered to an unwritten rule to that effect. Those who were interviewed about Skeeter's suspension sympathized with her but, careful not to criticize management, suggested that she should have known better. Management, however, was not careful in enforcing its unwritten rule. A *Billboard* magazine reporter based in Nashville told the *Tennessean* that he could remember at least three performers who spoke out from the planks of the Ryman: Billy Grammer, who preached a sermon; the Wilburn Brothers, who endorsed George Wallace; and Ernest Tubb, who touted other Democratic politicians; a more thorough survey would have revealed the *Opry* appearance of Nashville-area congressman Richard Fulton, who sang a song called "Poor Little Paper Boy" during an election year. When reporters asked Wendell about the Wilburns and Wallace, he refused to comment.

Years later, Wendell confirmed that he'd booted Skeeter because her remarks had shown disrespect for the police, who were working so hard to solve the Stringbean case. And Skeeter—who finally returned to the *Opry*—admitted to scheduling an apology to those police who had arrested the missionaries but had balked after reading about the indictment of five cops on vice charges. "Evidently these officers had been using their power and official capacity to solicit sexual favors," she wrote in her autobiography. "With this new development exposed, I found it impossible to apologize."

★　　★　　★

DURING SKEETER'S ABSENCE, the *Opry* had shown that the right kind of political posturing could always find a home on its stage. After closing down the Ryman Auditorium with the last *Friday Night Opry* on Friday, March 15, 1974, management unveiled the show on Saturday at the new Opryland digs. A front-row space awaited Alabama governor George Wallace, paralyzed in 1972 from an assassination attempt, who'd be watching the stage appearance as guest of honor President Richard Nixon.

The country music establishment had long ago embraced the nation's arch-segregationist Wallace. In 1966, Roy Acuff welcomed him onto the *Opry* stage, and in 1972, George Jones and Tammy Wynette hosted a huge fund-raiser to support his campaign. "During the 1968 Presidential campaign, Music Row was practically a battlefield command post for George Wallace, who drew supporters there while he ran . . . and mourners when he lost," noted Paul Hemphill in his classic 1970 meditation on country music, *The Nashville Sound*. Indeed, the stars merely reflected many in their southern audience, who plastered their cars with Wallace stickers and never failed to point out that his reported disdain for blacks was merely a newspaper exaggeration.

But Nixon? Yes, he won Nashville in 1972 and, yes, the town linked arms with his southern strategy. But in the spring of 1974, his presidency was in tatters. The Watergate scandal had become a national obsession and even Republican U.S. senator Howard Baker, from Huntsville, Tennessee, challenged the administration as vice chairman of the Senate Watergate Committee. Nixon was only months away from resigning when he showed up to christen the Opry House, but the city welcomed him as if it were 1972 all over again. And if the *Opry* still had an unwritten rule about politics and religion on its hallowed stage, it was thrown out the window. Skeeter Davis—still persona non grata on the broadcast—listened to the March 16 show in wonderment.

Before the night was over, Nixon banged out three songs on the piano, including "Happy Birthday" for his wife. Politicians in the front rows cheered him, fans pressed the stage as if he were Hank Williams come back, and wide-eyed cast members lingered in the wings watching his every move. The president couldn't have paid for a more radiant backdrop, one that he surely hoped would communicate the resilience of his "solid South" constituency. "Nashville and the Grand Ole Opry can be proud they brought happiness to the Nixons," gushed the *Banner* in a Monday morning editorial. "They can also be proud they gave the nation—and the world—an opportunity to see what's right in America—a positive look at what Mr. Acuff termed 'we working people'—the real America."

On the prairies and in the cities and towns, debate roared over the meaning of "real America." No doubt some decided that it didn't live in Nashville.

★   ★   ★

IN THE 1960S, northern writers had parachuted into town to swipe their fingers across Nashville's dusty surface. In 1974, the West Coast took its turn. Enter screenwriter Joan Tewkesbury and director Robert Altman, stage left.

A mother of two with some film school and stage appearances on her dossier, Tewkesbury had contributed to the screenplay of Altman's most recent film, *Thieves Like Us*, starring Keith Carradine and Shelly Duvall. The movie rang of Arthur Penn's *Bonnie and Clyde* and failed to impress the critics, but that didn't stop Altman from tapping Tewkesbury for his movie about country music; he dispatched her twice to Nashville to research the script.

The screenwriter found two Music Cities: the slick corporate town of Music Row and Opryland and the hip West End scene, which made room for rock and folk. She observed Loretta Lynn perform and found in her the inspiration for her script's Barbara Jean, the honey-sweet yet troubled singer whose negotiations with fame dominate the film. Tewkesbury hung out at the Exit/In, and wove into the script little scenes she observed there, including an encounter there with a man who was vamping on David Allan Coe's death-row shtick. Jan Stuart, in her book about the film, described it: "As Tewkesbury cocked an ear to filter the music and chatter, a middle-aged black man sidled up to her . . . extending a hand. [He] told her that he had recently gotten out of jail, where he had served twenty-six years for murder. He said he killed the man his wife had been sleeping with, then studied law in jail to help himself get out."

Harking back to John Frankenheimer's work in *The Manchurian Candidate*, Tewkesbury and Altman's characters indicted the nation's blind embrace of Nixon-style conservatism, gaudy consumerism, violence, and superficiality. "Nashville is a place where people get off the bus like Hollywood was many years ago," Altman told the *Washington Post*. "The money is generated and there's a crudeness to the culture. It just seems like the proper place for me to be able to equate the analogy of our elected officials and politicians—which in many ways, I think is a popularity contest—with the success of country and western music. It's a way of melding a whole view, my view, of that political climate in America today."

Nashville comes to Woodland Sound Studio. Standing, left to right: Geraldine Chaplin, Robert Altman, recording engineer David McKinley, and Lily Tomlin. Seated is studio owner Glen Snoddy.

Characters who seemed cribbed from a glossy *Grand Ole Opry* program mingled with cartoonish representations of West End hippies and National Life suits in various subplots that finally collided in Centennial Park, where a drifter shoots down Barbara Jean at a rally for the unseen political candidate Hal Philip Walker. It was the arrested promise of the Kennedys mashed with the cynicism of Nixon against the landscape of good ole American narcissism that no priest or politician can moderate. When the film opened in 1975, critics praised its allegorical message. "It's about ambition, sentimentality, politics, emotional confusion, empty goals and very big business in a society whose citizens are firmly convinced that the use of deodorants is next to godliness," observed Vincent Canby in the *New York Times*.

In Nashville, it became something of a parlor game to match the film's characters with the country music personalities who inspired them: Haven Hamilton, the self-satisfied elder statesman of the industry, smacked of Hank Snow; Tom Frank, the sexy singer-songwriter, brought to mind Kristofferson; Tommy Brown, the black country singer, had similarities to Charley Pride; and Connie White, the ambitious second to Barbara Jean, recalled Tammy Wynette. Industry insiders spotted cameo appearances by session guitarists Harold Bradley and Lloyd Green, songwriter-manager Merle Kilgore, and Elvis Presley's old drummer D. J. Fontana. Locals no doubt enjoyed seeing well-known spots around town, such as lower Broadway and the Parthenon in Centennial Park as well as the exteriors of the Old Time Picking Parlor and the Demon's Den, both downtown clubs.

But the fun ended there. Many refused to let the familiar scenery and faces, not to mention Altman's literary subtleties, excuse the ridiculing of their town and its industry. When it opened in Nashville on August 8, 1975—many weeks after its premiere in New York—the red-carpet audience rebelled. Spat Nashville's hottest producer Billy Sherrill, "When you show the anatomy of a man you should try to show something besides his tail."

AFTER THE SCREENING, partiers jammed the Exit/In for Paramount Pictures' official reception, where the debate no doubt continued. The club's interiors had been featured prominently by Altman, who cast it as Nashville's hip place, a star magnet. His portrait mirrored the truth: in four short years, the Exit/In had gone from earnestly wooing Vanderbilt students with eclectic tastes to hosting Hollywood post-screening parties and national rock acts for Nashville people with money to burn. Indeed, the vibe was changing across the West End, as if the neighborhood were waiting for the last of Vanderbilt's class of 1973 to leave town and corporate dollars to turn the seedy side streets and avenues into the music industry's very own gated community.

Behind doors from Division Street to Elliston Place, the dull smell of pot gave way to the sleek, odorless jolt of cocaine. Rodney Crowell, the young songwriter from Texas with some songwriting dollars newly stashed in his pocket, saw the new lines forming. "There's a famous drag race guy who was at the Exit/In with Guy Clark and me. And this guy says, 'Hey, I got some coke out in the car.' So we go out there, and the guy opens up his trunk and he's got, like, two and a half pounds in his trunk. And Guy and I look at each other and go, 'This guy's a coke dealer, geesh. Thought he was a race car driver.' Said, 'Man, what are you doing with all this?' And he says, 'It's my stash.' So this guy had two and a half pounds of coke that he wasn't even trying to sell. It was just what he had in the back of his car to go around and hang out with people. I mean, Jesus, cocaine."

CROWELL LEFT NASHVILLE in the wake of Nixon's *Opry* visit and Altman's filming to explore what he may have been missing down in Austin. The Willie Nelson phenomenon—not to mention the town's fabulous hippie chicks—was too irresistible to ignore. "Willie was a poet," he says. "He was a long-haired stoned hippie country-singing songwriter, but it was all the embodiment of poetry. Waylon was this long-haired outlaw, stoned poet. It was the embodiment of poetry that drew me. I went there and was going to be a poet. That's what I was going to do."

As it happens, Crowell was in Austin about one month when Emmylou Harris's luxury liner purred into town and he was tapped to play in her band. The placid songstress had first met Crowell while he was still based in Nashville and hired him in Austin, he says, "strictly for poetic reasons. It wasn't my musicianship at all. It was the conversation that Emmy and I were having about songs over and over again. We were having a dialogue on songs, and material. If I can claim any piece of that moment, it was that I was part of the discussion about the material that was being done. And that would go back to my early days in Nashville. My sensibility about that was formed, and Emmy was open to that, understood it."

Interestingly, the willowy songbird who had come of age in Washington, D.C., was living Willie and Waylon's dream to thrive artistically and commercially without Nashville interference. In 1975, her *Pieces of the Sky* LP, which included Crowell's "Bluebird Wine," floated near the top of the country music album charts and appeared on the pop side as well, without the benefit of Nashville's studios. Working with outside producer Brian Ahern and an army of polished sidemen, she recorded the collection in Los Angeles. And her label—which was not a big player in Nashville—lavished big bucks on her promotion. "She was with Warner Bros. Records then," says Crowell, "and they spent money to get her. That's how I wound up going on the road with her. I was lowly. I was her pal and her songwriter and harmony singer. But they coughed up money for James Burton and Glen Hardin and Emory Gordy. Basically, they hired Elvis Presley's backup band to go on the road with Emmy and kick people's ass with this Hot Band," as it was called.

Emmylou Harris with Mickey Raphael on harp.

"The Nashville establishment started considering Emmylou when she started making money," explains Crowell. "It's always that way. That's how that machine down there works. When money starts being generated, they cast an eye. I would say Emmy embodied the poet. She later became a songwriter, but in the beginning, her work embodied poetry. In some ways, you can look at Emmylou as coming from the female version of the Kris Kristofferson archetype. Which is poet makes market mainstream."

Emmylou's mainstream lifted Crowell's songs like "You're Supposed to Be Feeling Good" and "Till I Gain Control Again" to new prominence and cleared a way to his own recording contract. In time, he moved to Los Angeles, although connections remained strong in Nashville.

★   ★   ★

EMMYLOU MOVED SWIFTLY without the bonds of Nashville. And she was mostly without peers. Until Willie Nelson floated up from the dust cloud behind her.

Even while he was touring in the Austin-godfather glow and enjoying exuberant ink from the national press for his second go-round in Dripping Springs, his record sales remained moribund. Willie's two Atlantic albums—although critically praised—slumped commercially, and a third album of inspirational music languished in the can as Atlantic prepared to abandon its country music house.

Neil Reshen negotiated a deal for Willie at CBS Records, which did business in Nashville via its Columbia and Epic labels and had become the distributor of Fred Foster's Monument Records. Like the Atlantic contract, the deal gave Willie freedom to use his own musicians, but now he could record without the oversight of staff producers. It was like Waylon's deal, and he tucked it under his arm and retreated to Austin. "It was the first time that I had quote artistic control endquote," Willie told Chet Flippo in 2000. "So, I thought I would just start writing. And I was coming back from Denver to Austin. I had this song 'Red Headed

Stranger' in my life for so long that I always felt it was a great story and, if I ever got the chance, I would try to create what happened up to the beginning of that and what happened afterwards. So, on that trip from Denver to Texas, I had time to think about it. And [my wife] Connie was there with me and sat and rode shotgun and kept me awake while I wrote it."

CBS executive Rick Blackburn (left) and Neil Reshen.

The song, written in the 1950s by Edith Lindeman Calisch and Carl Stutz, profiles a widowed man desperate in his grief who shoots a woman trying to take his deceased wife's horse. Before Willie, John D. Loudermilk and Eddy Arnold had recorded it, but nobody thought to build an album around it. According to Connie Nelson, Willie hadn't, either—until *she* suggested it on that ride from Denver to Austin.

In the days ahead, Willie tinkered with the story, adding his own songs and a smattering of country chestnuts, including Wally Fowler's "I Couldn't Believe It Was True" and Fred Rose's "Blue Eyes Crying in the Rain." When he submitted *Red Headed Stranger* to Columbia, the instrumentation was so sparse and Willie's guitar playing so splintered that officials assumed it was unfinished. Bruce Lundvall, the chief of CBS Records in New York, who had veto power over any recording in the organization, thought as much when Neil Reshen brought him the album to preview. Waylon, who was visiting Reshen in New York at the time, came along for the ride. "They played the record in my office," he told Flippo. "And I said, 'This is pretty fascinating.' It's not what I expected for the first record and it's more like a collector's piece in terms of its commercial potential, I thought, when I heard it. With that, Waylon jumped up and said, 'That's what this is all about. That's what Willie's music is all about. He doesn't need a producer. This is the way it should go.'" Lundvall brought home the record and listened to it all weekend, wrote Flippo. On Monday, he conferred with Billy Sherrill, the head of CBS Nashville, who reluctantly endorsed it despite the absence of any mainstream hook.

In 1975, what counted as mainstream was the sleek child of Chet Atkins and Owen Bradley's Nashville Sound. Highly produced outings by Charley Pride and Conway Twitty skipped up the charts holding hands with perky numbers by B. J. Thomas and Don Williams while big pop-country smashes in the form Glen Campbell's "Rhinestone Cowboy" and Linda Ronstadt's "When Will I Be Loved" mingled with novelties such as Loretta Lynn's "The Pill" and C. W. McCall's "Convoy." All of which culminated in pop-country's John Denver capturing the Country Music Association's "Entertainer of the Year" honors in 1975, moving presenter Charlie Rich to burn the card announcing Denver's win on national television. Indeed, measured against the sugary sounds of Denver, Campbell, Ronstadt, and even Rich, Willie's new album seemed oblivious to the mainstream.

And oblivious to his RCA legacy. The lush background vocals, throbbing strings, and uneven song selection had disappeared in favor of economical instrumentation and ruddy vocals. And despite *Yesterday's Wine*, the concept album Willie so adored from his RCA days, this new album was his first true concept album, composed of new songs and old, arranged in a coherent sequence that told a fiercely emotional story.

Dan Beck, head of promotion at CBS Nashville at the time, recalled that *Red Headed Stranger* seemed so off-market that Lundvall needed more than Sherrill's assurances. Beck had first met Willie in the spring of 1973 at Glaser Sound Studios, when they, along with Waylon Jennings and Willie Fong Young, sang backup on Kinky Friedman's daring "They're Not Making Jews Like Jesus Anymore." That summer, Beck saw the excitement and chaos Willie inspired when he jetted down to Willie's second festival at Dripping Springs. "It was sex, drugs, and country music. You know, it was redneck rock, in a way. But a lot of pretty girls. It was a latter-day Woodstock sensibility. It was kind of the Texas bar scene, and there were people that did come in from outside, like Kathy Cronkite, Walter Cronkite's daughter. People were aware of something going on down there."

Two years later, Beck stared at his test pressing of *Red Headed Stranger* and saw more problems than Lundvall's comments to Chet Flippo revealed. "If you looked at [the album] from an A&R person's perspective, it was kind of a hodgepodge," says Beck. "It was completely stripped down at a time when these wall-of-sound country records were on the charts, ruling the charts!

"The record was delivered. And the one phrase I heard was 'This sounds like it was recorded in Willie's kitchen.' Nick Hunter [whom Neil Reshen had hired to do promotion] called me and said, 'Dan, you have to help me. Bruce has rejected Willie's album. You got to call him and tell him it's all right; you've seen the whole Texas thing!' And Nick proceeded to tell me, 'I think Bruce feels like Willie just gave up on Nashville, took the advance, cut something for a couple thousand bucks, and pocketed the rest and said, "The hell with my recording career! I'll just play in Texas."'

"I said, 'Nick, I wish I could help. If I can think of an idea, I'll get back in touch with you.' The next hour I got to thinking about the half a dozen press people in Nashville, and they had all been down to Texas, and they all kind of got it. So I called Nick back and said, 'Hey Nick, what if we got those people together and got them to listen to it off the record?' He said, 'That sounds like a great idea!' And Bruce said, 'I'd love to hear that; I'd love to get some feedback like that.'

Courtesy of Sony Music Entertainment

CBS executive Bruce Lundvall, Mark Rothbaum, and Willie.

"We hustled this thing up to get everybody to come over to the Exit/ In the next afternoon and listen to the record. I remember Ron Bledsoe came, who was VP of operations for CBS in Nashville. Bonnie Garner came, who was in A&R and a friend of Willie's. There were about a dozen of us. We went in, and it still smelled of stale beer from the night before. It was dark in there. I don't even think there was a waitress. When the first song finished, there was no comment. Nothing. Every band between songs, dead silence. You couldn't get a read from what was going on in the room. We put on 'Blue Eyes Crying in the Rain.' After that song played, Bill Littleton from *Performance Magazine* stood up very slowly and started very slowly applauding. And within a few seconds, everybody broke in. It was like, 'Oh my God, they love this record!'

"So we played the rest of the record, and I went back to the office. I called Bruce and told him what the reaction was. And I think it was the next day, Nick called me and said, 'Dan, he took it.' I think Bruce needed something to validate taking the record, because there was every reason not to."

RCA-Nashville must have scratched its head as *Red Headed Stranger* galloped up the charts past Don Williams and Charley Pride and lassoed reams of jubilant reviews. "This album reveals its treasures very slowly," wrote Ed Ward in *Country Music*. "As likely as not, you won't like it the first time through, but stick with it. It'll stick with you for a long time. Masterpieces are like that." *Rolling Stone*'s Paul Nelson saw in the new release a tableau of the archetypal lonely western outlaw, steeped in a new etherealness: "Hemingway, who perfected an art of sharp outlines and clipped phrases, used to say that the full power of his composition was accessible only between the lines; and Nelson, on this LP, ties precise, evocative lyrics to not quite remembered, never really forgotten folk melodies, haunting yet utterly unsentimental. That he did not write much of the material makes his accomplishment no less singular."

Nelson had fused the lonely western heroes of his youth—the Gene Autrys and John Waynes—with the complicated, ambiguous sort that novelists and filmmakers painted in the 1960s and 1970s. His redheaded stranger surely clung to the notion of forthright cowboy thinking, but he rode with an outlaw desperation that came right out of Sergio Leone's *A Fistful of Dollars*, Sam Peckinpah's *The Wild Bunch*, or Waylon Jennings's *Honky Tonk Heroes* album. After all, the cowboy of golden West would never shoot a woman.

Red Headed Stranger spent an astonishing 120 weeks on the charts and blazed a new trail for Willie Nelson, while reawakening CBS Records to the blockbuster potential of country music not seen since Johnny Cash's *At Folsom Prison* album of 1968 and Lynn Anderson's *Rose Garden* of 1970. And if Waylon's *Honky Tonk Heroes* was the outlaw movement's first album, Willie's proved to be its first smash. One of the haggard artists on the West End-to-Austin wire finally had broken through, setting the stage for Hazel Smith's chosen adjective to become a corporate marketing campaign.

*I've been called an outlaw, a renegade, and a son of
a bitch. But all we've been fighting for is artistic control.
Freedom is what it all boils down to,
having your own way.*

—**Waylon Jennings**

★ *Ten*

Wanted!

WHILE WILLIE COLLECTED laurels for *Red Headed Stranger*,
Waylon could proudly point to his two most recent albums, his strongest releases yet: *The Ramblin' Man* (1974) and *Dreaming My Dreams*
(1975). The former, which featured cover photos shot at Muhlenbrink's
(formerly the Red Dog Saloon) on Division, uncorked the number-one
title track written by RCA producer Ray Pennington and a gutsy cover
of Gregg Allman's "Midnight Rider," which, but for Ralph Mooney's
steel guitar licks, bled pure southern rock.

Dreaming My Dreams, too, flirted with southern rock, particularly
in the rollicking "Are You Sure Hank Done It This Way," a Waylon
composition that meditated on the state of modern country music and
predicted the big fuss over the outlaw movement. The song jetted to
number one in 1975, another exception to the silky, pop-oriented songs
of country music popular that year, much as Willie's "Blue Eyes Cryin'
in the Rain" was.

One of many hits from the storied country music catalog that cited

Hank Williams, Waylon's inspiration sprang from Ernest Tubb's band, of all places. The Texas Troubadour's men used to hang out on the bus during breaks on *The Midnight Jamboree*, a radio program that followed the *Grand Ole Opry* on Saturday nights, and which Ernest hosted from his record store on lower Broadway. According to Billy Ray Reynolds, who befriended Ernest's bass player Jack Drake, the musicians would emerge drenched from their shop performance, their gleaming suits sticking to their wet skin, and escape to the air-conditioned bus, all the while wondering out loud if "Hank done it this way." Reynolds brought the expression to Waylon's bus, where a big star emblazoned with Hank's name hung on the bathroom door. "Evidently, it became ingrained in Waylon's mind and that's where the song basically came from," says Reynolds.

Courtesy of Maryland Room, University of Maryland

Feeling free.

Jack Clement, who was married to Jessi Colter's sister Sharon at the time, produced the Hank song and the rest of the album *Dreaming My*

Dreams. They'd met years earlier, recalls Clement, in the RCA studios. "I was kind of a fan of him before I met him. And when I did meet him, he was in the middle of doing a session. He was in the control room and Johnny Cash was out there singing. He was going to go out there and sing with him in a minute or something. But I was kind of looking at Waylon, and that pissed him off! Like, 'If that guy looks at me again, I'm gonna kick his ass.'"

The tension eased when Waylon and Jack became brothers-in-law and Jack invited him to stop by his Belmont Boulevard studios on any given Thursday, when he always had musicians booked for routine work, such as demo sessions. "A few weeks later, he did," explains Clement. "I went down there that Thursday morning and he was waiting out back in his car. We went in, started cutting some stuff with him. We played 'Dreaming My Dreams,' and he fell in love with it."

Written by Clement protégé Allen Reynolds, "Dreaming My Dreams" was a tender waltz that must have enchanted the dancer in Clement and no doubt speared the "MacArthur Park" ballad lover in Jennings. But it was Waylon's "Are You Sure Hank Done It This Way" that soared to number one and defined the album. In the studio, the song came to life when Waylon invited Billy Ray's electric guitar to join his own for the opening measures, a common collaboration on the road, but rare in the studio. "That's when he pulled the piece of paper out of pocket that he'd written that morning," says Reynolds. "It was 'Hank Done It This Way.' Basically, what he started playing was what we'd do on the road. If he started a song, sometimes he'd do a vamp. He kicked off the vamp and we just started playing."

"That was one of the key tracks," agrees Clement. "We'd worked on it. I played something on it, guitar or something. Then he left, and I started mixing on it. And I mixed it in a whole different way. I brought them guitars way up there, and he came in the next day or whenever we got back there and listened to it and loved it. So if I could prove something to Waylon, we didn't have to argue about it. A lot of times, I have things in my head I want to hear, but I can't explain to you how it sounds, until you do it."

Photograph by Alan Mayor

Waylon, Jessi, and Jack Clement.

Drugs, breakdowns in communication, and innocent misunderstandings often left Clement and Waylon impatiently trying to read each other through the control room glass window. Says Richie Albright, "The thing Waylon figured out was—he said, 'If Jack is sitting behind the board and we're running the thing down, then we haven't got it yet. Once he gets up and starts dancing around the room, that's it, we're happening now.'"

Clement complains that Waylon often misread the control room body language. "We were there one time and Jessi was there, and Sharon was there, and I think maybe another person or two. And they were milling around the studio, and I was ready to get to work. He's out in the studio, and I was in the control room, kind of swarming around being dramatic or something, saying, 'Get out!' He's kind of looking at me. If he'd have heard what I was saying, he'd have understood it. It looked like I wasn't paying attention to him or something. He just saw it and just didn't understand it." The singer stormed out of the studio and stayed away for two weeks.

In the end, the uneasy foxtrot of egos sprinkled gold across the dance floor. Along with the title track and "Are You Sure Hank Done It This Way," they tacked on a live recording of "Bob Wills Is Still the King," which Waylon wrote and performed in Austin on September 27, 1974. It was another delightful example of Waylon's eagerness to poke fun at the highfalutin music industry, in this case Willie Nelson and the redneck rock thing down in Texas. *It don't matter who's in Austin / Bob Wills is still the king.* Fans gave Waylon his highest placement to date on the pop album charts as well as his longest run ever on the country charts.

But it was no *Red Headed Stranger.*

★   ★   ★

IF WAYLON'S LATEST albums failed to answer Willie's surge, then RCA-Nashville boss Jerry Bradley was going to find one. First, he repackaged some of Willie's old nuggets in an album that sold enough to recoup a few bucks of the company's seven-year investment in him. And then he got a bigger idea.

"Waylon was selling, if we were lucky, two hundred and fifty thousand albums," says Bradley. "Willie comes out with *Red Headed Stranger* and that took off and sold a million records. Jessi Colter put out 'I'm Not Lisa' on Capitol. That damn thing sold half a million, or a million, set our butt on fire. We're sitting over there, trying to sell two hundred and fifty thousand records, and we're still struggling. Tompall had a damn record, 'Put Another Log on the Fire.' I never was a big Tompall fan, I've said this from day one. I never could understand that one. Waylon liked him or liked what he did; they were buddies. 'Another Log on the Fire'

comes out, and they're booking out as the 'Outlaws.' I never went to one
of their concerts, but I can imagine what it looked like, they running up
and down the highway doing that."

Of course, Bradley had plenty of Willie's recordings in the vaults
and a session or two on Jessi Colter, too. He approached Waylon about
compiling an album with their tracks plus his and calling it *Wanted! The
Outlaws*, unaware of the southern rock band out there riding the rods
as the Outlaws. Waylon consented, provided that Jerry made room for
a few Tompall Glaser tracks. Bradley agreed, saying, " 'Life's a compro-
mise, and Waylon's part of it. You got to meet him halfway if you want
to do this job.' So I said, 'Okay. I'll do it.' "

Bradley hired *Rolling Stone*'s Chet Flippo to pen liner notes, and
looked to a Time Life book about the American West as inspiration
for the album's iconic cover, which featured photographs of Colter,
Glaser, Jennings, and Nelson on a parched, bullet-riddled wanted
poster. Bradley inflated Waylon's cover picture, but Waylon objected
again. "Waylon said, 'I really don't want my picture to be bigger.' I
said, 'Waylon, your picture has to be bigger. This is about you. I'm trying to get you to sell a million records. They're selling a million, and I
have to get your picture just a little bit bigger.' He said, 'Well, hell, do
what you want to do.' "

Nonetheless, Bradley still brought the album cover to Hillbilly Central for Waylon's approval, showing up one afternoon with his son and
daughter in tow. "All Waylon's men were sitting around the room," he
says. "Waylon's sitting behind the desk. I handed it to Waylon and he
said, 'Shut the door.' I shut the door. There was an ad from RCA sitting
up against the wall, just a Waylon ad. They had been throwing knives
at it. I'm sitting there with my kids and—thud!—the knife hit it. He
looked at [the cover], and handed it to the next guy, his entourage and
hangers-oners. They'd look at it and hand it to the next one, the next
one. Captain Midnight was in there. And [Waylon] said, 'What do y'all
think?' Before they had a chance to answer, he said, 'Well, hand it back

to me.' They handed it back and he said, 'It's your idea. If that's what you want to do, you run with it.' [I said,] 'Thank you Waylon!' And I walked out the door."

The album rolled out in February 1976 and quickly picked up endorsements from *Rolling Stone* and other publications. "Most of the tracks are from a period when the first seeds of experimentation began to spill in Music City," noted Joe Nick Patoski in *Country Music*. "Thus, a constant clash of traditional and innovative influences dominates each artist's selections, in most instances, finely woven lyrics hiding behind still slick studio concepts."

The album showcased Willie's smart poetry from the RCA years and a few gems from Waylon—"Honky Tonk Heroes (Like Me)" and the tender, newly recorded "My Heroes Have Always Been Cowboys"—but it was Waylon and Willie's "live" duet reprise of the warhorse "Good Hearted Woman," with its applause sounding suspiciously canned, that added up to big sales. On its wings, *Wanted!* became the first certified million-selling album in country music history and finally gave RCA an answer to Willie's bell ringer.

Like *Red Headed Stranger*, the album tapped into America's ongoing love affair with the western outlaw as well as each artist's growing stature in the music community. The glowering expressions of Waylon, Tompall, and Willie on the album cover recalled the outlaw biker on the dust jacket of Hunter S. Thompson's 1966 book *Hell's Angels*, while the rugged vocal delivery and pounding beat of "A Good Hearted Woman," made it an outlaw anthem and established the duo on top of the country-rock market. Talk of the pair joining Bob Dylan's Rolling Thunder Revue of 1976 buzzed around the music industry, while Willie's Fourth of July picnic that year resembled the chaotic rock convocations played by Janis Joplin, the Grateful Dead, and the Band on their fabled festival train ride across Canada in 1970. Gate crashers swarmed the picnic in Gonzales, Texas, and several rapes, stabbings, and robberies as well as the drowning of a young fan were reported.

Like a swift, dry wind, the new outlaw cacophony blew into Texas and swept up the redneck rock genre. All of a sudden, *outlaw* encompassed the whole lot of them—from Waylon, Tompall, and David Allan in Nashville to Willie, Jerry Jeff, and Billy Joe in Texas. It boiled down to this: country artists who chanced to be male and incorporated rock-and-roll ethos into their persona, if not their music, suddenly found themselves labeled "outlaw" by radio stations, record promoters, and journalists. The outlaw became one of country music's major archetypes, surviving into the next millennium, where it lives in artists such as Toby Keith, Jamey Johnson, Travis Tritt, and Hank Williams Jr.

Make no mistake, the outlaws communicated an image of pure Texas cussedness, but it was all routed through Nashville, "the store," as Willie Nelson referred to it. From their perches in Music City, marketers and promoters spun a standard narrative about the grizzled artists rebelling against music industry convention, which, though based in fact, quickly reverberated into redundancy. "It's just a lot of crummy jive," groused an anonymous observer in a 1976 magazine article. "As people feel more and more trapped in their lives in this country, with their dull lifeless jobs, boring family lives and hopeless inflation, the music industry tantalizes them with these images of fake rebels to look at." Even Neil Reshen, who had every reason to fuel the outlaw hype, chuckled publicly at the cowboy masquerade: "You couldn't find two guys who are less like outlaws than Waylon Jennings and Willie Nelson. . . . It's all horseshit really. But if the public wants outlaws, we'll give them outlaws."

Rhythm guitarist Gordon Payne, who had joined Waylon's group in 1974, recalls that Waylon and Willie went from playing smaller ballrooms left over from the western swing era and clubs on the coasts to capacity crowds in stadiums and indoor arenas. "We did gigs with Marshall Tucker and Lynyrd Skynyrd," adds Richie Albright. "We did shows with the Grateful Dead and New Riders of the Purple Sage. The crowd started getting more youngsters, more long-haired, you might say. Our production was pretty much like a rock show because of those guys coming over from the rock side [on our gigs] and they'd bring that attitude."

Courtesy of Sony Music Entertainment

"The outlaws strike gold!" Standing, left to right: Tompall, RCA's Harry Jenkins, Jerry Bradley, and Chet. Seated, left to right: Waylon, Jessi, and Willie. Closer inspection reveals they are holding Charley Pride albums.

As the concertgoers multiplied and demanded the heavy vibe that was part and parcel of Waylon's sound, Albright revamped the road show sonically and logistically. "When we were doing the *Are You Ready for the Country* album [in 1976], I remember Waylon came out and took one of my earphones off and said, 'I figured it out.' I said, 'What?' He said, 'You're going to run this thing.' I said, 'What do you mean?' He said, 'You know what I need done. The production end of it. So you're going to run it.' I said, 'Okay. I'm going to spend all of your money.' He said, 'I don't give a shit.' And that's when our productions started getting bigger."

When the Waylon Jennings show lurched out of Nashville its convoy looked like the Who's. Three or four tractor trailers lugged tons of sound and lighting equipment, and two buses carried roadies, technicians, and a band that had grown from four to nine, including background vocalists. The days of Waylors traveling in a station wagon pulling a small trailer seemed too obscure now to comprehend.

Gordon Payne watched the excitement multiply after the release of "Luckenbach, Texas," Waylon's latest single off the hit album *Ol' Waylon*, which pondered a mythical hippie lifestyle in small-town Texas. It was cowritten and produced by Chips Moman, who had brought his American Studio franchise from Memphis to Nashville, and included references to Waylon and Willie as well as a meaty vocal contribution by Willie himself. "We had just finished that recording and we went back on the road," says Payne. "And we were in Lakeland, Florida, at an arena there, probably held fifteen to eighteen thousand. A bunch of my buddies from the Miami Dolphins were there. And we were telling them about this song; we practiced it a bit in sound check. And we said, 'We're going to do it.' So that night, Waylon said, 'I got a new song I want to play for you. Tell me if you like it.' So we played it, and by the time we were singing the second chorus, the whole place was singing it with us. Unbelievable. I'll never forget it as long as I live. And Richie and I were just looking at each other going, 'Oh my God. This is huge.' After that, if you go and look at the *Billboard* grossing concerts, we were in there every week. After the show, we were all going, 'Oh my gosh, this is going to be big.' And it was. I mean, we started playing Shea Stadium. And Arrowhead Stadium. Eighty thousand. It just went nuts."

WILLIE SOARED IN the same updraft. His core audience in Texas, which had sustained him for so long, now merely became part of a wild national following. "Now he rules country music," proclaimed Chet Flippo in *Rolling Stone*.

But he more than ruled. He became something of a symbol to Americans still holding on to the hippie dream. His mellow demeanor, scruffy beard, and ubiquitous red bandana idealized the off-the-grid look that the college class of 1973, now on the job market, was fast abandoning for the polyester leisure suits and broad neckties of suburban America. On the other hand, the older set equated the look with cowboy style, a throwback to Gene Autry, although Willie often looked more like Gabby Hayes. Ultimately, as he had in Texas, the shopworn troubadour embodied the American crossroads where hippie, hillbilly, and, now, suburbia all met. Traveling with a band he called "family," the music flowing through him, he seemed to be living in a late-1960s, early 1970s place that America was fast leaving behind.

"There's just something real about Willie Nelson," adds Gordon Payne. "Yeah, he knows he's Willie Nelson, but he's still really, really kind. And he's a sweetheart of a guy. And I think that comes up. He's a real caring fellow. I think all of that comes across. The biggest thing about Willie was the music. He'd say, 'They've come to hear the music, so I'm going to play as much of it till I get tired!' Nobody'd ever done that! Willie's a character offstage. But the one thing you realize is he's just a nice guy. He doesn't fit the standard—he's not in your face. He knows who he is and he . . . just cares. Not that Waylon didn't! But Waylon was affected by his stardom. He was. I've never seen that out of Willie. Willie was just always Willie."

Willie earned Payne's undying affection in 1976, after his wedding. Waylon's guitarist and his new bride planned a ten-day honeymoon and told everybody to leave him alone. But on their wedding night, Waylon called. Payne recalls the conversation: "And he says, 'I know you're getting married tonight. I hate to make this call, but Willie called. He's out on the road with [the band] Poco. Their lead singer got laryngitis. He wants to know if we can come and substitute for Poco. I don't want to do it without you. I know I'm asking too much. I promise I'll make it up to you.' So we go, we get on the plane and go do the show. After the show, Willie comes over with his guitar. We're having a big party in the room, everybody comes by to say congratulations. Willie brings a bottle of champagne—about three feet tall and a foot across at the bottom. So we're drinking that champagne and having a nice party. Finally, about twelve-thirty or one, Willie ran everybody off and got him a little stool, and said, 'Now. What would you like to hear? I want to serenade you on your honeymoon.' So he sat there for about forty-five minutes, singing about every song he could pull out of the hat, just taking requests from my wife and me. That's the kind of guy Willie Nelson was. He wanted to say thank you."

Waylon and Willie with Jessi. Drummer Paul English is partially obscured behind Willie.

Photograph by Art Maillet, courtesy of Sony Music Entertainment

★　　★　　★

THE OUTLAW MOVEMENT offered little to fuel Kristofferson's record sales, although his name reverberated right alongside Waylon's and Willie's and he dependably showed up at the July Fourth picnics and toured with both of them from time to time. He had already accomplished an outlaw status independent of the industry's promotional engine by carving out a place for the earnest singer-songwriter in Nashville and introducing mature themes to country music. Perhaps if he'd been around town more often he might have shown up on the *Wanted!* album, but he had relocated to Malibu, where he spent more time in front of a movie camera than a studio microphone. "That was a good move for him, though," says Rosanne Cash. "Nashville was too small for him. He had a much bigger spirit."

Kris recalls artists who had big hits with his songs urging him to quit Hollywood. The implication, of course, was that his well had run dry. When Bob Beckham cracked that Kris might want to get back behind the throttle of a Gulf Coast helicopter, where he had strung together a lot of profitable verse, Kris replied that those days were long behind him. "But I'm sure that there were people that really started getting critical of what I was doing," says Kristofferson. "It was as if I were spending so much creative energy on the wrong thing, performing and movies, that my songwriting was suffering. I don't think it was. I don't think I'd have done any better if I'd been down there in the Gulf still. And certainly, the rest of my life was an exciting thing. I was doing movies, in the bathtub with Barbra Streisand! I said, 'What! Quit this?' I feel pretty blessed."

Courtesy of Maryland Room, University of Maryland

Kris as a truck driver in *Convoy*.

Indeed, Kris fashioned a new life in California. He had divorced Frances and married singer Rita Coolidge, who, like Jessi Colter, jostled with her husband on the pop charts, and together they were raising their daughter Casey. Journalists who visited with him juxtaposed a relatively stable family life with the demands of touring and starring in big films such as Lewis John Carlino's *The Sailor Who Fell from Grace with the Sea* and Frank Pierson's *A Star Is Born*. Between the lines, they suggested that Kristofferson's top billing in performing, acting, and songwriting was tenuous. In fact, at the first real flicker of Kris's film career in 1972, *Rolling Stone*'s Ben Gerson plunged a knife into his songwriting. "He's a fast-livin', hard lovin' dude who has just enough time between ballin' and brawlin' to jot down a tune or two. He's a cracker-barrel philosopher, able to sprout truisms grown from a life rooted in unadorned reality. He spars with the devil . . . and he and his women are forever falling into his snares. Kris' celebrations of machismo are his most patently stupid observations."

Gerson also complained that Kristofferson's music lacked a sense of place, an easy conclusion to draw when your target appears on the movie screen in all kinds of settings. But, to the contrary, his music remained very much anchored in the West End. His two albums released in 1972—*Border Lord* and *Jesus Was a Capricorn* (which contained the number-one pop hit "Why Me Lord")—included original band members, guitarist Bucky Wilkin (his old chauffer from the first day in town), and young Nashville cats like Charlie McCoy, Kenneth Buttrey, Mac Gayden, and David Briggs. Of course, Fred Foster produced.

The lyrical themes on both albums remained strongly individualistic and never failed to challenge Nashville's sensibilities. In addition, he remained true to his own definition of the singer-songwriter. By 1972, singer-songwriter meant James Taylor and Carole King, whose soft sounds and safe lyrics appealed to radio, while Kristofferson's music continued to mine the oil-stained streets for inspiration, producing ruminations on prostitution, dissipation, and getting high that proved too thorny for the broadcast airwaves.

His fellow recording artists continued to endorse his artistry by covering his songs. From the two 1972 albums, Johnny Cash plucked "Burden of Freedom" for his *Gospel Road* film and soundtrack, while no less than nine artists—including Elvis Presley—took Kristofferson's inspirational classic "Why Me" to the country charts during the course of the 1970s. Outside Nashville, Frank Sinatra picked "Nobody Wins" for his 1973 comeback album *Ol' Blue Eyes Is Back*.

The most arresting song from the two albums nobody picked: "Sugar Man," a noirish study of a woman prowling the streets, selling her body, and injecting heroin. Cast in a languid arrangement worthy of the incidental music in Billy Wilder's *Double Indemnity*, it remains one of Kristofferson's hidden treasures, dissecting the excesses of liberated culture when Sunday morning really does come down. But it was ignored. Critic Chet Flippo could only muster that it sounded like the blues standard "St. James Infirmary."

Musically, Kristofferson soldiered on through the 1970s, moving most of his sessions out to Los Angeles and making room for duets with Rita Coolidge, whose heavenly vocals softened his rugged edge. Despite shrinking sales and blistering reviews, he doggedly pursued his vision, exploring street life in verse and indulging his love of sprawling ballads that featured a colorful cast of characters embroiled in classic narrative conflict. "Silver (The Hunger)," from 1975's *Who's to Bless and Who's to Blame*, seemed inspired by William Blake's poetry or a Thomas Hardy novel, portraying in eight minutes a caddish buccaneer who confronts the awakening sensibilities of his naïve lover. Appealing characters had always populated Kristofferson's songwriting—think "Me and Bobby McGee" and "To Beat the Devil"—but Hollywood, not to mention the retreat of Fred Foster's influence, appears to have inspired him to let in more characters and extend his plotlines. Those songs became their own movies.

Kristofferson's freewheeling lyricism and mostly sparse instrumentation had inspired in one way or another Waylon's *Honky Tonk Heroes* and Willie's *Red Headed Stranger*. "He taught us how to write great poems," observed Waylon. "He changed the way I thought about lyrics, and he said one time that I was the only one that really understood his songs." But few connected Waylon's and Willie's celebrated new albums with Kristofferson. A review in *Country Music* of *Who's to Bless and Who's to Blame* that appeared just as RCA's *Wanted!* hit the market revealed the thick line between Kristofferson and his old friends, accusing him of retreading old ideas and weaving stilted social critiques. "What's sad and disturbing about this album is that it confirms that Kristofferson is no longer a force to be dealt with and that he has become, at least for the moment, irrelevant."

Kris's defection to Hollywood dominated the conversation about him in Nashville. He was always welcomed back cheerfully, but the town wondered why he'd ever left in the first place. "If he hadn't went to Hollywood, no telling how many songs he would have written," speculates Hazel Smith. "The only person Hollywood never ruined was Willie. But the rest of them . . . Mac Davis and Roger Miller . . . every last one of our wonderful songwriters. You just don't go to Hollywood. So Kris's stuff that was so great was written in Nashville, before Hollywood ever took a bite out of him."

A return trip to the South in the mid-1970s underscored the distance between Kris and the land where he had first struck prosperity. Explaining that the audiences were more in tune with his music than ever before, Kristofferson had persuaded Billy Swan to rejoin the band after a year or two away, during which time Swan scored a big pop-country hit with "I Can Help." But the first show with Swan back on board was a disaster. It was staged in Cumming, Georgia. "That's a mean-ass town," says Donnie Fritts, who was still playing piano for Kristofferson.

Folks with their picnic lunches had come out after church, but the sound system threatened to ruin the idyllic Sunday gathering. It coughed and wheezed, which irritated the band and drew an outburst of army vernacular from Kris. Behind the keyboard, Fritts winced. "When he said it," he recalls, "I knew we was in trouble." The males in the crowd, protective of their wives' and children's sensibilities, lay down their paper cups and sandwiches. Kris recalls infuriated men clambering up to the stage.

After the show, the scene in the dressing room was charged. The mayor of Cumming barged in screaming about Kris's language, and he wasn't alone. A group of snarling guys followed, who—Fritts's Alabama raising told him—were capable of trouble. Kris says guns appeared, but Swan merely recalls loud and heated language. In any case, the Georgians were not to be soothed, but neither was Kris backing down.

With the confrontation on the brink of turning physically violent, the band members were ushered to a police cruiser waiting outside to take them to safety. "We ended up getting in the car," says Kris. "We're driving away, and Billy said to me, 'Well, I can see what you mean about it being different now.' It's probably the roughest gig we ever had."

Eleven

Third Coast

ON THE BIG screen, Martin Scorsese's *Taxi Driver* of 1976 found a New York City not unlike Altman's Nashville. A tale of disaffection in a town whose romantic past is wilting in the shadows of post-Vietnam psychosis, the film bore into the heart of America's new self-doubt and arguably marked the high point of New Hollywood productions, garnering four Academy Award nominations. In a film sense, it was the place to be in 1976.

And Kristofferson was there. Not as part of the cast—he was keeping up with Barbra Streisand in *A Star Is Born*—but on the lips of *Taxi Driver*'s characters. Cybil Shepherd's Betsy tells Robert De Niro's Travis Bickel that he's a curious sort, like something out of Kristofferson's "The Pilgrim-Chapter 33."

"Sure, you know what you remind me of," she purrs.

"What?" he grunts.

"That song . . . by Kris Kristofferson."

"Who's that?'

"The songwriter. . . . He's a prophet and a pusher. Partly truth, partly fiction. A walking contradiction."

"Are you saying that about me?"

"Who else would I be talking about?"

"I'm no pusher. I never have pushed. . . ."

The scene cuts to the squirrely Bickel choosing *The Silver Tongued Devil and I* from a record bin, a gift for the sultry Betsy that she ultimately rejects.

In Malibu, Kristofferson appreciated Scorsese's tip of the hat. Forget the *New York Times* profiles or *Rolling Stone* record reviews; this was like Tom Wolfe quoting your poetry in a nonfiction novel. "I thought it was such a nice thing to do," says Kristofferson. "For him to give me a testimonial, that was very sweet. Everybody that does something nice like Scorsese did, the next thing you know, they've made you into something."

The sight of *Silver Tongued Devil and I* bobbing in Bickel's arms was more of a tribute to Kris's stature in the singer-songwriter community at large than a nod to Nashville's influence on his career. But anybody watching the film in Music City must have grinned like a proud papa: at least the prodigal son remained on the streets of popular culture, if not the West End.

Photograph by Alan Mayor

Chet Atkins, far left, with Paul and Linda McCartney in Nashville, 1974.

By 1976, discerning Nashville's impact on popular culture was as easy as peeling open an issue of *Time* or *Newsweek*. What began with *The Johnny Cash Show* in 1969 and all of his guests who hung around and came back to record in the Nashville studios had grown into full-blown cultural influence. Paul McCartney, Ringo Starr, France's Johnny Hallyday, and others led a new wave of artists tapping the city's recording magic and pointing the world to its door. Kristofferson's film career fueled the aura and so did Altman's *Nashville*, despite its indictment of the city's values. Following Altman's lead and enchanted by the new outlaw movement, filmmakers set their productions in contexts that involved country music and crime, though none rose to the level of Altman's classic. *Outlaw Blues* (1977), starring Peter Fonda, jostled with Lynda Carter's cheesecake debut in *Bobbie Joe and the Outlaw* (1976), which featured a Bobby Bare song and, in deference to the Burger Boy, a half-baked pinball machine competition. It didn't get much better than that: films such as *Nashville Girl* (1976) and *Smokey and the Good Time Outlaws* (1978) hewed to thin plots and poor production values that would be scrapped and reshaped for the hopeless *Smokey and the Bandit* franchise and television's *Dukes of Hazzard*, for which Waylon would sing the theme song.

Nashville's music and culture came off considerably better in the national press, which had needled the city so unmercifully in the 1960s. Big newspapers and magazines, impressed by the rock-influenced outlaw hits, found that country music had finally grown up. "The outlaws and the redneck rockers, dealing with new mores and formerly taboo subjects, have won powerful cults who fill up the halls to hear them perform—and who buy their records even if they receive fewer deejay spins than the old country traditionalists," wrote Larry L. King in 1976. "There is a grand mixture now of styles and content, and while it may lead to disputes among modernists and traditionalists over matters of purity, there's an overall higher degree of tolerance for musical diversity."

Chet Flippo of *Rolling Stone*, Robert Hilburn of the *Los Angeles Times*,

Patrick Carr, who contributed to the *New York Times* and was an editor at *Country Music*, and a host of other national journalists reported on the big names and developments in Nashville, stirring the city's Third Coast aura. Closer to home, the Nashville press finally splashed the music industry with deserving ink after years of treating it with aristocratic disdain. Writers such as the *Tennessean's* Laura Eipper and Jerry Bailey as well as the *Banner's* Bill Hance revealed that the country music beat demanded more than stories about, say, Willie Nelson's pig farming; it was now necessary to cover the industry's links to the economy, crime, fashion, and politics.

However, the beacon of such writing was *Country Music* magazine, which combined celebrity glitter with more-than-capable reporting and satire. Debuting in the fall of 1972, the magazine was based in New York, but you'd never know it by the editorial content's strong Nashville flavor and relentless coverage of Johnny Cash, Waylon Jennings, Kris Kristofferson, and Willie Nelson. And so well documented was the interplay between Nashville and Austin that the publication might as well have been the outlaw movement's very own house organ. Writers Dave Hickey (who dated Marshall Chapman), Bob Allen, Michael Bane, Martha Hume (who was married to Chet Flippo), and others burrowed so deeply into country music's inner sanctums that one could almost smell the dirty fryer at the Burger Boy or the smoldering weed at Dripping Springs. Hazel Smith, while working at the Glaser Brothers Studio, dished gossip in her "Hillbilly Central" column, and the inimitable Nick Tosches banged out lively record reviews. In the space of one issue, *Country Music* could communicate the clamminess of the Ryman Auditurium's backstage or the flash of the Exit/In. At its best, it lampooned the conservatism of Nashville or the hype of the outlaw movement without giving its readers reason to be ashamed of the music they loved.

The monthly periodical zealously covered radio stations that switched formats to country music, giving special prominence to the "progressive country" format pioneered by KOKE in Austin, which featured heavy doses of Willie, Waylon, and Kris. The rise of such stations, like the popularity of *Country Music* magazine, measured Nashville's growing stature as well as the outlaws' surging appeal; KAFM in Dallas, KLAC in Los Angeles, KWAM in Memphis, WCRP in Philadelphia, KFDI in Wichita, Kansas, and a few others blended country and rock, although their numbers never equaled that of traditional country formats that stuck to Charley Pride, Loretta Lynn, and Tammy Wynette. KWAM changed its format in 1975 to let in Emmylou Harris, Jerry Jeff Walker, Linda Ronstadt, and "lots of Waylon Jennings and Willie Nelson," noted Michael Bane in *Country Music*. "The most requests," he continued, "are for early Willie Nelson ('Yesterday's Wine' and 'Phases and Stages') with western rocker Gram Parsons following close behind."

Like anywhere in 1970s America, Nashville and country music were populated by plenty of frosted hairdos and clownish plaid suits, but in the wake of Kris, Willie, and Waylon, a Texas-style chic invaded the fashion world, particularly Nashville's. "The town has gone funky!" exclaimed Dave Hickey. "It's really wonderful. One year ago Kristofferson scandalized the town by showing up at a black tie banquet in blue jeans—the next year everyone looks like extras in a rodeo movie." Indeed, the Nudie-styled rhinestone suits and heavily embroidered costumes that had long defined style in Music City made room for the cowboy boots and leather vests that harked back to the country music idols of the late 1940s and early 1950s, albeit with a disheveled 1970s twist. "In Nashville these days, you just *caint git* outlaw enough," cracked Hickey. "All the bars look like the Last Chance Saloon and there are two pairs of Lucchese Boots and three Stetsons per capita here on Muzak Row." The obsession bled out of Nashville into the wardrobes of hipsters everywhere, who snatched up the outlaw belt buckles, gambler's hats, and Willie Nelson bandanas advertised in country music publications and sold in western stores everywhere.

Indeed, it was as cool to be from Nashville as it was to be from Austin. A young player with a country band who might have stammered explaining his job to rock people he met on the road in the late 1960s now had nothing to hide; after all, the icons of his genre toured with Lynyrd Skynyrd and received glowing affirmation in *Taxi Driver*. "Anymore you don't have to be ashamed to like country music," explained Willie Nelson in 1975. "I remember when some people didn't want their friends to know they dug it. Now, it's okay and I think a lot of it has to do with our changing styles, not just in music but dress. The world, at last, has accepted longer hair. The long-haired person can do anything he wants now whereas in the past, much of his actions were limited. I feel the novelty of the cowboy, the way he dresses, the way he thinks and where he lives also has had something to do with the surge in my kind of music which, basically, is country and western."

Some linked the popularity of country music and its outlaw movement to the revival of the South, which saw big manufacturers abandoning the Snowbelt for the Sunbelt, the rise of Jimmy Carter, and the decline of civil rights unrest. "The old South had died, and few Americans—southerners included—would have wanted it back if they could only remember it as it truly was," posited scholar Bruce J. Schulman. "Yet 'redneck culture,' in a commercialized form, thrived and spread in the 1970s. . . . Country music culture, cowboy boots, pickup trucks, and even the Confederate flag became familiar badges of an influential American subculture. Millions of middle-class and upper-class Americans became 'half a redneck.' Along with boots and trucks, these demi-rednecks also brandished a set of shared political attitudes: they resented government interference, although they excluded military procurement from their hit list of despised government programs. They disliked bureaucrats, pointy-headed intellectuals, and 'welfare Cadillacs.'" In other words, soldiers in Richard Nixon's silent majority had outlived Nixon and looked to the South for redemption.

Of course, many of them found Jimmy Carter, who seemed to be the antithesis of Nixon. Carter, like Nixon, surmised that the path to political acceptance snaked through Nashville and its country music.

The former Georgia governor's courtship of the Athens of the South and its music, even its outlaw music, would prove to be yet more evidence of the city's new cultural influence.

Born in Plains, Georgia, Carter grew up listening to country music on the radio, so he was no stranger to the genre when he began reaching out to major figures such as Johnny Cash, Charlie Daniels, and Willie Nelson. He insisted that Johnny's wife, June Carter, was kin, and grinned widely whenever artists like Billy Joe Shaver performed for his campaign. "If Carter makes it to the White House maybe then people will stop making fun of the way I talk," cracked Loretta Lynn, another supporter.

Turning to rock and roll, Carter recruited Allman Brothers band alumnus Dickey Betts and the Marshall Tucker Band, who cranked up the buzz around his presidential campaign. "I think that was one of the reasons I won," Carter told author Chris Willman, "because I *did* align myself with characters like these, who were admired by millions of people around the world. It was a very popular thing to do. I knew Bob Dylan quite well. . . . Dylan had visited me at the governor's mansion and spent the night there with us. And of course the Allman Brothers were special friends, as well. Tom T. Hall was a very strong supporter and still is a good friend."

In his book *Rednecks and Bluenecks*, about national politics and country music, Willman called out the unusual pairing of long-haired singers and a presidential candidate. Indeed, Carter was unusual in more ways than one. He confessed to *Playboy* magazine that he lusted after women; he let his blow-dried hair drop below the top of his ears; and he planned to abolish federal laws against possession of small amounts of marijuana. "Now, Jimmy Carter—some of those who say they're voting for him are doing it because they believe what he believes," said Johnny Cash in the midst of the 1976 campaign, "and some of them are voting for him because he believes in *something*. Whether *they* do or not, they're voting for him because *he* believes in something."

Photograph by Don Foster, courtesy of Nashville Public Library, The Nashville Room

Jimmy Carter hits the ground in Nashville. From left to right: U.S. Senate candidate Jim Sasser, local attorney John Jay Hooker, Carter, Nashville mayor Richard Fulton, and U.S. House candidate Al Gore Jr.

In the homestretch of Carter's campaign to unseat President Ford, he swooped into Nashville on his chartered jet, *Peanut One*, to spirit the faithful in an airport hangar rally. Country music acts Eddy Raven and Larry Gatlin performed, and Georgia native Brenda Lee sang "Happy Birthday" to the fifty-two-year-old candidate. Young Al Gore, who was running for the U.S. House of Representatives, showed up to hear Carter pledge that his next birthday would be in the White House. Fifteen hundred people cheered, and when his plane pulled out onto the runway for Pittsburgh, it was clear Nashville had found its alternative to Richard Nixon. Weeks later, the Carter juggernaut edged out Ford in national polling, but in the Nashville area the vote was decisive: Carter trounced Ford by more than 50 percent.

Throughout Carter's rocky term he continued to groom his relationship with the music world, staging country concerts at the White House and slipping away from his burdens to catch Willie Nelson shows. When

Nelson paid a visit to Carter in Washington, legend tells that the outlaw lit up on the roof of the White House.

Later, Willie visited again when both he and Waylon trundled through town, but he left Waylon in the hotel. "We had done one of the arenas there the night before," recalls Gordon Payne. "And [Waylon] and Willie stayed up pretty late, and Willie had told one of our guys that Waylon had been up for three days and he was bouncing off the wall. And so that morning, we get a call from the president's office, and they want Waylon and Willie to come to the White House. I really think it was Jimmy Carter calling Willie. So, anyway, Jessi and Willie and Connie, and myself ended up going, but Willie was the only one who knew where Waylon was. The only one. He wasn't about to take Waylon to the White House, the way he looked and was acting. Been up for three or four days. And Willie says, 'I'll take his rap. He can even hit me, but I ain't calling him.' So we went to the White House without him! Waylon was pissed! But we talked about it years later. He said, 'You know, it probably saved me more grief than I could ever imagine at the time.'"

Willie and the president.

★   ★   ★

BOTH WAYLON AND Willie got plenty of grief over drugs during the mid-1970s, mostly because of the creeping influence of cocaine, although Willie claims he stuck with pot. "The speed and the weed didn't mix, especially when you're up there trying to get a feeling going, get the dynamics going," he told biographer Joe Nick Patoski. "Nobody's thinking that way. They're just playing. I could handle the weed, but I couldn't handle the speed. I didn't want to be around people who were doing it, even my band." But he couldn't get away from it, whether dealing with Waylon's antics or the addiction of friends and family members. In 1976, authorities subpoenaed Willie twice in the case of a car dealer accused of leading an international narcotics ring, and one year later, three of Nelson's entourage were handcuffed after police sniffed out 1.12 grams of "unusually high grade cocaine" in a traffic stop.

Nashville authorities watched uneasily as the number of cocaine arrests increased. Moreover, they estimated that about three pounds of the drug—with a street value approaching one hundred thousand dollars—was snorted each week in the city, although Waylon and his people might have alone accounted for that amount. "It was everywhere," says Gordon Payne. "It was the cool thing. People on Music Row, on the record labels had it. Promoters had it. Everybody had it."

If Nashville boasted Third Coast status, it had to have its cocaine. "The early seventies were pretty gentle—grass and alcohol," says Rodney Crowell, who continued to come in and out of Nashville. "And then somewhere in there cocaine came in. And that was—whew—insidious stuff. But it was around. It was everywhere. [There was a] phone number on the bulletin board of the studio. You just call and they'd deliver. 'We deliver!' Like pizza delivery! I never did like cocaine. I tried to shovel as much of it as I could at times, but never liked it.

"I would generally become crippled with self-loathing if I got too far into that stuff," continues Crowell. "Which I did a few times. And I got to say most of the people that I observed . . . I just saw this really exclusive, greedy, hipper-than-thou behavior that came with who was holding [the parties]. Parties back then were with whoever had the most blow. Everybody hung around, like they were the cash cow. I didn't like it."

Waylon loved it. He had encountered cocaine for the first time after complaining to Richie Albright that his amphetamine suppliers were drying up. Albright—always familiar with the latest forms of recreation in the music business—pointed the way. And it was like unleashing a wild dog. Waylon claimed to spend twenty thousand dollars each time he scored, which was an awful lot of *Wanted!* albums, and stories abounded about bowls of the stuff cranking up the parties at his home. "I wasn't just doing a little drugs," confessed Waylon, years later. "I was doing them constantly. . . . I'd do them until I collapsed, then I'd get up and start right doing them again. I was killing the people around me, because they had to watch me destroy myself. I'd definitely hit bottom with it. I would never sleep. I'd stay up six or seven days or nights at a time, and I wouldn't go home. My health was bad, I had dizzy spells where I couldn't hardly drive, I had cars strewed all over this town, because I'd get somewhere, and I'd have to leave 'em and have somebody else take me home."

If Waylon had a reasonably good handle on what he was spending on coke—and he probably didn't—nobody could estimate what it was costing him in missed opportunities and lost work. Although, according to people around him, he had the constitution of a bull and rarely missed shows like Johnny Cash had in the 1960s; he was sometimes too messed up to do anything beyond his shows, like big interviews or potentially profitable TV appearances.

Jack Clement nudged him toward regular network television work in 1976, but the results were infuriating. He'd shot test video of Waylon and Jessi at the new Opry House and used it to pitch a weekly show to television producer Pierre Cossette, father of the Grammy Awards broadcast. According to Clement, Cossette had sponsorship money from Ford Motor Company that he was ready to spend on Waylon. They dubbed the show *Brand New Opry*. "Or something like that," murmurs Clement. "It was going to be a country show. Good music. Lots of fun stuff. And he was going to let me produce it. And then Waylon was playing in Amarillo, Texas; Pierre came out to see the show before the TV thing. And he kind of disappeared. Pierre's sitting there, waiting for him in this big restaurant or something, you know. Waylon shows up kind of high and takes off. Then Pierre came to Nashville to meet him, went to the house, and it was a go-deal. And then what really blew it was he was doing the Grammy show that year [in Los Angeles], and he had Waylon and Jessi on it as presenters."

Waylon, says Clement, was stoned on the broadcast. The next day they were all to meet to discuss the proposed show, despite whatever Cossette's reaction had been to the night before. "Pierre's tired," explains Clement. "He's been up all night, and then waiting on Waylon to get up at three or four in the afternoon. And he's enduring this shit. We drop by Andy Williams's house, hung out there for a while, then we rode around Hollywood Hills, then went back to the hotel. Waylon came down, stayed about five minutes and then took off!" Naturally, the show died right there.

★　　　★　　　★

THE CAUTIONARY TALE for all of the country music users should have been Elvis Presley, who consumed prescription medication as if it were peanuts and popcorn. Of course, he assumed godhead stature in the mind of every hillbilly singer who dreamed of stardom and embodied rock and roll's embrace of country music, a union that thrived in Waylon's artistry during the 1970s. Waylon's friend Bobby Bare never saw much distance between the King's music and the styling that he and Waylon and the boys unleashed on Nashville. "To me it was country, and I loved it," said Bare. " 'That's All Right Mama' and 'Blue Moon of Kentucky,' to me, that was country. Anything that had an open chord guitar was country. *High* energy." Said Waylon, "Most of us marked time Before Elvis and After Elvis."

And on the gilded stages of Las Vegas, Elvis reflected back the adoration, anointing more than a few of the outlaws' creations. Most concerts in the 1970s drew from Kristofferson's well—"For the Good Times" and "Why Me"—and spun dramatic performances of Willie's "Funny How Time Slips Away." And when the King churned out Tony Joe White's "Polk Salad Annie," as he did frequently, he connected to the heartbeat of the West End, Combine Music, which had championed some of the best Nashville-bred music ever. He even covered Waylon and Billy Joe Shaver's "You Asked Me Too," straight from *Honky Tonk Heroes*, the first outlaw album.

In 1975, Elvis's cover of Billy Swan's "I Can Help" earned Kristofferson's bass player an audience with the singer. Kristofferson drooled over Swan's meeting with royalty, wondering what he was like. "I remember Billy telling me about it," says Kris, "and I said, 'Well, geez, is he fat now?' And Billy gets his Billy look on his face and says, 'Well, yeah.' But then he started to smile and said, 'But he was Elvis.' I'll never forget that."

Elvis had always inspired whispers in Nashville, mostly over his covert visits from Memphis to record at RCA, which had begun in 1956 and continued into the 1970s. He often crept into RCA late at night and escaped before first light, igniting talk on Music Row about the publishers who had gotten cuts on his sessions and karate demonstrations that he'd given when he should have been singing. Staff producer Ronny Light might turn a corner or open a door to find Elvis on the premises, but he got a truer picture of the big fellow from chats with Felton Jarvis, who exclusively produced Elvis. In conversations, Jarvis marveled at Elvis's Graceland world, where servants made any dessert he wanted at any time of the day or night. But desserts, Jarvis would tell friends, were merely the low-hanging targets of Presley's whims.

When it looked like Jarvis might be leaving RCA to work independently as Presley's producer, he scooted down to Memphis to measure Elvis's feelings about the deal. "I talked to him when he got back," says Light, "and he had this look like he didn't quite know what to think. I said, 'Did everything go okay?' He said, 'Yeah, I've got a story I got to tell somebody. You can't tell anybody this. The strangest thing happened. I was down in the music room and we were talking about artists.' Felton had done an album on Fats Domino and he'd done Tommy Roe. They talked about different things they'd done and music they liked. Elvis was playing albums. This could have been like three o'clock in the morning. He said, 'Do you like guns, Felton?' And Felton said, 'Oh, yeah.' He said, 'I got to show you my guns.' And he brings out a pearl-handle. So he had three TVs in this little room with a low ceiling down in the basement, and then all of a sudden he's shooting up the walls and the TVs. He said, 'I'm thinking my hero's gone crazy. I got to do something. What do I do? I can't call the police. I'm frozen and then Elvis says, 'I'm tired. I'm going to bed. I'll see you in the morning.' And Felton knew where he was going to sleep. It was upstairs. So here he is in the shot-up room that smells like gun powder. He doesn't know what to do. He goes up to his bedroom and he lays there and looks at the ceiling and thinks, 'What am I going to do?' He lay there for hours, and he finally went to sleep.

"So Felton wakes up hours later. It was almost daylight before they went to bed. The sun's coming in the window and Felton says, 'I can't believe what happened last night. I must have dreamed it. It can't be true.' He goes downstairs to see it. The TVs are fine. The room is fine. It's not shot up. But he could smell fresh paint and plaster. Somebody [had come] in the hours they had slept."

The only story more mind-boggling was the death of Felton's charge after years of drug abuse. It hit Nashville like a thunderclap. On the steamy afternoon of August 16, 1977, as the news flew around the world, Nashville donned its mourning clothes. Fans emptied record stores of Elvis albums, and movie theaters booked his old films, while music industry veterans recalled the artist's long-ago visits to the *Grand Ole Opry* and his many Music City recording sessions. "Oh, everybody was crying!" remembers Hazel Smith. "Everybody was brokenhearted. Elvis belonged to us."

On August 16, Gordon Payne pulled up to the traffic light at the intersection of Thompson Lane and Nolensville Road, near the Woodbine neighborhood south of Nashville, when the news crackled on the radio. A few blocks away, in Berry Hill, Elroy Kahanek—who'd been fired from RCA—left an audio store with a stylus he'd bought for his new boss, Jack Johnson, who managed Charley Pride and Ronnie Milsap. "It wasn't a half a mile back to the office, and when I pulled into the parking lot, the sky turned dark and it just started thundering and lightning. And I walked into the office and Jack was there and he said, 'Guess what?' I said, 'What?' He said, 'Elvis just died.' "

Willie Nelson wasn't in Berry Hill or Austin or Conifer, Colorado, where he and Connie had moved in the summer of 1976. He was in Memphis, Tennessee, preparing for a show with Emmylou Harris at the Mid-South Coliseum. Rodney Crowell was flying in from Nashville to meet the rest of Emmylou's band at the airport, and he figures Elvis died while he was still in the air. When the plane landed, some Memphis reporters arrived hoping to interview James Burton, Glen D. Hardin, and Emory Gordy, who split their time between Elvis and Emmylou. "I don't know how they got there so fast," marvels Crowell. "They descended on the guys from the band. It was a dark night, but I'll never forget it."

The big venues of Memphis would shutter their doors two days later for Elvis's funeral, but, strangely, Willie's show carried on against the eerie mood that drifted across Memphis that night. A spectator later recalled that Emmylou took the stage and never mentioned the King, and then Willie, too, performed without acknowledging the obvious. While the music played, a thin figure swayed in the wings, stepping into the stage lights only when Willie summoned him. It was Jerry Lee Lewis.

He crooned behind Willie on a few numbers, and then the headliner motioned to his sister Billie to move from the piano. Lewis sat down and dove into a set of gospel music, the night's benediction for the King.

But Crowell read the Killer differently, spying a swagger in the old boy's step. "Looked to me like he was celebrating," he says. "He's the king now."

★   ★   ★

CROWELL, TOO, HAD reason to celebrate in 1977, although not over Presley's death. Since running away and joining Emmylou's travelers, he'd been at the core of her first two number-one albums: *Elite Hotel* (1976) and *Luxury Liner* (1977). His "Till I Gain Control Again" on *Elite Hotel* proved a wondrous vehicle for her soaring vocals as did *Luxury Liner*'s "You're Supposed to Be Feeling Good"; both songs landed on the B sides of top-ten country hits, and were some of Crowell's first big paydays since lighting out of Houston in 1972, a young outlaw in the shadow of Kris Kristofferson.

During those days with Emmylou, Crowell showed enough potential that her manager took over his career and helped him win a contract at Warner Bros., which spawned his first album, *Ain't Living Long Like This*. The project was a pure spin-off of the Emmylou phenomenon: Brian Ahern, Emmylou's husband, produced the album and the heart of her Hot Band dished out the instrumentation. Willie Nelson added background vocals, and Willie's harpist, Mickey Raphael, served up a large helping of funky licks.

Far from a commercial success, the album nonetheless gave Crowell another showcase and formed a bridge between the gritty West End street life of the early 1970s and then-current commercial country music, particularly the outlaws' music. Certainly other men and women who immigrated to the West End in the late 1960s and early 1970s, whether to attend Vanderbilt or to find cheap rents, climbed into the recording industry by the late 1970s: Paul Worley was playing sessions and producing and Marshall Chapman signed with Epic, for example. But Crowell mingled with country music's biggest commercial forces. Willie's appearance on Crowell's album was obviously meaningful, but by 1977, when it hit the stores, Waylon, too, was connecting with the Houston kid. The top-dog outlaw recorded "Till I Gain Control Again" for his *Ol' Waylon* album of 1977 and later turned to "Even Cowgirls Get the Blues," "Ain't Living Long Like This," "Old Love, New Eyes" (cowritten with Hank DeVito), "Song for the Life," and "Angel Eyes." On the road, Crowell slipped away from Emmylou's band and with his own small group opened a few dates for Willie, and, then, Willie, too, dipped into the young artist's well, taking his turn at "Till I Gain Control Again" and "Angel Eyes." Johnny Cash soon discovered Crowell and presently became his father-in-law, but Waylon's and Willie's attention to the singer as he graduated from Emmylou helped steady his legs in the country music business.

Crowell's relationship with Waylon particularly rang of that old West End magic, although the old outlaw and the young outlaw had never crossed paths there in the early days. In the innocent neighborhood, Crowell had shuffled from bar to bar in search of tips and experience, while Waylon had found risk personified at Hillbilly Central. In them, the Professional Club gamblers and the Bishop's Pub ramblers had joined forces at the forefront of country music in the late 1970s, helping to propel the new and invigorating singer-songwriter phenomenon of the 1980s, over which Crowell and his then-wife Rosanne Cash reigned.

BUT THERE WAS still the matter of cocaine, which had taken root in that same West End habitat. When Rodney and Waylon finally sat down to discuss a direct collaboration, this in the wake of Rodney's magic production of his wife, Rosanne, a snowdrift seized up their wheels. "The head of RCA says, 'I want you to do with Waylon what you've done with Rosanne,'" remembers Rodney. "So Waylon was already a friend of mine, but we go to have this meeting. And it turns out Waylon's all gacked on coke, and I'm all gacked on coke, and we come to this meeting and I start posturing around like a know-it-all asshole, telling Waylon what we're going to do. And Waylon just says, 'Fuck you! Get the fuck out of here!' Waylon was a sweet guy, but he basically just said, 'You asshole. Who do you think you are, coming in here, telling me you're going to change my music?' I went, 'Oh . . . who do I think I am? He's right.' He nailed it. Later on I called him and said, 'I'm so sorry, I was loaded.' He says, 'I was, too.' I could have had a run producing Waylon Jennings records, but I was just a frozen-brained idiot."

*Even with its present day vulgar, ugly, plastic look and
sound there is a little something else left for anybody who
was once under Nashville's spell. As one walks or rides
down any street in Nashville one can feel now and again
that he has just glimpsed some pedestrian on the sidewalk
who was not quite real somehow, who with a glance over
his shoulder or with a look in his disenchanted eye has
warned one not to believe too much in the plastic present
and has given warning that the past is still real and
present somehow and is demanding something of all men
like me who happen to pass that way.*

—**Peter Taylor**

 Twelve

Ain't Living Long Like This

THE TWENTY-THIRD OF August in 1977 found Nashville still pondering the death of Elvis, but Waylon and Willie conspired to puncture the downcast mood. It was time again to play outlaw, so in front of an entertainment press corps still very much in Elvis mode, they demanded that the Country Music Association (CMA)—the industry's top trade association—withdraw their names from 1977 award contention. Despite whatever private competiveness that may have existed between them, they did not wish to see their solo recordings up against each other in categories such as Single of the Year, Album of the Year, and so on. Furthermore, they believed the large number of votes controlled by big record labels undermined the integrity of the honors. "These awards are like the Academy Awards to some extent," said a statement issued by Bill Conrad, Waylon's publicist. "A lot of unnamed people who are privileged to vote, vote for their own camps. Show business politics are like any politics, and Waylon is just not interested."

The CMA and Waylon, specifically, had sparred throughout the 1970s: Waylon had refused invitations to attend the organization's awards show in previous years and when he did accept, the show's producers ordered him to restrict his "Only Daddy That'll Walk the Line" to one verse, which moved Waylon to storm out of rehearsals. In the wake of Waylon and Willie's announcement, the CMA nominated them for Best Vocal Duo of the Year, which meant they wouldn't be in competition against each other, but the men stayed home anyway and continued to smear the CMA. In the end, the disheveled duo never forced change at the organization, if that was their aim, but the controversy slung them back into the newspapers, until the next time they tangled with authority.

In the midst of the storm over Elvis's demise and while Waylon and Willie planned their protest, an extraordinary streak of vice squad activity targeting illicit alcohol sales cut across Nashville. Early in August, police had raided an unlicensed private club called Top of the Block, on Elliston Place near the Exit/In, arresting gamblers, drug users, and the manager. According to the *Tennessean*, police confiscated "six pistols, four decks of poker cards, a pair of brass knuckles, several bottles of pills, and several packets of white powder believed to be cocaine." Seven days later, the coppers again stormed the Top of the Block before invading two other joints: the Varsity Club on Fourth Avenue South and the King of Clubs on Thomson Place. And then four days after Elvis died and three days before Waylon and Willie hollered about the CMA, the vice unit netted one more private club, walking nonchalantly into One-Eyed Jack's on Edmondson Pike and ordering drinks without as much as producing a membership card. "They served us, took our money, and then we arrested them," declared one of the detectives.

Just when it seemed that Metro police might seize the governor's very own liquor cabinet, federal narcotics agents elbowed aside local authorities on the city's front pages. In late August, they followed a package of cocaine into the heart of Music Row and prepared to arrest its intended recipient, the outlaw Waylon Jennings.

★   ★   ★

WHILE WAYLON'S PUBLICIST faced reporters over the CMA controversy on August 23, Waylon headed to the American Sound Studios, located in a Romanesque house on Seventeenth Avenue South, right next door to his office, where he was coproducing a Hank Williams Jr. album. It was one of those sessions that epitomized West End attitude: loose, unpredictable, and studded with characters. Of course, Waylon and Hank amply filled the center, but they were joined by Jack Routh, Johnny Cash's son-in-law, who was pitching his songs, and the L.A. disc jockey Hugh Cherry, who had emceed Cash's Folsom Prison show back in 1968 and was producing a radio documentary on Waylon. You never knew who else might show up.

Earlier in the day, Mark Rothbaum, an aide to Neil Reshen, had slipped twenty-three grams of cocaine into an envelope addressed to Waylon's office and dispatched it by courier to Nashville. At the airport in New York, a suspicious clerk unsealed it and found the white substance tucked in a sheet of yellow legal paper. When federal drug enforcement officers arrived, they confiscated twenty-two grams and sent the rest on to Waylon, tipping off agents in Nashville that his secretary, Lori Evans, would be collecting the package at the airport.

In Nashville, the G-men watched a cabdriver retrieve the package from the courier counter and hand it to Evans, who slipped into a Ford Bronco and sped off to Music Row. Unaware of the eyes watching her, she cruised past the old homes in the neighborhood, pulled into the back parking lot, and walked into the studio, where the session was in full swing. Waylon stood in the vocal booth preparing to overdub harmonies to Hank's lead on "Storms Never Last," while Evans stepped into the control room and dropped the package on a chair near Richie Albright, who was behind the board that night.

Waylon hustled into the control room, snatched the package, checked the contents, and headed back to the booth. Albright cued up "Storms Never Last," which Jessi Colter had written, and Waylon tackled his vocals. Meanwhile, the feds gathered at the back entrance, where a security guard pointed them to Albright. When they approached the control room, the drummer-producer quietly bore down on the talkback button so Waylon—who was out of sight in the booth—could hear everything.

"They said they were there because they knew a package had come in, and they were there to investigate," says Albright. "I said, 'Show me your search warrant.' Well, they had a search warrant for the office, which was next door to the studio. They had the wrong number. I said, 'This won't work because it's the wrong address.' They said, 'We can get another one.' I said, 'Okay. But that takes a little while, to get the judge and all of that stuff.' They said, 'We're going to stay here.' I said, 'We're going to go ahead and record because this is costing [hundreds] an hour.' They said, 'We'll just stand back here but we'll be in every room.' I said, 'Every room except [the studio]. We're going to keep working. Those microphones are so sensitive that they pick up every move.' So they bought that."

Waylon nervously left the booth and approached the agents in the control room, playing dumb and listening intently while they explained that more agents would be returning soon with another warrant. Albright told Waylon they needed to get back to work. He played a track at high volume so he could escort Waylon, and now Hank, back to the vocal booth and find out where the coke was. It was on the floor in the booth, said Waylon.

Putting Hank in the booth gave Albright an excuse to set up another microphone, which got him close to the powder-filled bags. Ever the fixer, he grabbed them, stuffed them in his pants, and finished with the microphones. He wadded up the courier envelope and threw it deep into an opening in the wall before returning to the control room. Who knows if Albright actually recorded the harmony vocals that the men sang, but by the time they finished, the agents had returned with their warrant and prepared to search. Just then, as if on cue, one of Neil Reshen's lieutenants in Nashville burst into the studio, and Waylon tore into him. The lawmen turned toward the flare-up, while Albright stole into the bathroom and flushed the evidence down the toilet. "They were banging at the door, and I came out and said, 'I had to pee.' Boy, that guy's face was as red as a beet.

"This one agent said, 'What's downstairs?' And I said, 'It's a tape vault, but you got to be careful.' And he said, 'Well, you go with me.' So I go down there and he's walking through all these tape boxes." As the flashlight darted around in the darkness, they approached the space where Albright thought the courier pouch might have landed. "I said, 'I seen the biggest rat you've ever seen down here the other day.' He said, 'Really?' And we turned around, and he said, 'Let's go.'"

At a few minutes after midnight, an agent found two wet plastic bags in a trash can in the studio bathroom. A Drug Enforcement Administration detective later reported that they matched the description of those in the courier envelope and contained trace amounts of cocaine. Small stashes of pot and cocaine, though none tied to Waylon's package, turned up in searches of various people in the studio, but not in searches of Waylon and Lori Evans. Despite that, agents arrested both of them on charges of conspiracy to possess and distribute cocaine.

The next morning, Waylon, his face cast down, negotiated a throng of press outside the federal courtroom while Richie Albright thrust his open hand into the lenses of swarming photographers. One newsman rose above the clicking cacophony to ask the singer how he felt.

"I'm hangin' in there," muttered Waylon.

Richie Albright runs interference for Waylon as he enters
federal court after his arrest on drug charges in 1977.

★   ★   ★

IN THE WAKE of Waylon's arrest, *outlaw* may have taken on darker
tones in the public's eye. Maybe there was something to this Bumpy
Jonas act, a tantalizing possibility in the halls of the music industry.
The singer's troubles, the speculation went, could only rev up his album
sales, predicting the huge sales that rappers enjoyed twenty years later
whenever they tussled with the law. "Waylon'll have a whole new following now," trumpeted an anonymous Music Row figure in the *Banner*. "I'll bet he does another million dollars' worth of business next
year. . . . There's no stopping him now."

Jerry Bradley had a similar view from his office at RCA. "A little bit
of drugs was selling records for Waylon in my mind," he says. "Maybe
a rebellious attitude, along with the *Outlaw* album, didn't hurt. I'm not
trying to be mean when I say that, but the mafia didn't hurt Sinatra. I
never had a discussion with Waylon about drugs. Hell, I was a three-
hundred-pound guy. I didn't want nobody discussing weight with me. I

knew it was bad, wasn't good for your health, but wasn't a hell of a lot I could do about it at the time."

Waylon, too, let the bust run down his collar. The evening of his first court appearance, when charges were lodged, he strutted on to Willie Nelson's show at Nashville's Municipal Auditorium, "looking decidedly unbowed and seemingly of extreme good cheer," noted Laura Eipper of the *Tennessean*. The two outlaws sliced through "Good Hearted Woman" and then "Pick Up the Tempo," a Willie number that Waylon had included on his *This Time* album. He smirked and ad-libbed its third line: *People are saying that I'm living too fast, and they say that I can't last much longer / Little they know that I don't give a damn.*

Weeks later, a judge threw out charges against Waylon and his secretary, leaving only Mark Rothbaum, who had dispatched the drugs to Nashville, to face prosecution. In April 1978, he pleaded guilty to one count of distributing cocaine and served a short prison sentence. The plea prevented a trial that might have exposed Waylon's long drug history, so Rothbaum is widely viewed as having taken a bullet for the singer, leaving the outlaw singer free to revert to his old ways.

Guitarist Gordon Payne, who sat next to Richie Albright at the console that night when the feds invaded, observed a post-bust wariness in Waylon but no change of heart for his darling cocaine. "Everywhere we went we were looking over our shoulder," he recalls, "looking for cop cars. We were really careful after that. And we literally would have rooms swept for bugs when we went to certain places, where we knew there was a big [police] presence. It changed a lot of things. We just had to be more careful. I mean, none of us were going to quit! That wasn't the answer! The logical answer did not come up!"

It wasn't long, though, before Payne observed that the drugs were telling on Waylon. "You'd see Waylon stay up for seven days and he wouldn't look well. There were conversations about it: 'He's partying too hard.' So there was a bit of a cloud, and it was becoming a problem.

Before then, we were doing our job. Nobody missed a call; nobody missed a sound check. But there were little things in the organization that started happening.

"What I noticed was people started getting into Waylon's inner circle that never should have been. People conning him, making him believe that his best interest was at heart, when they were really just taking advantage of him. People kissing his ass. None of us ever did that. If he was wrong, we'd tell him!

"I come to the bus one day, and he was sitting there with Kristofferson. He smacked me in the balls, and I just knocked the shit out of him! It was just a quick reflex. As soon as I did it, I'm sure my mouth dropped and my eyes went up. I looked at him and said, 'I'm sorry; it was just a freak accident.' He said, 'I don't blame you; no problem, hoss. I'll never hit anybody in the balls again as long as I live.'"

Observers say that by 1978 manager Neil Reshen was less and less attentive to business and quickly falling out of favor in Waylon's and Willie's camps. Waylon claimed that Reshen was poisoning his relationship with RCA and had gone missing when the singer needed help with finances. On Willie's side of the house, the singer blamed Reshen for an unpaid tax bill and for Rothbaum's conviction, believing rightly or wrongly that the manager had let his assistant go to jail, so he rewarded Rothbaum with Reshen's job once the prison term ended. Waylon never made such a public gesture of gratitude or solidarity, strangely omitting Rothbaum's name from a detailed accounting of the coke bust in his 1996 autobiography, but soon, he, too, split with Reshen, citing his inattention to business matters. "Neil had helped me and Willie in the beginning, but now it was going nowhere," complained Waylon. "My damn business was screwed up."

Waylon discharged Neil in 1980.

But the cocaine proved more resilient, dominating Waylon for another four years.

★   ★   ★

AS WAYLON'S EXCESSES snagged him deep in the 1970s, the recklessness of Music Row's real criminal outlaw was fast catching up with him. Lee Emerson emerged from prison in Memphis just in time to catch the wild Hillbilly Central days and sign with Combine Music in hopes of churning out another "Ruby Ann" or "I Thought I Heard You Callin' My Name." But son Rodney Bellamy recalls that bad luck soon descended. "[Emerson] was eating a Hostess Twinkie, and he swallowed his dentures. He had to go into the hospital and have his stomach operated on to get them out. He came to live with us right after that, and [my wife] Marilyn made a comment that [his wound] was smelling bad. Well, he took it all wrong and got mad because she was telling him that if it's smelling bad it might not be healing up right. He stunk. So he up and packed his stuff together and left."

Later Rodney learned that Lee moved in with a new girlfriend, Darlene Sharpe, who was recovering from a cataclysmic auto accident that had left her disfigured and blind in one eye. Sharpe later claimed that Lee frequently assaulted her. "No one realized that Lee was really doing these things to me," she said, "until he broke into my apartment and told me and my sister that he was going to kill me. I picked up the telephone to call the police and he jerked the cord out of the wall. . . . Another time he took a piece of firewood and busted my leg muscle, and he told me he was going to poke my other eye out so that I would be blind." When Emerson and Sharpe finally parted ways, he hounded her for song lyrics he had left at her home while she took up with Barry Sadler, the famous army man whose "Ballad of the Green Berets," a 1966 hit, briefly made him a national hero.

Sadler had settled in Nashville some years after leaving the army, his patriotic ballad then a past glory. He wrote songs, authored historical fiction, and compiled a sloppy book on the music business, but his biggest audience hung out in the bars of Nashville, where he spun tales about mercenary adventures and his service in the jungles of Vietnam. According to Nashville legend, Sadler once treated a knife wound inflicted by a country-music-playing American Indian with a few shots of whiskey and did a home-stitch job. He liked to be feared, and he could be as mean as Lee Emerson. "I think he was one of those people who really doesn't care," said a Nashville woman who knew him.

Courtesy of Nashville Public Library, The Nashville Room

Barry Sadler, the balladeer of the Green Berets.

One night out on the streets of town, Emerson saw Sharpe with her new boyfriend and again demanded his lyrics. "Sadler stepped up to him," recounts son Bellamy. "Well, Dad flattened him. There was that left hand out of nowhere that could do it and he done it." Sadler later claimed Emerson began harassing the couple, jeering him about the sissy Green Berets and running her off the road with his van. There was little question that Emerson was unhinged. He'd become disheveled in his appearance and refused to communicate with his son. "He had a side of him that was kind of ingrained in him, to do something when it was wrong when it was easier to do something right," says his friend Donnie Fritts.

On December 1, 1978, just before midnight, Emerson appeared in the parking lot outside Sharpe's apartment. Sadler later claimed that Emerson had made threatening phone calls from a local bar earlier in the night and showed up to make good on them, but Bellamy's son charged that he'd been lured there. What happened next is not disputed. While Emerson sat in his van, Sadler emerged from the darkness with his .32-caliber pistol and shot him between the eyes. The former Green Beret hurried to the van and placed a .38-caliber piece on the floor in front of his victim's seat; he then called police to report that he'd just shot at a man in self-defense. Emerson would hang on until early the following morning, finally breathing his last at St. Thomas Hospital.

When police arrived at the crime scene, they dug through Emerson's wallet looking for identification but only found four prescriptions for amphetamines. Meanwhile, Sadler stood by spewing a litany of fantastic theories: perhaps Emerson's own gun had fired a bullet into his head or maybe Sadler's shot ricocheted off the glass and hit Emerson. "I'm a weapons expert and there's no way my little .32 could have made the kind of wound they're talking about," lied Sadler in conversation with a *Banner* reporter. "I fired to miss him by two feet and I'm a damn good shot. If I'd been trying to kill him, I could have put a bullet in his ear. But I shot to miss and I've never heard of a bullet making a 90 degree turn." Nor had anybody heard such fanciful storytelling.

Sadler retained one of Nashville's superstar attorneys, Joe Binkley, who had represented Douglas Brown in the Stringbean killings. He needed him—police detectives in their investigation were learning that the gun in Emerson's car was registered in the former Green Beret's name. There had been no shot from Emerson's car nor had the rough-edged victim even brandished a weapon. In June 1979, the district attorney's office charged Sadler with second-degree murder. Less than a year later, he pleaded guilty to voluntary manslaughter and received a four-to-five-year prison term.

Strangely, a judge reduced the sentence four months after it was imposed, giving the killer thirty days in the Nashville workhouse and two years' probation. Today, decades after Sadler's own death in 1989, the files in the case are missing from the criminal court archives.

★   ★   ★

TRUE TO JERRY Bradley's predictions, Waylon's public cocaine troubles only fueled his record sales. His five solo singles after the arrest rushed to the top five, and his albums sailed just as swiftly. On the surface, his two solo albums released after the bust—*I've Always Been Crazy* and *What Goes Around Comes Around*—communicated defiance. He appeared scowling on the covers and belted out strutting anthems, such as Crowell's "Ain't Living Long Like This" and his own "I've Always Been Crazy." But underneath the bluster, Waylon had mellowed. As the 1970s dwindled, he covered old rock and country songs and unfurled deeply sentimental ballads, including Tony Joe White's "Billy" and Mickey Newbury's "If You See Her." And then he dusted off Bob McDill's "Amanda," which he originally recorded in 1974, and watched it shoot to number one in 1979. The volume now turned down on the outlaw bad man narrative, the critics applauded. "Side two consists of ballads the likes of which Jennings hasn't sung in some time," observed Martha Hume of 1979's *What Goes Around Comes Around*. "In the hands of lesser talent, a few of these songs . . . would sound overly sentimental. But Jennings' rough baritone can handle a soulful ballad, and his masculine style just makes him seem all the more vulnerable." Nick Tosches went as far as to suggest that 1978's *I've Always Been Crazy* tolled Waylon's "farewell to outlawry."

If Waylon was trying to cut the stitching in the outlaw label, he still hovered near the Waylon-and-Willie franchise, which lived on the road and in occasional recorded duets. In 1978, RCA released the duo's eponymous album collaboration, which charged through the country and pop markets like an angry steed.

The way Bradley tells it, Waylon's nose for ideas had dulled in the wake of the cocaine arrest, so he approached the RCA executive looking for another magical concept like *Wanted! The Outlaws*. Bradley had promised never to reprise the outlaw packaging, but he had cooked up an album idea pairing the country's most famous bearded Texans. In the wake of so many concert tours and one-off collaborations in the studio, it was only a matter of time before the two got behind the microphone for an album. "I turned around and I got this small [mock-up] copy of *Waylon and Willie*, the embossed album," says Bradley about his meeting with Waylon. "I said, 'How do you like that?' He said, 'I love that. How we gonna do that?'"

Bradley directed Waylon to select a few Willie tracks in the RCA vaults and add his vocals, but the singer ultimately struggled to meld with his friend's recordings, so with Bradley's blessing he went to Rick Blackburn, who ran CBS Records in Nashville, and asked to sing real duets with Willie. "So they went and recorded in-the-business, drug songs," says Bradley, probably referring to "Gold Dust Woman," written by Stevie Nicks of Fleetwood Mac. "Waylon come to play those for me. He looked at me and said, 'You don't really like them?' I said 'Well, we'll do well with them, but I don't think there's one as good as what we had with the *Outlaws*.' He said, 'What about this one?' And that's when he played 'Mammas.'"

It was "Mammas Don't Let Your Babies Grow Up to Be Cowboys," written by Ed and Patsy Bruce. The lilting ode to the cowboy's destiny was a natural for the two old outlaws and a sure enough winner in a nation that adored the Dallas Cowboys football team and still romanced history's range riders. Bradley knew from the minute he heard Waylon play the song that it was as good as Elvis rising up from the dead. It shot to number one in March 1978 and stayed there four weeks, longer than any other single released by a country act that year.

The album itself, made up of mostly new recordings, stopped at every depot on their 1970s outlaw journey, featuring two Kristofferson

tracks, one by the outlaw writer Lee Clayton, and a cowritten piece by
the old Hillbilly Central denizen Shel Silverstein. Reliable Chet Flippo
turned in dynamic liner notes as if to summon the fair winds of *Wanted!
The Outlaws*, and Waylon and Willie rounded out the set with a few
recordings from their early 1970s sessions at Hillbilly Central. The al-
lure of the outlaw reunion coupled with "Mammas," which fathers and
sons could sing together like Cash's "Folsom Prison Blues," prepared
the way for a 126-week stay on the country charts; nobody in country music—not Tammy Wynette, Johnny Cash, Dolly Parton, Charley
Pride, or Loretta Lynn—mustered that kind of staying power. "The
album is rarely as good as its creators can be, but it's more than respectable," noted writer Patrick Carr. "As Willie points out, the mere fact
that RCA and CBS were persuaded to let it happen is something close
to a miracle. And, as *I* point out, it beats most everything else on the
record racks right now."

Waylon and Willie even moseyed into Manhattan's Rainbow Room
to promote their new collaboration. It was a high perch atop Rockefeller
Center. But greater heights towered in country music's sight. And Willie
Nelson was about to scale them alone.

★   ★   ★

WILLIE—LIKE WAYLON—WOULD ALWAYS embody the
outlaw ethos, but by 1978, he was quickly cresting the outlaw river-
banks. Plainly, he had become more appealing to mass audiences than
Waylon Jennings, continuing to ride the wave of hillbilly and hippie acceptance, but now diving into the deep eddy of middle-American suburbia, whose denizens—despite his rowdy picnics—found him as safe
to love as Roy Rogers. Unlike Waylon, who snorted that cocaine and
appeared as menacing as the guys in Black Oak Arkansas, Willie smiled
and shook your hand, sipped at the beers fans handed him outside the
bus, and rarely said no. On the other outlaw hand, Waylon frequently
said no. "Waylon was a little paranoid, and he didn't trust people," says

Hazel Smith. "Therefore, I felt like Waylon would have been a much bigger star than he was, [but] he hadn't been able to trust people. Willie never had no trouble trusting the media, and he always would give an interview to anybody that he had time for." However, Waylon despised the media, feeling patronized by reporters, and for a time only granted interviews to those who submitted their finished articles for his approval. Waylon was the sullen guy on the corner, undeniably appealing, but not one to invite home for dinner with the family. So it was Willie who became the darling, an American legend.

In 1978, the redheaded stranger consolidated an audience that would fill his concerts for decades to come. The catalyst was the album *Stardust*, a collection of American pop standards that Willie had recorded with producer Booker T. Jones, the Memphis soul legend who also happened to be married to Rita Coolidge's sister. "I remember the first night I sang 'Stardust' with my band at the Austin Opera House," wrote Willie. "There was a kind of stunned silence in the crowd for a moment, and then they exploded with cheering and whistling and applauding. The kids in the crowd thought 'Stardust' was a new song I had written. The older folks remembered the song well and loved it as much as I did."

When Willie brought the album idea to Rick Blackburn, the executive reacted a lot like Bruce Lundvall when he first heard *Red Headed Stranger*. Blackburn, who'd proven his mettle as CBS's man at Monument Records when the company bought Fred Foster's baby in the mid-1970s, scratched his head and thought wistfully about the chunky duets with Waylon Jennings that sold so well. Blackburn: "He said, 'I'm going to go [to California] and we're going to cut this album on these old standards.' And I said, 'Hold it! Wait, wait, wait, wait.' I said, 'People don't want that. Give me more of what you're doing.' He said, 'Well, I don't want to be predictable and these are good songs.' I said, 'Booker T.'s an organ player.' I didn't know him as a producer, and I didn't know the project was going to be that simple. I mean it was a very simple project with voice out front. 'No, no,' he said. 'I'm going to go do it. And you have a nice day.'

"When that album came in, I sat my whole staff down and I said, 'All right, listen up. This is Willie's next project.' And I started playing the roughs on it. They were presentable. They weren't finely mixed, but enough to tell. My promotion department went nuts. They said, 'What are you doing? How can you allow this? How can [we] get *Stardust* played on the radio?' But I have to defend it. It's already committed. I mean, the ship has sailed. And it's not like I didn't have reservations. There was almost a mutiny in my conference room to throw me overboard. . . . And when it came out, radio was reluctant, too."

But, like water, *Stardust* found a channel. The first single, "Georgia on My Mind," peaked at number one in the spring of 1978 and the follow-up "Blue Skies" fared just as well. "All of a sudden," says Blackburn, "everybody looked right. I learned that sometimes artists have a better feel about where they are going than record companies or, certainly, corporations." Just like *Waylon & Willie*, the album camped for eleven weeks at number one, but then it became a monument that stood for 551 weeks on the album charts. That's more than ten years in Willie time. Critic John Morthland pointed out that Willie had introduced his "pop tastes to country fans," but "reintroduce" may be more accurate. In the 1960s, Willie freely dropped pop standards into his album repertory, and then, as on *Stardust*, performed them with little hint of country inflection. In a way, the smash album freed Willie to liberally indulge his pop leanings, and over the next decade he returned to the standards again and again for album content while also exploring pop music of the 1980s. On his 1984 album *City of New Orleans*, with Chips Moman producing, he recorded and released "Wind Beneath My Wings," made popular by Bette Midler, and Michael Jackson's "She's Out of My Life." Call it an extension of *Stardust*, but many listeners gagged. *Rolling Stone* gave it two stars.

Emerging on the heels of the big outlaw albums, *Stardust* ushered in an era of unparalleled prosperity in Nashville's music business. Record companies now figured that every country artist could sell millions, so, as the 1970s petered out, singular artistic vision began to fade in the glare of marketing aspirations. For a time, American country audiences had accepted outlaw artists who looked and sang as if they'd just tumbled out of a Mexican whorehouse, but the courtship of large audiences, particularly in the prepped-out era of Ronald Reagan, refused to suffer such suggestions. Even Rosanne Cash, whose maverick singing and songwriting rebelled against corporate country music, was told by CBS executives that on her album jackets she must always appear ripe for sex, though in a chaste sort of way. The greasy, edgy likes of David Allan Coe and Waylon Jennings would find themselves turned out of the herd by the end of the 1980s, for they were too old and offensive to middle-of-the-road sensibilities. Accordingly, the whole outlaw sales vehicle was dismembered and its pieces appropriated for the time being by the brief and vacuous Urban Cowboy fad, where disco met outlaw fashion.

To his credit, Waylon probably recognized that the industry was turning to a new sales strategy that would soon relegate him to "legend" status. He had always known that even the outlaw bit was nothing more than another way to sell country music and soon it would be replaced by another hook. Indeed, he had delighted in exposing the marketing apparatus and his own participation in it by writing songs like "Bob Wills Is Still the King" and "Are You Sure Hank Done It This Way?" which cut down outlaw-era pretentions. In 1978, his hit "Don't You Think This Outlaw Bit's Done Got Out of Hand" chronicled his cocaine bust and detailed his disgust with the media and recording industry's construction of the outlaw myth. *Someone called us outlaws in some ole magazine / New York sent a posse town like I ain't never seen.* If Willie's *Stardust* closed the outlaw chapter in country music, "This Outlaw Bit" wrote its epilogue.

The spirit of early 1970s musical progressivism that lived in *The Johnny Cash Show* and in the characters of the West End limped toward 1980. Long about 1976 Cash had become more concerned with finding hits than pursuing a musical vision, while he reclined comfortably as a patriotic American symbol. National fast-food restaurants and Vanderbilt annexes now dotted the West End, and rents there soared as Music Row prosperity and the university's expansion drew moneyed young urbanites and drove out bohemian culture.

Until his dying day in 2002, Waylon never stopped grumbling about authority, even while cashing big record company checks, and Willie rarely appeared without blue jeans and a retinue of hippie fans still looking for carefree days at Centennial Park or the Armadillo World Headquarters (which closed in 1980, followed into oblivion a year later by the Exit/In). However, the Littlefield boy and his Abbott brother now seemed far removed from their outlaw days at the Professional Club and Hillbilly Central, where they had dreamed of recording music according to their own rules. Waylon tangled with Tompall Glaser in a lawsuit over publishing, which had ended their friendship and removed Waylon from the curbside madness of Glaser's recording studios. Meanwhile, Willie hewed toward more music that sounded like the *City of New Orleans* album and jetted to Hollywood, where he appeared in *The Electric Horseman* (1979) with Robert Redford and Jane Fonda and *Honeysuckle Rose* (1980) with Dyan Cannon and Amy Irving. "Film projects immediately began stacking up," wrote Michael Bane in a friendly early 1980s biography. "He starred in a special CBS presentation of 'Coming Out of the Ice,' the story of two Americans imprisoned in Siberia. Journalists on the set in Finland reported there was no sign of Willie the musician."

There would be one more attempt to revive the outlaw juggernaut, at least as it lived in Waylon and Willie and Kris: when the three men joined Johnny Cash in the studio to record an album titled *Highwayman*. Together, the quartet embodied the transformational winds that had swept through Nashville in the late 1960s and early 1970s. They were outlaws, even Cash, who never appeared on the marketing label but who resolutely pursued his own vision in the studio and on his television show. Remove them from the chapters that cover Nashville in the late 1960s and early 1970s and the city's music industry would have clung indefinitely to old formulas.

Their first album, released in 1985, birthed the number-one hit "Highwayman," which portrays four lives cut from the fabric of America and links them in an unending wire. The singers' pocked voices and the song's historical patina echoed outlaw, but it was only a revival. Two subsequent albums failed to transcend the men's weighty legends, and the franchise crumbled in the 1990s when Cash became ill.

★   ★   ★

THE END OF the 1970s found Kris Kristofferson in a personal and professional tailspin. His latest album, *Easter Island*, looked back on his prime and engaged his beloved wordplay, particularly in a song called "The Fighter."

> *We measured the space between Waylon and Willie*
> *And Waylon and Willie and me*
> *But there wasn't nothing like Billy Joe Shaver*
> *The way Billy Joe Shaver should be*

But despite the outlaw ballad, the critics sneered. *Rolling Stone* complained that it was "barely a mediocre record, one short step up from the bottom." When Kristofferson's new material failed to move critics and fans, Willie Nelson entered the corral to remind them of his friend's greatness. A year after *Stardust* shook up Nashville, he released *Willie Nelson Sings Kristofferson*, which surged on the album charts and boasted arrangements of the songwriter's hits that were among the best ever. "Kris Kristofferson's songs were easy; that's one of the reasons I did it," he said. "It didn't require a lot of teaching of the band or anything. We'd known those songs for years."

But Kris could not capitalize on Willie's gesture. And from 1981 to 1986, he released no solo work. Even his film career teetered on the cliff's edge, pushed there by poor scripts and the devastating failure of 1980's *Heaven's Gate*, in which he starred and which rudely shut down the age of the director in Hollywood. An *Esquire* reporter who visited him at the time wrote that he was carrying the flagging *Heaven's Gate* to the Cannes Film Festival "like a reheated enchilada no one wants." For two years in the early 1980s, he made no films for theatrical release.

At home, there was only more uncertainty. In 1980, Rita Coolidge left him in a house on top of a parched hill in Malibu, where their daughter Casey's stuffed animals lounged on every sofa and chair. *Esquire* noted that he was smoking copious amounts of mind-smacking weed and reliving scenes from his collapsed marriage, all while juggling part-time care of Casey and the regimen of staying physically fit for the movies.

Obviously, the magazine correspondent and, indeed, the new decade observed him negotiating something of a midlife crisis, but unbeknownst to the press and many people around him, Kris had already formulated a remedy. The man who landed in Nashville in 1965 to explore his impulse to write woke up to a new impulse, the prickling of his social conscience. In the early 1980s, he rediscovered the flame of promise and possibility that once burned in the West End, applying it exclusively to a host of political aims. Indeed, the spirit of Nashville's civil rights protestors and antiwar demonstrators had settled into Kristofferson.

With little concern about his failure to conjure another "Me and Bobby McGee" or "For the Good Times," Kristofferson found satisfaction tramping stages and picket lines in support of the United Farm Workers (UFW), led by Cesar Chavez, who advocated for perennially undercompensated produce workers, particularly those in California. "I think it all probably started in the Rio Grande valley [as a child]," he says. "I identified with Mexicans. And Cesar Chavez . . . I got to meet him several times, and I just had more respect for him than when I first heard about him. He was a great human being." He told writer Peter Cooper that in the Texas of his childhood light brown was black: "It was Mexicans that there was prejudice against, and my mother made sure we knew that was wrong. One example I remember of it is when a Mexican from Brownsville won the Medal of Honor and they had a parade for him, and we were the only Anglos at the parade."

But when Kris arrived in Nashville for the first time in 1965, his political point of view hinged on his army past and upper-middle-class values. He backed the war in Vietnam and only casually followed the civil rights protests that had surged through the city like a summer thunderstorm. The songwriters he ran with were similarly oriented. "I don't think anybody was pushing any particular political direction," he says. "A lot of the songs that came out were just the truth [about living] as we perceived it."

His take on the war shifted as the 1960s spiraled to an end. Fellow oil-rig helicopter pilots and old friends with whom he'd served in Germany had gone to Southeast Asia and returned with a new perspective. "They were telling stories about what was going on in Vietnam that were chilling: taking people up in choppers and interrogating them, then throwing them out," he told *The Progressive* in 1991. "One boy told me about kicking the hands of this man who was holding on to the skids, holding on for his life. I got to thinking that if you could make nineteen-year-old kids do that, you could make them do anything."

Kris's new skepticism of power delivered him to Chavez, whom he recalls meeting on the set of Scorsese's *Alice Doesn't Live Here Anymore*. The UFW faced an uncertain road, he learned from the Arizona-born activist: legislators were chipping away at labor laws, and big growers, mostly in California, were trying to neutralize the UFW, primarily by cozying up to the friendlier Teamsters union. In response, Kris, in his words, "aligned with them," uncorking a lifelong commitment to the farmworkers' movement; for years, he played benefit concerts and lent his music and name to other activities.

Kris greets Cesar Chavez.

By the early 1980s his political activities—which also included appearing in concert for UNICEF and stridently protesting U.S. policy
in Central America—overshadowed his music. And they certainly dis-
tinguished him from his outlaw buddies. Waylon's rabble-rousing remained encased in the lyrics of some songs he sang and mostly bubbled
over in interviews when he attacked corporate influence in the music
business. And Willie was still a few years from taking up Farm Aid in
support of the American family farmer and wading into the murky water of Native American activist Leonard Peltier's legal defense, a cause
that Kristofferson, too, adopted.

At a Grammy Awards show press conference in 1981, the former
army captain, without so much as a cue or a provocation, issued one of
his first loud condemnations of U.S. involvement in Central America.
"Let's get the hell out of El Salvador," he blurted as the paparazzi and
fellow actors looked on. Throughout the decade, he did not relent. In
1986, his album *Repossessed*, his first on Mercury Records, took aim at
the sitting president as well as his policies on El Salvador. And then he

targeted the U.S. government's support of the Contra rebels in Nicaragua, traveling there in 1988 to show support for peace talks between the Contras and President Daniel Ortega, where he received a dignitary's welcome. At home, he rarely let an interview or concert pass without speaking out on the issue. "We have such a sorry history in Nicaragua," he told a reporter. "Most Americans don't know that for forty-five years we supported the most hated dictatorship in the hemisphere; somehow, they finally threw that son of a bitch [Anastasio] Somoza out despite our support. I can't believe that most Americans would be comfortable knowing they're paying to kill children."

Kristofferson earned the venom of the right and the praise of the left. Somewhere in the middle, a few people remained who still embraced his art. He had paid for his activism. He struggled to find major label support (Mercury promptly dropped him after *Repossessed*), and one might have been forgiven for assuming that Cash, Nelson, and Jennings, as the Highwaymen, scooped up their friend from the picket line just to keep his career going. On the screen, his film appearances no longer made the A-list, and he appeared more often in TV movies, anyway. Out on the road, some concertgoers lugged placards to his shows deriding his causes and accusing him of being a communist or, worse, the Antichrist. When he turned up the political rhetoric onstage, a certain percentage of the audience could always be counted upon to demand their money back. Not surprisingly, one of the biggest outcries against his politics rose up in Georgia, where his bad language had sparked a near riot in the 1970s. Playing Atlanta during the 1987 Oliver North hearings in Washington, Kristofferson complained that the spectacle in the congressional chamber was little more than an advertisement for the Contras and implored the audience to reevaluate these "freedom fighters" whom North assisted; they were anything but, insisted Kristofferson, and had targeted schools, medical centers, and farmers—not soldiers. When he finished, the stirring in the audience was palatable. Fans, who evidently were fans no longer, dusted off their own First

Amendment rights and demanded the singer's removal. "Get that communist off the stage!" they yelled. Three hundred people marched to the ticket window for a refund.

Today the old outlaw chuckles at the memory of such confrontations. And then he pauses again. "I knew that some of my audience at the time thought I was a communist or something. But I had a thing about the truth, you know. I felt, ever since I had gone to be a songwriter, that I was trying to tell the truth."

★　　★　　★

WILLIE NELSON'S MERCURIAL ascent and Waylon Jennings's deepening cocaine habit coincided with the death of the outlaw movement and ushered to an end the decade of Nashville's young adulthood. The West End blush of 1970 had faded as drug-dimmed eyes and the hunger for big money replaced the optimism of those who believed the mood of the 1960s would flourish in the 1970s. Jimmy Carter, whom Nashville had entrusted to erase the blemish of its Nixon infatuation, hobbled into the 1980 election, his presidency smoldering in the wreckage of military aircraft in the Iranian desert. Former mayor Beverly Briley, who ruled Metro government in 1970, finally admitted to the alcoholism that many had long suspected, after he drunkenly rammed a car carrying two elderly people. The looming National Life company, five years after trying to tear down the Ryman Auditorium and sparring with Skeeter Davis, still advertised its narrowness, censoring a news director at its WSM-TV subsidiary who tried to report on a multimillion-dollar lawsuit stemming from a child's injury at Opryland. And in 1980, toxic shock syndrome, the infection that defined American consumer culture, crept into Tennessee, sending a twelve-year-old girl to Vanderbilt University Hospital for a long stay.

But while the outlaw decade gracelessly retreated, Waylon—battling at least three lawsuits over business matters—saw clearly for a moment. In the Spanish Revival manse on Seventeenth Avenue that housed his office, he often lingered when the night was closer to dawn than midnight, phoning friends or employees who'd gone to bed hours earlier. This night somebody called him. The voice on the other end of the line described a cancer-ridden man in Raleigh, North Carolina, whose last wish was to meet him. When the sun came up, Waylon told Richie Albright to arrange it. They'd soon be in Charlotte for a show and afterward could head over to Raleigh before traveling to another gig in Grifton, North Carolina, in the eastern part of the state.

So on May 24, 1980, Waylon's bus eased down the residential street where the failing Joel Jackson lived. Accompanied by Albright, Ralph Mooney, and Gordon Payne, Waylon—in his usual vest, boots, and gambler's hat—eased into the living room where Jackson was sleeping on the couch. "I was just standing back," recalls Albright, "and Waylon was standing next to him. His wife woke him up and said, 'Waylon's here.' And the guy opened his eyes and said, 'I'll be God-damned.'"

For a half hour, the visitors popped open beers and chatted about music. And Waylon, like a southern politician, spun around the room, signing albums for friends and family who'd come to visit and gathering up in his arms the dying man's four-year-old daughter. Says Payne, "The thing I remember is the guy held Waylon's hand with both of his hands. 'Can't believe you're here!' He was real drugged. 'Can't believe you're here!' And then he would nod off. The guy's wife, she sat back there with the biggest smile on her face the whole time. It was really something."

When Joel Jackson finally fell into a deep sleep, Waylon and the boys stepped one by one onto the bus and rolled south to their next show. Seven hours later, the stricken man died.

★ Notes

A Note about Sources

As I researched and wrote *Outlaw*, I tapped several indispensable periodicals: *The Tennessean* (known before 1970 as the *Nashville Tennessean*), *Nashville Banner*, *Nashville Scene*, the *Nashville Retrospect*, and the *Vanderbilt Hustler*. The value of the monthly magazine *Country Music*, which featured the work of Dave Hickey, Martha Hume, Michael Bane, Patrick Carr, Bob Allen, and others, is self-evident in this narrative. So is the writing and reporting of Chet Flippo, who rarely let the outlaws stray from his radar during the 1970s. My treatments of Waylon, Willie, and Kris were supplemented by several books: *Waylon: An Autobiography*, by Waylon Jennings with Lenny Kaye; *Waylon: A Biography*, by R. Serge Denisoff; *Willie Nelson: An Epic Life*, by Joe Nick Patoski; *Willie: An Autobiography*, by Willie Nelson with Bud Shrake; and *Kristofferson: The Wild American*, by Stephen Miller. In addition, my discussion of Robert Altman's *Nashville* was helped by Jan Stuart's *The Nashville Chronicles: The Making of Robert Altman's Masterpiece*. Patrick Allen's *Literary Nashville* provided a delightful introduction to fiction writers based in or passing through the Athens of the South, and David Halberstam's *The Children* and Don H. Doyle's *Nashville Since the 1920s* offered concise accounts of various important chapters in the history of the city.

Introduction

1   "I just don't think": Author interview with Dianne Davidson, July 12, 2011.

1   "It was like, everybody": Author interview with Kris Kristofferson, November 16, 2010.

2   "I wish I could": Ibid.

5   His gutsy, throbbing sound: In 2011, debate over current outlaws showed up in two much-discussed essays: Peter Cooper, "Country Boys Are Wearing Out Calling Cards," available at http://blogs.tennessean.com/tunein/2011/07/11/country-boys-are-wearing-out-calling-cards/, and Chet Flippo, "Nashville Skyline: So, Is Justin Moore Really an Outlaw? Time for a Reality Check," available at www.cmt.com/news/nashville-skyline/1666703/nashville-skyline-so-is-justin-moore-really-an-outlaw-time-for-a-reality-check/.

6   By the late 1960s: I've broadly defined a two-square-mile area of Nashville's near southwest side as the West End. Much of the area is, in fact, known by Nashvillians as the West End, but my more liberal boundaries include other named neighborhoods, such as Music Row and Hillsboro Village.

6   "The thing about the Exit/In": Author interview with Davidson.

8   "To me, the best thing": Author interview with Kristofferson.

Chapter One: The Newcomers

9   "How remarkably lucky": Robert Penn Warren, "A Reminiscence" in John Edgerton, ed., *Nashville: The Faces of Two Centuries, 1780–1980* (Nashville: PlusMedia, 1979), 205–20.

9   "Nashville is a pallid": Gene Lees, "Nashville: The Sounds and the Symbols," *High Fidelity Magazine*, April 1967.

9   When veeps from RCA: Author interview with Johnny Rosica, November 4, 1996.

10   "It is located in a section": Larry L. King, "The Grand Ole Opry," *Harper's*, July 1968.

10   Young people who showed up: Author interview with Lewis Shiner, August 2, 2010.

10   "Nashville certainly was no hotbed": Author interview with Michael Minzer, August 2, 2010.

11   "was largely a soft kind": David Halberstam, *The Children* (New York: Random House, 1998), 110.

12   Alarmed by the violence: Ibid., 234.

13   "I had eleven years": Author interview with Kris Kristofferson, June 14, 2011.

14   "I checked into this hotel": Author interview with Kristofferson, November 16, 2010.

14   "It was his first record": Ibid.

14   "After everybody else fell": Ibid.

15   "It seemed like every place": Ibid.

15   It was "poetical stuff": Author interview with Jack Clement, July 21, 2010.

15   "We happened to be the": Robert Oermann, *Behind the Grand Ole Opry Curtain: Tales of Romance and Tragedy* (New York: Center Street, 2008), 296–97.

16   "The way I looked at it": Willie Nelson with Bud Shrake, *Willie: An Autobiography* (New York: Simon & Schuster, 1988), 117.

17   "I didn't get to tell him": Author interview with Fred Foster, May 17, 2011.

18   "I couldn't get anybody": Ed Ward, "Willie Nelson: Breakthrough of A Lone-Star Legend," *Rolling Stone*, January 15, 1976.

18   "I went to catch": Nelson with Shrake, *Willie*, 117.

18   "He was just king": R. Serge Denisoff, *Waylon: A Biography* (New York: St. Martin's Press, 1973), 103–5.

19   "Waylon played lead": Author interview with Richie Albright, July 20, 2010.

19   "My reputation was growing": Waylon Jennings with Lenny Kaye, *Waylon: An Autobiography* (New York: Warner Books, 1996), 92–93.

20   "Herb kept looking": Ibid, 95.

20   "Well, he always had": Grant Alden, "Bobby Bare/Bobby Bare, Jr.: Bobby Bares, All," *No Depression*, July–August 2002.

22   Rather, it prided itself: "The Gold Guitars," *Newsweek*, April 4, 1966.

22   When fifteen compositions: This statistic was noted in an obituary of Howard on the BMI website by Robert K. Oermann, available at www.bmi .com/news/233082.

23   "That's the biggest": Author interview with Chet Atkins, May 16, 1996.

23   "Chet was so secure": Author interview with Jim Malloy, September 22, 1995.

23   Although Chet never objected: John Grissim, *Country Music: White Man's Blues* (New York: Paperback Library, 1970), 67.

25   "When we'd get to Nashville": Rich Kienzle. *Southwest Shuffle: Pioneers of Honky-Tonk, Western Swing, and Country Jazz* (New York: Routledge, 2003), 246–47.

25   "I worked for Steve": Author interview with Atkins.

25   "I spread myself too thin": Author interview with Chet Atkins, August 28, 1995.

Chapter Two: Nashville Sounds

27   "A quiet place": O. Henry, "A Municipal Report," in *The Complete Works of O. Henry*, vol. 2 (Garden City, NY: Doubleday, 1953), 1554.

28   Kris's memories of childhood: Author interview with Kristofferson, June 14, 2011.

28   "He was really a highly": Ibid.

28   "I thought I was special": Sally Quinn, "Kristofferson: Hits and Myths," *Washington Post*, May 18, 1971.

29   "But I didn't want to do": Author interview with Kristofferson.

30   "It's never been easy": Waylon Jennings with Lenny Kaye, *Waylon: An Autobiography* (New York: Warner Books, 1996), 19.

30   The moment she and Monroe: Monroe apparently enjoyed such reactions from the younger generation, as a meeting with Jerry Lee Lewis at one of Nashville's Fan Fair conventions illustrated. "We went on down there, there's a lot of stars there and stuff," describes Hazel Smith. "And so [Bill] just took hold of my hand and put it through this arm of his, and he said, 'Watch this.' And he walked into the middle of the room—I didn't know who it was—and he touched this guy on his shoulder. And this guy whirled around like he was just going to knock somebody one. Well he looked at Bill straight in the face, and he bowed three times to the floor! And Bill had to reach out and grab his hand. It was Jerry Lee. Jerry Lee was so honored to see Bill, and Bill made him shake his hand. He could not shake Bill's hand; Bill had to make him. He was just so honored to see Bill Monroe. Are you believing that now?" Author interview with Hazel Smith, July 21, 2010.

32   "He was easy to get along with": Patrick Carr, "Waylon Jennings," *Country Music*, April 1973.

32   "They were remarkably": Denisoff, *Waylon*, 56.

32   "I heard him say": Author interview with Gordon Payne, August 2, 2010.

33   "I didn't like picking": Michael Bane, *Willie: An Unauthorized Biography of Willie Nelson* (New York: Dell, 1984), 36.

34   "I remember when we": Bill DeYoung, "Willie Nelson: Funny How Time Slips Away," *Goldmine*, January 6, 1995.

34   "We went to a very small": Michael Hall, "Willie's God, Willies God," *Texas Monthly*, May 2008.

35   Willie graduated from high school: Bane, *Willie*, 50.

37   When Chet learned: Author interview with Bill Pursell, February 20, 1997.

37   In a conversation in the mid-1990s: Author interview with Atkins.

38   "It had it all": Jennings with Kaye, *Waylon*, 143.

38   "He was like an idol": Author interview with Reynolds, January 27, 2012.

41   "I just didn't": Irwin Stambler and Grelun Landon, *The Encyclopedia of Folk, Country and Western* (New York: St. Martin's Press, 1984), 501–2.

41   As Chet once said: Nelson with Shrake, *Willie*, 178.

42   One night, he sat: Author interview with Billy Swan, November 5, 2010.

42   "I suddenly felt like": Author interview with Kristofferson.

42   "At about twelve o'clock": Author interview with Swan.

44   "So I walk out of his office": Ibid.

45   "He went in": Author interview with Kristofferson, November 6, 2010.

45   "I talked to his wife": Ibid.

45   "[They thought] I'd gone down": Ibid.

45   "It was like a two-page": Author interview with Clement.

46   "He was born with his": Tom Burke, "Kris Kristofferson's Talking Blues," *Rolling Stone*, April 25, 1974.

46   Often, he fell in: Author interview with Reynolds.

47   "I was trying to make": Author interview with Kristofferson.

47   "They wouldn't let me demo": Peter Cooper, "Freedom's Still the Most Important Thing for Me," *No Depression*, January–February 2005.

Chapter Three: Let a Flower Be a Flower

49   "I know a lot of times": Author interview with Kristofferson, November 6, 2010.

50   "What was coming back": Author interview with Swan.

51   "They all wanted to be around": Author interview with Jim Casey, October 29, 2010.

51   "I got out of the car": Author interview with Albright.

52   "Jack had enough": Author interview with Casey.

53   "Monument had sort of": Author interview with Foster.

53   "You've got to let a": Ibid.

53 "Kris always wrote alone": Philip Self, *Guitar Pull: Conversations with Country Music's Legendary Songwriters* (Nashville: Cypress Moon, 2002), 34.

54 "I couldn't carry him": Ibid., 35.

54 "He was a super-likable": Author interview with Swan.

54 "I stayed out there": Michael Kosser, *How Nashville Became Music City U.S.A.: 50 Years of Music Row* (Milwaukee: Hal Leonard, 2006), 176.

55 "It was Beckham": Author interview with Kristofferson.

55 "That was our world": Author interview with Swan.

55 "I don't know what": Author interview with Foster.

55 Kristofferson recalls singing: Author interview with Kristofferson, June 14, 2011.

56 "He sang the first song": Author interview with Foster.

56 "He just has such a way": Ibid.

56 Indeed, nursery-rhyme-simple: Tom T. Hall's "Margie's at the Lincoln Park Inn" was a top-ten country hit for Bobby Bare in 1969. Like Kristofferson, Hall injected smart lyrics into country music, but a reading of his 1979 memoir *The Storyteller's Nashville* suggests that he thinks Kristofferson got too much credit.

56 That day in Hendersonville: Author interview with Foster.

57 "I had no idea": Ibid.

57 "I went down and hid": Michael Simmons, *Please Don't Tell Me How the Story Ends: The Publishing Demos, 1968–72* (Light in the Attic Records, 2010).

57 "When I showed it": Ibid.

57 "Beckham was a big": Author interview with Kristofferson, November 6, 2010.

59 "The thing about": Author interview with Smith.

59 "Waylon had a": Author interview with Reynolds.

59 One night after a concert: Author interview with Albright.

60 "For a lot of people": Author interview with Berger.

61   "So we are having": Patrick Thomas, "Ex-GI Folkie Kris Kristofferson,"
Rolling Stone, March 18, 1971.

62   "We went out": Author interview with Donnie Fritts,
November 15, 2010.

62   "We'd all sit around": Johnny Cash with Patrick Carr, *Cash: The Autobiography* (New York: HarperCollins, 1997), 205.

62   In the autumn of 1970: Steve Pace, "Cash and Easy Rider Hopper,"
New Musical Express, October 17, 1970.

62   "It made everybody": Author interview with Kristofferson,
June 14, 2011.

63   Jack Clement had told: Author interview with Clement.

64   "It was a beautiful": Author interview with Casey.

64   "The breezy twang": John S. Wilson, "Newport Folk Festival Becomes
Music Bazaar," *New York Times*, July 19, 1969.

65   "If there was one thing": Author interview with Kristofferson,
November 6, 2010.

65   "It was six o'clock": Author interview with Swan.

65   "He was going to make": Author interview with Foster.

Chapter Four: Nothing Left to Lose

67   "Some unlikely fare": Alice Alexander, "Exit the Red Dog," *Vanderbilt
Hustler*, November 10, 1971.

68   "Danny and I": Jennings with Kaye, *Waylon*, 170.

69   "Waylon liked Danny": Author interview with Reynolds.

69   In his autobiography: Jennings with Kaye, *Waylon*, 168.

72   "I didn't know": Author interview with Paul Worley,
November 8, 2010.

73   "I started taking": Ibid.

74   "The courts should": LaWayne Satterfield, "School Integration Court
Order Study Looms Next Week," *Nashville Banner*, December 19, 1970.

74 When federal investigators: Edmund Willingham, "18-Year Corruption Laid to City Police," *Nashville Banner*, June 4, 1969.

76 In 1969, the Vanderbilt: "SDS Plans 'Peaceful' Protest at VU," *Nashville Tennessean*, May 8, 1969.

76 "The students were": Author interview with Worley.

76 "They were going to": Author interview with Shiner.

76 Within days, hundreds: Peter Brush, "Another Faraway War Got a Different Response at VU," *Vanderbilt Register*, May 3–9, 1999.

77 "We did a lot of": Author interview with Shiner.

78 "The entire campus": Author interview with Worley.

78 "Since I had a car": Author interview with Minzer.

78 "There were musicians": Ibid.

79 Just Friends sponged: Author interview with Worley.

81 "It was pretty much": Author interview with Dick Bay, September 18, 2010.

82 "I remember him as a very nice": Email to author from Darrell Berger, September 5, 2010.

82 The Exit/In had opened: The club advertisement referred to appeared in the *Vanderbilt Hustler* on October 22, 1971.

82 "We were playing": Author interview with Bay.

85 "He was my milepost": Author interview with Guy Clark, July 29, 2010.

85 "Suddenly, I was a performer": Author interview with Kristofferson, November 6, 2010.

85 "*Kristofferson* is a superb": Ray Rezos, "Records," *Rolling Stone*, November 12, 1970.

86 "One day Kris": Author interview with Swan.

87 "That was the place": Author interview with Fritts.

87 "The lines were": Ibid.

87 "I had been out": Gary Cartwright, "A Star Is Reborn," *Texas Monthly*, March 1997.

87   A *New York Times*: Paul Hemphill, "Kris Kristofferson is the New Nashville Sound," *New York Times Magazine*, December 6, 1970.

87   "We weren't prepared": Author interview with Fritts.

88   "I lived with her": Cartwright, *Texas Monthly*.

88   "He listened to it": Author interview with Fritts.

89   "There has never been": Dave Hickey, "Notes on Kris Kristofferson, 1968–1974," *Country Music*, October 1974.

89   "I can't really remember": Author interview with Kristofferson.

90   "Kris Kristofferson surprised": Ralph J. Gleason, "Perspectives: Kristofferson's Fine Flick," *Rolling Stone*, April 13, 1972.

91   Young musicians in Nashville: Chet Flippo, "Dylan Meets the Durango Kid," *Rolling Stone*, March 15, 1973.

91   "I'll never forget seeing": Author interview with Fritts.

91   It also gave him: Author interview with Foster.

Chapter Five: With Purpose Down There

93   "As my country": David Crockett, *The Life of Davy Crockett* (New York: A. L. Burt, 1903), 251.

93   "Chet knew I wanted": Jennings with Kaye, *Waylon*, 168.

94   "I'd mix his sessions": Author interview with Jerry Bradley, May 17, 2011.

94   "About twelve o'clock": Author interview with Bradley, July 11, 2010.

94   "The minute he came": Author interview with Ronny Light, November 7, 2010.

95   "Chet used to have": Author interview with Bradley.

95   "I was hoping": Author interview with Light.

96   He and his brother: Ibid.

96   "He had tons of cuts": Ibid.

96   "It's this album": J. R. Young, "The Monster Voice of Waylon Jennings," *Rolling Stone*, September 9, 1971.

97   "The next day or so": Author interview with Reynolds,
        January 28, 2012.

97   On record, the rollicking: Email to author from Wayne Stevens,
        March 10, 2011.

97   "Ronny was young": Jennings with Kaye, *Waylon*, 184.

97   "When I produced": Author interview with Light.

98   "I was in an office": Author interview with Bradley, May 17, 2011.

98   In the spring of 1971: Author interview with Reynolds,
        January 27, 2012.

98   "Somebody sent out for some hamburgers": Ibid.

99   "At the time": Jennings with Kaye, *Waylon*, 161.

99   "It was a great record": Ibid.

99   "It wasn't the normal": Author interview with Elroy Kahanek,
        May 15, 2011.

99   "They would press": Author interview with Light.

100   "Waylon walked into": Author interview with Kahanek.

100   "One day in my office": Ibid.

101   "One tour would": Author interview with Reynolds, January 28, 2012.

102   He was run-down: Jennings with Kaye, *Waylon*, 176.

102   "This town ran": Author interview with Albright, July 20, 2010.

102   Suffering from hepatitis: Robert Hilburn, "The Ballad of A Nashville
        Outlaw," *Washington Post*, December 24, 1978.

102   "He was just fed up": Author interview with Albright.

102   "He looked like a": Author interview with Albright, November 4, 2010.

103   "Neil and I talked": Ibid.

103   "I think it's one": Nelson with Shrake, *Willie*, 167.

104   One last album on RCA: Chet Flippo, "Records," *Rolling Stone*,
        November 23, 1972.

104   "Chet liked me": Joe Nick Patoski, *Willie Nelson: An Epic Life* (New York: Back Bay Books, 2008), 249–50.

105   Ronny Light argues: Author interview with Light.

105   "They were just off-the-wall": Author interview with Kahanek, October 8, 2010.

105   "I was in sort of": Nelson with Shrake, *Willie*, 167.

105   "Lynn Anderson was": Author interview with Reynolds, January 28, 2012.

106   "I was at a Christmas": Ed Ward, "Willie Nelson," *Rolling Stone*, January 15, 1976.

106   "I knew I only": Patrick Carr, "The Man Who Beat the System," *Country Music*, February 1976.

107   Willie reckoned that: Oermann, *Behind the Grand Ole Opry Curtain*, 298.

107   "Threadgill's was the first": Jack Hurst, "The Pickin's Pickin' Up in Austin," *Chicago Tribune*, March 31, 1976.

108   "But the obvious plus": Jan Reid, *The Improbable Rise of Redneck Rock* (Austin: University of Texas Press, 2004), 68.

108   "The manager was real": Oermann, *Behind the Grand Ole Opry Curtain*, 298–99.

108   "There was hippies": Author interview with Albright, July 7, 2010.

109   "Going back to Texas": Dave Hickey, "In Defense of the Telecaster Cowboy Outlaws," *Country Music*, January 1974.

110   "He got on the stool": Susie Nelson, *Heart Worn Memories: A Daughter's Personal Biography of Willie Nelson* (New York: Pocket Books, 1987), 218.

111   On the first day: Ed Ward, "Troublemaker: My Contribution to Willie Nelson's 'Complete Atlantic Sessions,' " *Austin Chronicle*, December 29, 2006.

111   And when the last inch: Chet Flippo, "Willie Nelson's New York Country Sessions," *Rolling Stone*, April 12, 1973.

111   "With this flawless album": Steve Ditlea, "Records," *Rolling Stone*, August 30, 1973.

Chapter Six: The West End Watershed

113   "Nashville's a great": Jack Bernhardt, "'Like Paris in the Twenties,'" *Journal of Country Music* 13, no. 3 (1990).

114   "We were all hippies": Author interview with Davidson.

114   "This was post Flatt-Scruggs": Author interview with Dan Beck, September 28, 2010.

115   "We could afford": Ibid.

115   He couldn't have picked: Marshall Chapman, *Goodbye, Little Rock and Roller* (New York: St. Martin's Griffin, 2003), 140.

115   "The girl, all 6 foot 2": Louis Vodopya, "Memories of Nashville," available at www.nashlinks.com/memories.htm.

115   "They used to": Author interview with Beck.

116   "All the session guys": Ibid.

117   Each and every evening: Ibid.

118   Characters such as: Ibid.

118   "I remember when": Author interview with Berger.

118   "He was about my age": Ibid.

118   "Somebody must have got": Ibid.

119   A girl simply known: Joyce Wadler, "Making It and Making Do in Nashville," *Country Music*, August 1973; author interview with Hugh Bennett, May 16, 2011.

119   "There's a wonderful": Author interview with Minzer.

119   "The Exit/In was": Author interview with Berger.

122   "Vince was the guy": Author interview with Casey.

122   "There was a doctor": Ibid.

123   "Nobody knew what": Ibid.

123   "I used to take": Author interview with Kristofferson.

124   "This time, I": Gail Buchalter, "Vince Matthews Sings about Kingston Springs," *Country Music*, March 1973.

124   "The Cashes sat": Author interview with Casey, October 29, 2010.

124   "By this time": Author interview with Kristofferson.

124   Jim Casey remembers: Author interview with Casey.

124   "Vince was never": Author interview with Kristofferson.

125   "All of a sudden": Author interview with Casey.

125   "That signaled the end": Ibid.

125   He eventually returned to: Peter Cooper, "Matthews, Who Wrote Songs Including 'Love in the Hot Afternoon,' Dies at 63," *Tennessean*, November 26, 2003.

126   "In that east-side": Author interview with Rodney Crowell, July 19, 2010.

127   "We were all young": Author interview with Clark.

128   With that "L.A. Freeway": Ibid.

128   "Basically, it's busking": Author interview with Crowell.

130   "Unbeknownst to me": Ibid.

Chapter Seven: Hillbilly Central

131   "Paris of the thirties": Reid, *The Improbable Rise of Redneck Rock*, 188.

131   "She had separated": Jennings with Kaye, *Waylon*, 164.

132   "He was a typical": Author interview with Reynolds.

133   According to Waylon's biographer: Denisoff, *Waylon*, 184–85.

133   In a statement to the press: Ibid., 187.

133   "While Steve Young": Vladimir Bogdanov et al., *All Music Guide to Country* (San Francisco: Backbeat Books, 2003), 377.

134   "It was after five o'clock": Author interview with Bradley, July 22, 2010.

134   RCA rushed out: "RCA Reshuffles Personnel," *Billboard*, December 6, 1972.

135   "You'd look out there": Author interview with Fritts.

135   "Everywhere now there": Grover Lewis, "Hillbilly Heaven: Take the Money and Go Limp," *Rolling Stone*, April 27, 1972.

136   Onstage, Tex Ritter: Reid, *The Improbable Rise of Redneck Rock*, 245.

136   Earl Scruggs generously: Lewis, "Hillbilly Heaven"; Dave Hickey, "Waylon: More and Better, Faster Stronger," *Country Music*, December 1974.

136   When the last tones: Lewis, "Hillbilly Heaven."

137   "I was just worn-out": Author interview with Reynolds.

137   Lewis followed Shaver: Ibid.

137   In his autobiography: Billy Joe Shaver, *Honky Tonk Hero* (Austin: University of Texas Press, 2005), 32–33.

139   The often butted singer: Author interview with Casey.

139   "Tompall was pretty much": Author interview with Reynolds, January 27, 2012.

140   On March 15, 1968: David N. Meyer, *Twenty-Thousand Roads: The Ballad of Gram Parsons and His Cosmic American Music* (New York: Villard, 2007), 232.

140   "It was just people": Author interview with Fritts.

140   "They had an extension cord": Author interview with Stevens.

141   "I discovered two principles": Dave Hickey, "A Night of 'Hillbilly Reality' with Tompall Glaser," *Country Music*, December 1973.

141   Tompall had encountered: Denisoff, *Waylon*, 218.

141   "We wound up in England": Author interview with Reynolds.

142   "You know, before": Dave Hickey, "Waylon: More and Better, Faster and Stronger."

142   In his autobiography, Shaver: Shaver, *Honky Tonk Heroes*, 33.

142   According to Waylon's drummer: Author interview with Albright.

143   "I'd leave messages": Shaver, *Honky Tonk Heroes*, 33.

143   "That just pissed": Ibid., 34.

143   "We were doing the album": Author interview with Albright.

144   When it came time to pick: Author interview with Kahanek, October 8, 2010.

144   "That was really weird": Author interview with Fritts.

145   "Their attitude then was": Author interview with Kahanek.

145   "After many years": Steve Ditlea, "Records," *Rolling Stone*, November 22, 1973.

146   In an interview with the *Tennessean*: "Jennings Severing His RCA Ties," *Tennessean*, September 6, 1973.

146   "He tried to get": "Jennings Has Obligation, RCA Says," *Tennessean*, September 7, 1973.

146   During the *Honky Tonk Heroes*: Jennings with Kaye, *Waylon*, 192.

146   "I'm in the middle": Author interview with Bradley, July 11, 2010.

147   "I was in the studio": Author interview with Kyle Lehning, July 20, 2010.

148   "I was at a Shel Silverstein show": Author interview with Mayor.

149   "Jessi was opening": Author interview with Lehning.

149   "It started with a couple": Author interview with Reynolds, January 28, 2012.

149   "I refuse to be two different people": Bill Hance, "Wax Fax," *Nashville Banner*, November 16, 1973.

150   "Waylon had this tough-guy image": Author interview with Lehning.

150   "Every time we played": Author interview with Reynolds.

Chapter Eight: Burger Boy Outlaws

151   "You walk down": Robert Penn Warren. *At Heaven's Gate* (1943; reprint, New York: New Directions, 1985), 225.

152   Repeated tellings: Richard E. Meyer, "The Outlaw: A Distinctive American Folktype," *Journal of the Folklore Institute* 17, no. 2/3 (May–December 1980), 99.

153   "They are serious people": Nicholas Von Hoffman, "How Columbia Pulled Down Its Pillars," *Washington Post*, June 16, 1968.

153   In 1973, a North Carolina: Author interview with Smith.

154   In January 1974: Hickey, "In Defense of the Telecaster Cowboy Outlaws."

155   For a while, major publications: Martha Hume, "David Allan Coe's Strange Saga," *Country Music*, March 1976.

155   "According to people": Marshall Fallwell, "Watch This Face: David Allan Coe," *Country Music*, May 1974.

156   "You'd have a beginning-of-the-year convention": Author interview with Beck.

156   "Now he seems": John Rockwell, "David Coe on Way to Strong Career as a Song Stylist," *New York Times*, May 24, 1974.

156   "In a way": Author interview with Beck.

156   "A great, great songwriter": Author interview with Albright.

157   "Waylon was nice enough to play guitar": Ibid.

157   "His need to be looked upon": Author interview with Mayor.

157   "We were loading David": Author interview with Bennett.

157   "He wouldn't go to bed": Author interview with Albright.

158   "They'd play [pinball]": Author interview with Smith.

158   "They are all-business": Rich White, "Pinball Wizards Say, 'Go for Broke,'" *Vanderbilt Hustler*, October 29, 1971.

159   The manager of the Burger Boy: Author interview with Terry George, September 14, 2010.

159   "mental masturbation": Author interview with Albright.

159   "Sometimes he'd get": Author interview with George.

159   "The atmosphere in the restaurant": Ibid.

159   "You had people": Ibid.

160   "Next to the pinball": Ibid.

160   "One morning I came in": Ibid.

160   Like George, Albright: Author interview with Albright.

161   "Waylon one day": Author interview with George.

161   "We tried to bar her": Jennings with Kaye, *Waylon*, 247.

161   "I came in the Burger Boy": Author interview with George.

162   Waylon wrote later: Jennings with Kaye, *Waylon*, 247.

162   "He was doing a lot of pills": Author interview with Albright.

163   "When Lee smiled": Author interview with Cowboy Joe Babcock,
           October 28, 2010.

163   "One time we were playing a dance": Author interview with Babcock.

164   "One time when Lee": Ibid.

164   He saw sadness: Author interview with Fritts, June 27, 2011.

164   Three years later, Emerson shot: Official court records, Shelby County
           (Tenn.) Criminal Court, *State of Tennessee v. Lee E. Bellamy*.

164   "I know that he hung with": Author interview with Smith.

165   "John was not writing": Author interview with Casey,
           October 22, 2010.

165   Fritts warned Emerson: Author interview with Fritts.

Chapter Nine: Between Worlds

167   "We in Nashville": Ralph McGill, "Formaldehyde and Poetry," in
           Patrick Allen, ed., *Literary Nashville* (Athens, GA: Hillstreet Press, 1999), 88.

168   "The counterculture": Author interview with Rosanne Cash,
           May 17, 2010.

169   Newspapers reported: Gene Baker, "Prince Foiled in Marriage,"
           Nashville Banner, June 4, 1969; "No Sale," *Tennessean*, September 6, 1973;
           "Nashvillian Charged in Dice Game Death," *Nashville Tennessean*, June 4,
           1969.

170   "Why, I've stood": Jerry Thompson, "Acuff Says Ryman Should Go
           'Before It Falls Down,'" *Tennessean*, March 15, 1974.

170   "That probably takes first prize": Ada Louise Huxtable, "Only the
           Phony Is Real," *New York Times*, March 13, 1973.

171   National Life blinked: *Music*: Patrick Carr, "One Year's Grace for the Ryman Auditorium," *Country Music*, August 1973.

171   Skeeter Davis, known: John McLemore, "Cult Dramatizes 'Brothers' Arrest," *Nashville Banner*, December 10, 1973.

171   A *Billboard* magazine reporter: Jerry Bailey, "WSM Policy Scalds Skeeter," *Tennessean*, December 18, 1973; Larry L. King, "The Grand Ole Opry," *Harper's*, July 1968.

171   When reporters asked: Patrick Thomas, "Christ Group Picket in Support of Skeeter," *Tennessean*, December 22, 1973.

171   Years later, Wendell: Stacy Harris, "Bud Wendell: Company Man," available at http://stacyharris.com/bud.html.

172   "Evidently these officers": Skeeter Davis, *Busfare to Kentucky: The Autobiography of Skeeter Davis* (New York: Birch Lane Press, 1993), 267.

172   In 1966, Roy Acuff: Peter McCabe, "The Wallaces Are Keeping Country Music in the Family," *Country Music*, October 1973; Jimmy McDonough, *Tammy Wynette: Tragic Country Queen* (New York: Viking, 2010), 187.

172   "During the 1968": Paul Hemphill, *The Nashville Sound: Bright Lights and Country Music* (New York: Simon & Schuster, 1970), 153.

172   The Watergate scandal: Hays Corey, "The Nation: Goldwater on Nixon's Prospects," *Time*, May 28, 1973.

173   "Nashville and the Grand Ole Opry": "That Piano Player 'Felt at Home,'" *Nashville Banner*, March 19, 1974.

174   "As Tewkesbury cocked an ear": Jan Stuart, *The Nashville Chronicles: The Making of Robert Altman's Masterpiece* (New York: Limelight Editions, 2000), 47.

174   "Nashville is a place": Gary Arnold, "Altman's Nashville: An American Allegory on Film," *Washington Post*, June 29, 1975.

175   "It's about ambition": Vincent Canby, "Lively Film of Many Parts," *New York Times*, June 12, 1975.

176   "When you show the anatomy": Bill Hance, "Nashville Premiere Churns Sour Response," *Nashville Banner*, August 9, 1975.

177   "There's a famous drag race guy": Author interview with Crowell.

177   "Willie was a poet": Ibid.

178   "She was with Warner Bros.": Ibid.

179   "The Nashville establishment": Ibid.

180   "It was the first time": Chet Flippo, *Red Headed Stranger* (Sony Music
           Entertainment, 2000).

180   According to Connie Nelson: Ibid.

180   "They played the record": Ibid.

182   "It was sex, drugs, and country music": Author interview with Beck.

182   "If you looked at [the album]": Ibid.

184   "This album reveals": Ed Ward, "Records," *Rolling Stone*, August 1975.

184   "Hemingway, who perfected": Paul Nelson, "Willie Nelson's Phono-
           graphic Western," *Rolling Stone*, August 28, 1975.

Chapter Ten: Wanted!

185   "I've been called an outlaw": Daniel Henninger, "The Outlaws Take
           Aim at the Nashville Sound," *National Observer*, August 7, 1976.

186   According to Billy Ray Reynolds: Author interview with Reynolds,
           January 28, 2012.

187   "I was kind of a fan of him": Author interview with Clement.

187   In the studio, the song came to life: Author interview with Reynolds.

187   "That was one of the key tracks": Interview with Clement.

188   "The thing Waylon figured out": Author interview with Albright.

188   "We were there one time": Author interview with Clement.

189   "Waylon was selling": Author interview with Bradley.

191   "Most of the tracks": Joe Nick Patoski, "Records," *Country Music*,
           May 1976.

191   Talk of the pair joining Bob Dylan's: Peter Doggett, *Are You Ready for
           the Country: Elvis, Dylan, Parsons and the Roots of Country Rock* (New York:
           Penguin, 2000), 366; Denisoff, *Waylon*, 264; Nelson Allen, "Is It Goodbye
           to Willie's Picnics?," *Country Music*, November 1976.

192   "It's just a lot of crummy jive": Robert Ward, "Redneck Rock," *New Times*, June 25, 1976.

192   Rhythm guitarist Gordon Payne: Author interview with Payne.

192   "We did gigs": Author interview with Albright, July 20, 2010.

193   "When we were doing": Ibid.

194   "We had just finished": Author interview with Payne.

194   "Now he rules country music": Chet Flippo, "The Saga of Willie Nelson: From the Night Life to the Good Life," *Rolling Stone*, July 13, 1978.

195   "There's just something real": Author interview with Payne.

196   "That was a good move for him": Author interview with Cash.

197   When Bob Beckham cracked: Author interview with Kristofferson.

198   "He's a fast-livin' ": Ben Gerson, "Kristofferson: Goin' Down Slow," *Rolling Stone*, April 27, 1972.

199   Critic Chet Flippo could only muster: Chet Flippo, "Records," *Rolling Stone*, January 4, 1973.

200   "He taught us how to write great poems": Jennings with Kaye, *Waylon*, 211.

200   A review in *Country Music*: Kit Rachlis, "Records," *Country Music*, May 1976.

200   "If he hadn't went to Hollywood": Author interview with Smith.

200   A return trip to the South: Author interview with Fritts; author interview with Swan; author interview with Kristofferson, June 14, 2011.

Chapter Eleven: Third Coast

203   "The constant bustle": Allen Tate, "The Migration," in Patrick Allen, ed., *Literary Nashville* (Athens, GA: Hill Street Press, 1999), 35.

203   "Sure, you know what you remind me of": *Taxi Driver*, directed by Martin Scorsese, Columbia Pictures, 1976.

204   "I thought it was such a nice thing to do": Author interview with Kristofferson.

205   "The outlaws and the redneck rockers": Larry L. King, "The Passions of the Common Man," *Texas Monthly*, August 1976.

206   Closer to home: *Hank* magazine was another Nashville publication that lasted for a few years in the mid-1970s and reliably covered the city's underground music scene.

207   KWAM changed its format in 1975: Michael Bane, "KWAM: Memphis Goes Progressive Radio," *Country Music*, July 1976.

207   "The town has gone funky!": Hickey, "Notes on Kris Kristofferson, 1968–1974."

207   "In Nashville these days": Hickey, "Outlaw Blues," *Country Music*, February 1977.

208   "Anymore you don't have to be ashamed": Bill Hance, " 'T' for Texas . . . , 'T' for Tennessee," *Nashville Banner*, September 20, 1975.

208   "The old South had died": Bruce J. Schulman, *The Seventies: The Great Shift in American Culture, Society and Politics* (New York: Da Capo Press, 2001), 117.

209   "If Carter makes it": Ed Kiersh, "What's Jimmy Carter Doing in This Magazine Anyway?," *Country Music*, December 1976.

209   "I think that was one of the reasons": Chris Willman, *Rednecks and Bluenecks: The Politics of Country Music* (New York: New Press, 2005), 77.

209   "Now, Jimmy Carter": Patrick Carr, "Cash Comes Back," *Country Music*, December 1976.

210   In the homestretch: Tom Ingram, "Carter Visit 'Just Great' for Sasser," *Nashville Banner*, October 2, 1976.

211   "We had done one of the arenas": Author interview with Gordon Payne.

212   "The speed and the weed": Patoski, *Willie Nelson*, 328.

212   In 1976, authorities: "Willie Nelson Subpoenaed in Hicks Narcotics Trial," *Nashville Banner*, August 25, 1976; "3 Willie Nelson Aides Charged on Cocaine," *Nashville Banner*, November 19, 1977.

212   "It was everywhere": Author interview with Payne.

212   "The early seventies": Author interview with Crowell.

213   He had encountered cocaine: Author interview with Albright.

213   He claimed to spend twenty thousand dollars: Jennings with Kaye,
         Waylon, 253.

213   "I wasn't just doing a little drugs": Bob Allen, "Waylon Jennings:
         Steady as She Goes," *Country Music*, May/June 1986.

213   Jack Clement nudged him: Author interview with Clement.

214   "To me it was country": Alden, "Bobby Bare/Bobby Bare, Jr.: Bobby
         Bares, All."

215   "Most of us marked time": Jennings with Kaye, *Waylon*, 257.

215   "I remember Billy telling me": Author interview with Kristofferson.

215   In conversations, Jarvis marveled: Author interview with Light.

217   "Oh, everybody was crying!": Author interview with Smith.

217   On August 16, Gordon Payne: Author interview with Payne.

217   A few blocks away: Author interview with Kahanek.

217   "I don't know how": Author interview with Crowell.

217   A spectator later recalled: Richard Irby, "Heartbreak Hotel Is Still
         Open," August 19, 2010, available at www.areawidenews.com.

218   "Looked to me": Author interview with Crowell.

219   "The head of RCA": Ibid.

Chapter Twelve: Ain't Living Long Like This

221   "Even with its present day": Peter Taylor, *A Summons to Memphis* (New
         York: Knopf, 1986), 23–24.

221   "These awards are": Laura Eipper, "2 'Outlaws' Don't Want on Ballot,"
         Tennessean, August 24, 1977.

222   Early in August: Dwight Lewis and Frank Cason, "17 Arrested as Vice
         Unit Raids Top of Block Club," *Tennessean*, August 8, 1977; Pat Alexander,
         "8 Arrested in After-Hours Raids," *Tennessean*, August 15, 1977; Katherine
         Freed, "2 Released Following Club Raid," *Tennessean*, August 21, 1977.

224   "They said they were there": Author interview with Albright.

225   The next morning, Waylon: Larry Brinton, "Waylon Faces Federal Cocaine Charge," *Nashville Banner*, August 24, 1977.

226   "Waylon'll have a whole new following": Bill Hance, "Coke Bust Could Boost Outlaw Singer's Pot," *Nashville Banner*, September 2, 1977.

226   "A little bit of drugs": Author interview with Bradley, July 22, 2010.

227   The evening of his first court appearance: Laura Eipper, "Outlaws and Emmy Lou Triumph," *Tennessean*, August 25, 1977.

227   In April 1978: Kirk Loggins, "Waylon Manager Aide Pleads Guilty," *Tennessean*, April 26, 1978.

227   "Everywhere we went": Author interview with Payne.

228   Waylon claimed that Reshen: Jennings with Kaye, *Waylon*, 264.

228   On Willie's side of the house: Patoski, *Willie Nelson*, 334.

228   "Neil had helped me and Willie": Jennings with Kaye, *Waylon*, 293.

228   But the cocaine proved: Ibid., 304.

229   "[Emerson] was eating": Author interview with Bellamy.

229   "No one realized": Adell Crowe, "Court Slashes Sadler's Term in Gun Death," *Tennessean*, September 29, 1980.

230   "I think he was": Bob Sipchen, "The Ballad of Barry Sadler," *Los Angeles Times*, January 27 1989.

230   "Sadler stepped up to him": Author interview with Bellamy.

230   "He had a side of him": Author interview with Fritts.

231   "I'm a weapons expert": Hunt Helm, "Sadler Involved in Songwriter's Shooting Death," *Nashville Banner*, December 2, 1978.

232   "Side two consists": Martha Hume, "What Goes Around Comes Around," *Rolling Stone*, December 13, 1979.

232   "farewell to outlawry": Nick Tosches, "Lunchtime," *Rolling Stone*, February 8, 1979.

233   "I turned around": Author interview with Bradley.

234   "The album is rarely": Patrick Carr, "Waylon and Willie Go to a Party," *New Times*, February 20, 1978.

235   "Waylon was a little paranoid": Author interview with Smith.

235   "I remember the first night": Nelson with Shrake, *Willie*, 147.

235   Blackburn, who'd proven his mettle: Author interview with Rick Blackburn, January 21, 2005.

236   Critic John Morthland: John Morthland, *The Best of Country Music* (Garden City, NY: Doubleday, 1984), 412.

237   *Rolling Stone* gave it two stars: Christopher Connelly, "City of New Orleans," *Rolling Stone*, August 30, 1984.

237   Even Rosanne Cash: Paul Kingsbury and Alanna Nash, eds., *Will the Circle Be Unbroken: Country Music in America* (London: Dorling Kindersley, 2006), 336.

238   Until his dying day: The Exit/In later reopened and would close and reopen in the future. It remains in operation today.

238   "Film projects immediately": Bane, *Willie*, 226.

239   "barely a mediocre record": Paul Nelson, review of *Easter Island*, *Rolling Stone*, April 20, 1978.

240   "Kris Kristofferson's songs": Bane, *Willie*, 240.

240   "like a reheated enchilada": Laura Cunningham, "The Very Long Nights of Kris Kristofferson," *Esquire*, November 1981.

241   "I think it all probably started": Author interview with Kristofferson, June 14, 2011.

241   "It was Mexicans": Peter Cooper, *The Pilgrim: A Celebration of Kris Kristofferson* (American Roots, 2008).

241   "I don't think anybody": Author interview with Kristofferson.

241   "They were telling stories": Rosa Jordan, "Kris Kristofferson," *Progressive*, September 1991.

241   Kris's new skepticism: Author interview with Kristofferson.

242   And Willie: In 1975, Native American activist Peltier shot and killed two FBI agents at the Wounded Knee reservation in South Dakota. Many of his advocates believe that he did not receive a fair trial.

242   At a Grammy Awards: Cunningham, "The Very Long Nights of Kris Kristofferson."

243   "We have such a sorry history": Jay Scott, "Kristofferson All Fired Up About Politics," *Globe and Mail*, May 7, 1988.

243   Playing Atlanta during: Ibid.; Jordan, "Kris Kristofferson."

244   "I knew that some of my audience": Author interview with Kristofferson.

244   Former mayor Beverly Briley: Frank Gibson, "Briley, in Tears, Admits He Has Alcohol Problem," *Tennessean*, June 2, 1979.

244   The looming National Life: Gene Wyatt, "WSM Exec Fights Order on Opryland," *Tennessean*, June 2, 1979.

244   And in 1980, toxic shock syndrome: Bill Snyder, "Toxic Shock Hits 5 Tennesseans," *Nashville Banner*, September 27, 1980.

245   This night he picked up: Author interview with Albright.

245   So on May 24, 1980: "Singer Waylon Jennings' Visit Dying Man's Dream Come True," *Tennessean*, May 25, 1980.

245   "I was just standing back": Author interview with Albright.

245   "The thing I remember": Author interview with Payne.

★ Sources

References

Bogdanov, Vladimir, Chris Woodstra, and Steve Erlewine, eds. *All Music Guide to Country*. 2nd ed. San Francisco: Backbeat Books, 2003.

Bufwack, Mary A., and Robert K. Oermann. *Finding Her Voice: Women in Country Music, 1800–2000*. Nashville: CMF/Vanderbilt Press, 2003.

Cantwell, David, and Bill Friskics-Warren. *Heartaches by the Number: Country Music's 500 Greatest Singles*. Nashville: Vanderbilt University Press/Country Music Foundation Press, 2003.

Collins, Ace. *The Stories Behind Country Music's All-Time Greatest 100 Songs*. New York: Boulevard Books, 1996.

Federal Writers' Project of the Works Progress Administration for the State of Tennessee. *Tennessee: A Guide to the State*. New York: Viking Press, 1939.

Guralnick, Peter, and Ernst Jorgensen. *Elvis Day by Day: The Definitive Record of His Life and Music*. New York: Ballantine Books, 1999.

Heylin, Clinton. *Bob Dylan: A Life in Stolen Moments: Day by Day, 1941–1995*. New York: Schirmer Books, 1996.

Kingsbury, Paul, ed. *The Encyclopedia of Country Music*. New York: Oxford University Press, 1998.

Kingsbury, Paul, and Alanna Nash, eds. *Will the Circle Be Unbroken: Country Music in America*. New York: Dorling Kindersley, 2006.

Larkin, Colin. *The Virgin Encyclopedia of Country Music*. London: Virgin Books, 1998.

McCloud, Barry, ed. *Definitive Country: The Ultimate Encyclopedia of Country Music and Its Performers*. New York: Perigee, 1995.

Meade, Guthrie T., Jr., with Dick Spottswood and Douglas S. Meade. *Country Music Sources: A Biblio-Discography of Commercially Recorded Country Music*. Chapel Hill: University of North Carolina Press, 2002.

Nashville City Directories. Detroit: R. L. Polk, 1965–80.

Opdyke, Steven. *Willie Nelson: Sings America!* Austin, TX: Eakin Press, 1998.

Pruett, Barbara J. *Marty Robbins: Fast Cars and Country Music*. Lanham, MD: Scarecrow Press, 2007.

Sanjek, Russell (updated by David Sanjek). *Pennies from Heaven: The American Popular Music Business in the Twentieth Century*. New York: Da Capo Press, 1996.

Seigenthaler, John M., and Curtis Allen. *Nashville: City of Note*. Memphis: Tower, 1997.

Smith, John L. *The Johnny Cash Discography*. Westport, CT: Greenwood Press, 1985.

———. *The Johnny Cash Discography, 1984–1993*. Westport, CT: Greenwood Press, 1994.

———. *The Waylon Jennings Discography*. Westport, CT: Greenwood Press, 1995.

Whitburn, Joel. *Top Country Albums, 1964–1997*. Menomonee Falls, WI: Record Research, 1997.

———. *Top Country Singles, 1994–1993*. Menomonee Falls, WI: Record Research, 1994.

———. *Top Pop Singles, 1955–1993*. Menomonee Falls, WI: Record Research, 1994.

General

Allen, Patrick, ed. *Literary Nashville*. Athens, GA: Hill Street Press, 1999.

Amburn, Ellis. *Buddy Holly: A Biography*. New York: St. Martin's Press, 1995.

Bane, Michael. *The Outlaws: Revolution in Country Music*. New York: Country Music Magazine Press, 1978.

———. *Willie: An Unauthorized Biography of Willie Nelson*. New York: Dell, 1984.

Bart, Teddy. *Inside Music City USA*. Nashville: Aurora, 1970.

Biskind, Peter. *Easy Riders, Raging Bulls: How the Sex-Drugs-and-Rock 'n' Roll Generation Saved Hollywood*. New York: Simon & Schuster, 1998.

Bland, Mary Ruth Jackson. *The Autobiography of Mary Ruth Jackson Bland*. Unpublished manuscript, n.d.

Blumstein, James F., and Benjamin Walter, eds. *Growing Metropolis: Aspects of Development in Nashville*. Nashville: Vanderbilt University Press, 1975.

Brown, Jim. *Emmylou Harris: Angel in Disguise*. Kingston, Ontario: Fox Music Books, 2004.

Buffett, Jimmy. *A Pirate Looks at Fifty*. New York: Random House, 1998.

Busby, Mark, and Terrell Dixon. *John Graves, Writer*. Austin: University of Texas Press, 2007.

Carter, Jimmy. *An Hour Before Daylight: Memories of A Rural Boyhood*. New York: Simon & Schuster, 2001.

Cash, Johnny, with Patrick Carr. *Cash: The Autobiography*. New York: HarperSanFrancisco, 1997.

Cash, Rosanne. *Composed: A Memoir*. New York: Viking, 2010.

Cason, Buzz. *Living the Rock 'n' Roll Dream: The Adventures of Buzz Cason*. Milwaukee: Hal Leonard, 2004.

Causey, Warren B. *The Stringbean Murders*. Nashville: Quest, 1975.

Chapman, Marshall. *Goodbye, Little Rock and Roller*. New York: St. Martin's Griffin, 2003.

———. *They Came to Nashville*. Nashville: Country Music Foundation Press/Vanderbilt University Press, 2010.

Ching, Barbara. *Wrong's What I Do Best: Hard Country and Contemporary Culture*. New York: Oxford University Press, 2001.

Cobb, James C. *Redefining Southern Culture: Mind and Identity in the Modern South*. Athens: University of Georgia Press, 1999.

Conkin, Paul. *Gone with the Ivy: A Biography of Vanderbilt University*. Knoxville: University of Tennessee Press, 1985.

Connelly, Thomas L. *Will Campbell and the Soul of the South*. New York: Continuum, 1982.

Davis, Clive, with James Willwerth. *Clive: Inside the Record Business*. New York: Ballantine Books, 1976.

Dawidoff, Nicholas. *In the Country of Country: A Journey to the Roots of American Music*. New York: Pantheon Books, 1997.

Denisoff, R. Serge. *Waylon: A Biography*. New York: St. Martin's Press, 1984.

Denisoff, R. Serge, and Richard A. Peterson, eds. *The Sounds of Social Change*. Chicago: Rand McNally, 1972.

Doggett, Peter. *Are You Ready for the Country?* New York: Penguin, 2001.

Doyle, Don H. *Nashville Since the 1920s*. Knoxville: University of Tennessee Press, 1985.

Egerton, John. *Nashville: The Faces of Two Centuries, 1780–1980*. Nashville: PlusMedia, 1979.

Einarson, John. *Desperados: The Roots of Country Rock*. New York: Cooper Square Press, 2001.

Eng, Steve. *Jimmy Buffett: The Man from Margaritaville Revealed*. New York: St. Martin's Press, 1996.

————. *A Satisfied Mind: The Country Music Life of Porter Wagoner*. Nashville: Rutledge Hill Press, 1992.

Escott, Colin. *Lost Highway: The True Story of Country Music*. Washington, DC: Smithsonian Books, 2003.

Faragher, Scott. *Music City Babylon: Inside the World of Country Music*. New York: Birch Lane Press, 1992.

Fong-Torres, Ben. *Hickory Wind: The Life and Times of Gram Parsons*. New York: St. Martin's Press, 1991.

Friedman, Kinky. *'Scuse Me While I Whip This Out*. New York: HarperCollins, 2004.

Gaillard, Frye. *Watermelon Wine: The Spirit of Country Music.* New York: St. Martin's Press, 1978.

Goldfield, David R. *Promised Land: The South Since 1945.* Arlington Heights, IL: Harlan Davidson, 1987.

Goldrosen, John, and John Beecher. *Remembering Buddy: The Definitive Biography of Buddy Holly.* New York: Penguin Books, 1986.

Green, Douglas B. *Singing in the Saddle: The History of the Singing Cowboy.* Nashville: Vanderbilt University Press/Country Music Foundation Press, 2002.

Grissim, John. *Country Music: White Man's Blues.* New York: Paperback Library, 1970.

Guralnick, Peter. *Careless Love: The Unmaking of Elvis Presley.* Boston: Little, Brown, 1999.

————. *Last Train to Memphis: The Rise of Elvis Presley.* Boston: Little, Brown, 1994.

————. *Lost Highway: Journeys and Arrivals of American Musicians.* New York: Vintage, 1979.

Haggard, Merle, with Peggy Russell. *Sing Me Back Home: My Life.* New York: Times Books, 1981.

Halberstam, David. *The Children.* New York: Random House, 1998.

Hall, Tom T. *The Storyteller's Nashville.* New York: Doubleday, 1979.

Hardy, Robert Earl. *A Deeper Blue: The Life and Music of Townes Van Zandt.* Denton: University of North Texas Press, 2008.

Hemphill, Paul. *The Nashville Sound: Bright Lights and Country Music.* New York: Simon & Schuster, 1970.

Honey, Michael K. *Going Down Jericho Road: The Memphis Strike, Martin Luther King's Last Campaign.* New York: Norton, 2007.

Horenstein, Harry. *Honky Tonk: Portraits of Country Music, 1972–1981.* San Francisco: Chronicle Books, 2003.

Hoskyns, Barney. *Say It One Time for the Brokenhearted: Country Soul in the American South.* London: Bloomsbury, 1987.

Jarrett, Ted, and Ruth White. *You Can Make It if You Try: The Ted Jarrett Story of R&B in Nashville.* Nashville: Country Music Foundation Press and Hillsboro Press, 2005.

Jennings, Waylon, with Lenny Kaye. *Waylon: An Autobiography.* New York: Warner Books, 1996.

Kienzle, Rich. *Southwest Shuffle: Pioneers of Honky-Tonk, Western Swing, and Country Jazz.* New York: Routledge, 2003.

Killen, Buddy, with Tom Carter. *By the Seat of My Pants: My Life in Country Music.* New York: Simon & Schuster, 1993.

Kosser, Michael. *How Nashville Became Music City USA.* Milwaukee: Hal Leonard, 2006.

Koster, Rick. *Texas Music.* New York: St. Martin's Griffin, 2000.

Kreyling, Christine, Wesley Paine, Charles W. Warterfield Jr., and Susan Ford Wiltshire. *Classical Nashville: Athens of the South.* Nashville: Vanderbilt University Press, 1996.

Kruth, John. *To Live's to Fly: The Ballad of the Late, Great Townes Van Zandt.* New York: Da Capo Press, 2007.

Lee, Brenda, with Robert K. Oermann and Julie Clay. *Little Miss Dynamite: The Life and Times of Brenda Lee.* New York: Hyperion, 2002.

Lomax, John, III. *Nashville: Music City USA.* New York: Harry N. Abrams, 1986.

Malone, Bill C. *Country Music USA.* Rev. ed. Austin: University of Texas Press, 1985.

————. *Don't Get above Your Raisin': Country Music and the Southern Working Class.* Urbana: University of Illinois Press, 2002.

Malone, Bill C., and Judith McCulloh. *Stars of Country Music: Uncle Dave Macon to Johnny Rodriguez.* Urbana: University of Illinois Press, 1975.

McAlexander, Hubert H., ed. *Conversations with Peter Taylor.* Jackson: University Press of Mississippi, 1987.

McDonough, Jimmy. *Tammy Wynette: Tragic Country Queen.* New York: Viking, 2010.

McGee, David. *Steve Earle: Fearless Heart, Outlaw Poet.* San Francisco: Backbeat Books, 2005.

McGuire, Jim. *Historic Photos of the Opry.* Nashville: Turner, 2007.

Meyer, David N. *Twenty Thousand Roads: The Ballad of Gram Parsons and His Cosmic American Music.* New York: Villard, 2008.

Miller, Stephen. *Kristofferson: The Wild American.* London: Omnibus Press, 2010.

Morris, Charles R. *A Time of Passion: America, 1960–1980.* New York: Penguin, 1986.

Morthland, John. *The Best of Country Music.* Garden City, NY: Doubleday, 1984.

Murphy, Reg, and Hal Gulliver. *The Southern Strategy.* New York: Scribner, 1971.

Nash, Alanna. *Behind Closed Doors: Talking with the Legends of Country Music.* New York: Knopf, 1988.

———. *Dolly: The Biography.* Updated ed. New York: Cooper Square Press, 2002.

Nashville: Conserving A Heritage. Nashville: Historical Commission of Metropolitan Nashville-Davidson County, 1977.

Nelson, Susan. *Heart Worn Memories: A Daughter's Personal Biography of Willie Nelson.* New York: Pocket Books, 1987.

Nelson, Willie, with Bud Shrake. *Willie: An Autobiography.* New York: Simon & Schuster, 1988.

Norman, Jack. *The Nashville I Knew.* Nashville: Rutledge Hill Press, 1984.

Patoski, Joe Nick. *Willie Nelson: An Epic Life.* New York: Back Bay Books, 2008.

Powell, Austin, and Doug Freeman, eds. *The Austin Chronicle Music Anthology.* Austin: University of Texas Press, 2011.

Reid, Jan. *The Improbable Rise of Redneck Rock.* New ed. Austin: University of Texas Press, 2004.

Sadler, Barry. *Everything You Want to Know about the Record Industry.* Nashville: Aurora, 1978.

Schimmenti, Mark, and Gary Gaston. *The Plan of Nashville: Avenues to a Great City.* Nashville: Vanderbilt University Press, 2005.

Schulman, Bruce J. *The Seventies: The Great Shift in American Culture, Society and Politics.* New York: Da Capo Press, 2001.

Scobey, Lola. *Willie Nelson: Country Outlaw.* New York: Zebra Books, 1982.

Self, Philip. *Guitar Pull: Conversations with Country Music's Legendary Songwriters.* Nashville: Cypress Moon Press, 2002.

Sewall-Rushkin, Yvonne. *High on Rebellion: Inside the Underground at Max's Kansas City.* New York: Thunder's Mouth Press, 1998.

St. John, Lauren. *Hardcore Troubadour: The Life and Near Death of Steve Earle.* London and New York: Fourth Estate, 2003.

Smith, Richard D. *Can't You Hear Me Callin': The Life of Bill Monroe.* Boston: Little, Brown, 2000.

Stuart, Jan. *The Nashville Chronicles: The Making of Robert Altman's Masterpiece.* New York: Limelight, 2003.

Stuart, Marty. *Pilgrims: Sinners, Saints, and Prophets.* Nashville: Rutledge Hill Press, 1999.

Tichi, Cecelia, ed. *Reading Country Music: Steel Guitars, Opry Stars, and Honky-Tonk Bars.* Durham, NC: Duke University Press, 1998.

Tosches, Nick. *Country: The Twisted Roots of Rock 'n' Roll.* New York: Da Capo Press, 1998.

Townsend, Charles R. *San Antonio Rose: The Life and Music of Bob Wills.* Urbana: University of Illinois Press, 1976.

Trevino, Geronimo, III. *Dance Halls and Last Calls: A History of Texas Country Music.* Plano: Republic of Texas Press, 2002.

Wexler, Jerry, and David Ritz. *Rhythm and the Blues: A Life in American Music.* New York: Knopf, 1993.

Wilentz, Sean, and Greil Marcus. *The Rose and the Briar: Death, Love and Liberty in the American Ballad.* New York: Norton, 2005.

Willman, Chris. *Rednecks and Bluenecks: The Politics of Country Music.* New York: New Press, 2005.

Wolfe, Charles. *Classic Country: Legends of Country Music.* New York: Routledge, 2001.

Wolfe, Charles E., and James Akenson, eds. *Country Music Goes to War.* Lexington: University Press of Kentucky, 2005.

Yetnikoff, Walter, with David Ritz. *Howling at the Moon: The Odyssey of a Monstrous Music Mogul in an Age of Excess.* New York: Broadway Books, 2004.

Zimmerman, Keith, and Kent Zimmerman. *Sing My Way Home: Voices of the New American Roots Rock.* San Francisco: Backbeat Books, 2004.

Zollo, Paul. *Songwriters on Songwriting.* 4th ed. New York: Da Capo Press, 2003.

Websites

billdeyoung.com

cmt.com

davehoekstra.com

encyclopediaofalabama.org

secondhandsongs.com

tennesseeencyclopedia.net

tshaonline.org

uselectionatlas.org

Films

The Electric Horseman. Dir. Sydney Pollack. Columbia Pictures, 1979.

Heartworn Highways. Dir. James Szalapski. Crimson Productions, 1976.

Nashville. Dir. Robert Altman. Paramount, 1975.

The Nashville Sound. Dirs. Robert Elfstrom and David Hoffman. Amram Nowak Associates, 1970.

The Other Side of Nashville. Dir. Etienne Mirlesse. Transfilm Productions, 1983.

Pat Garrett and Billy the Kid. Dir. Sam Peckinpah. MGM, 1973.

Taxi Driver. Dir. Martin Scorsese. Columbia Pictures, 1976.

Liner Notes

Cooper, Peter. The Pilgrim: *A Celebration of Kris Kristofferson*. American Roots, 2006.

Flippo, Chet. *Red Headed Stranger*. Sony Music Entertainment, 2000.

————. *Wanted! The Outlaws*. 20th Anniversary. BMG, 1996.

George-Warren, Holly. *Dolly*. Sony Music Entertainment, 2009.

Gray, Michael and Ron Wynn. *Night Train to Nashville: Music City Rhythm and Blues, 1945–1970*. CMF Records/Lost Highway, 2004.

————. *Night Train to Nashville: Music City Rhythm and Blues, 1945–1970*. Vol. 2. CMF Records/Lost Highway, 2005.

Kaye, Lenny. *The Journey: Six Strings Away*. Bear Family Records, 1999.

Kienzle, Rich. *Are You Ready for the Country*. BMG Heritage, 2004.

————. *Dreaming My Dreams*. Buddha Records, 2001.

————. *Lonesome, On'ry & Mean*. BMG Heritage, 2003.

————. *Ol' Waylon*. BMG Heritage, 2003.

————. *The Ramblin' Man*. Buddha Records, 2000.

————. *This Time*. Buddha Records, 1999.

————. *The Troublemaker*. Sony Music Entertainment, 2004.

————. *Waylon & Willie*. BMG Music, 2000.

————. *Waylon Live: The Expanded Edition*. BMG Heritage, 2003.

————. *Waylon: Nashville Rebel*. Sony BMG Music Entertainment, 2006.

————. *Yesterday's Wine*. BMG Heritage, 2003.

Morthland, John. *The Best of Billy Swan*. Sony Music Entertainment, 1993.

Schutt, Roger. *Honky Tonk Heroes*. Buddha Records, 1999.

Simmons, Michael. *Please Don't Tell Me How the Story Ends: The Publishing Demos, 1968–72*. Light in the Attic Records, 2010.

★ Acknowledgments

THE LIST IS always long, the journey filled with friends, family, happy coconspirators, and reluctant accomplices. Thanks to you: Rosanne Cash, Dianne Davidson, Kris Kristofferson, Lisa Kristofferson, John Leventhal, Richie Albright, Billy Ray Reynolds, Jesse Reynolds, Rodney Crowell, Kyle Lehning, Jerry Bradley, Gordon Payne, Hugh Bennett, Jack Clement, Fred Foster, Don Davis, Guy Clark, Carl Knight, Ralph Mooney, Earl Sinks, Rodney Bellamy, Girl George, Donnie Fritts, Billy Swan, Alan Mayor, Hazel Smith, Ray Pennington, Ronny Light, Elroy Kahanek, Dan Beck, Inez Johnson, Chris Leuzinger, Bill Walker, Rick Blackburn, Cowboy Joe Babcock, Steve Shoen, Mike Farrell, Jim Casey, Even Stevens, Jim Malloy, Mary Matthews, Ranger Doug Green, Terry George, Dick Bay, Joe Nick Patoski, Mark Rothbaum, Harry Warner, Paul Worley, Ernie Winfrey, Robert Ogles, Don Boner, Richard Weize and Andy Merck at Bear Family Records, Tommy Wayne Burlett, Rick Trunfio, Carolyn June Lallemand, Rochelle Bilow. The office of the Criminal Court Clerk of Metropolitan Nashville and Davidson County. The staff of the Nashville Room at the Nashville Public Library. The office of the Criminal Court Clerk of Shelby County, Tennessee. Steve

Andreassi and Cindy Baffa of the IUP Lodge and Convocation Center, Hoboken, New Jersey. Chris Ratliff in Special Collections at the University of Memphis, Deborah O. Cox at the Metropolitan Government Archives of Nashville and Davidson County. Michael McCall and John Rumble at the Country Music Hall of Fame and Archives. My agent, Jim Fitzgerald. Publisher Cal Morgan at It Books, who championed this book from the very start. And editors Jennifer Schuster and Mark Chait, who helped mold *Outlaw* into a more effective narrative. Thanks also are due to Trina Hunn at HarperCollins. John Jackson, Che Williams, Matt Kelly, Tom Tierney, Rob Santos, Toby Silver, and Jim Parham at Sony Music. Danelle Moon in Special Collections and Archives at San Jose State University. Henry Shipman and other staff members of the Jean and Alexander Heard Library at Vanderbilt University. The staff of Ridgetop (Tennessee) City Hall. The staff of the Maryland Room at the University of Maryland. At Le Moyne College: Carrie Carpenter, Linda LeMura, Julie Grossman, Wayne Stevens, Phil Novak, Melissa Short. The Commodores: Darrell Berger, Lewis Shiner, Michael Minzer. Two angels in Nashville: Ruth White and Tamara Saviano. My wife, Leslie, and our children, Emily, Cate, and Will.

★ Index

Page numbers in *italics* indicate photographs.